CASTE
CLASS
AND POWER

ANDRÉ BÉTEILLE

CASTE, CLASS, AND POWER

Changing Patterns of
Stratification in a Tanjore Village

1971

Berkeley, Los Angeles, London
UNIVERSITY OF CALIFORNIA PRESS

University of California Press
Berkeley and Los Angeles, California
University of California Press, Ltd., London, England
© 1965 by The Regents of the University of California
Second Printing, 1969
First Paperback Printing, 1971
ISBN: 0-520-02053-7
Library of Congress Catalog Card Number 65-25628
Printed in the United States of America

For Meenakshi, Babu, and Kausalya

ACKNOWLEDGEMENTS

This is a revised version of a thesis submitted to the University of Delhi for the Ph.D. degree. I should like here to record my thanks to the authorities of the University for having allowed me to take a term off in order to complete my field work. My thanks are due in particular to Professor M. N. Srinivas, who helped in a multitude of ways to bring this work to fruition.

I owe a special debt of gratitude to the people of Sripuram who made many concessions so that I might live with them as a member of their community. I should like to express my thanks in particular to Shri C. R. Raghavachar, Shri P. T. Gaudapadah, Shri R. Varadachari, Shri N. Ramachandran and his family, Shri Narayanaswami Nayudu, and Shri Kanakasabhai Pillai. My thanks are also due to Shri T. V. Naganathan and his family; their house at Tanjore was a second home for me.

I have benefited from the criticisms of many people while preparing this study, among whom I should like to mention Shri R. Jayaraman and Dr. P. C. Joshi. I should also like to thank Professors N. K. Bose and David G. Mandelbaum for helpful suggestions as well as other acts of kindness.

Finally, I owe a debt to Dr. R. N. Konar, but for whose organisational help the work might have been delayed by several months. I would also like to thank Miss Aneeta Ahluwalia and Miss Mohini Budhraja for preparing the index.

ANDRÉ BÉTEILLE

CONTENTS

Chapter I

Introduction

This study has grown out of field research conducted in a village, here called Sripuram, of Tanjore District in South India. Although most of the primary data were collected in Sripuram, many of the observations made in the course of the study relate to a wider area. These observations, thus, have necessarily a tentative character, although the utility of intensive case studies for illuminating problems of a wider scope has now come to be generally recognised. The studies of the Coorgs by Srinivas (1952), of an Orissa village by Bailey (1957), and of a Tamil subcaste by Dumont (1957a) offer cases in point.

The relations between a single village and the wider social system of which it forms a part are complex, and very little will be gained by discussing at the outset these relations in abstract and formal terms. Suffice it to say that it is possible to study within the framework of a single village many forms of social relations which are of general occurrence throughout the area. Such, for instance, are the relations between Brahmins, Non-Brahmins, and Adi-Dravidas (Untouchables) and between landowners, tenants, and agricultural labourers.

These relations are governed by norms and values which have a certain generality. This can be verified by making even casual comparisons in adjacent villages, or villages in adjacent districts. No doubt the norms do not operate in identically the same manner in each particular instance, but much can be learnt about the relationship between principle and practice by making detailed observations in a single village.

Many of the rules governing the relations between different sections of people in the village apply to the state as a whole. Some of these rules carry legal sanctions. Such, for instance, are the rules governing the relations between landowners and tenants. There are also organs and institutions created by state legislation whose principles of operation are the same in every village. The statutory *panchayat* provides an example of this. Intensive field study in a single village provides crucial evidence regarding the manner in which rules having general validity operate in concrete situations.

The outside world enters into the life of the villager in a multitude of ways. What happens in the state capital and in other urban centres is often discussed with keen interest by the residents of Sripuram. The village, being situated in the delta of the Kaveri River, is particularly exposed to external forces. Thus, in studying the social life of the village it is extremely difficult to separate what is internal to it from what belongs to the milieu of which it is a part. The village, in fact, may be viewed as a point at which social, economic, and political forces operating over a much wider field meet and intersect.

Social relations overflow the boundary of the village easily and extensively. Ties of kinship and affinity link members of every caste to people in other villages or towns. Many of the members of the older families and lineages have become scattered. But they continue to retain some contact with those who have stayed behind in the village. Although kinship and affinal ties did cut across the boundary of the village even in traditional society, subcastes, lineages, and families have become much more dispersed today. What happens to the villager when he goes to live in a town or a city? We get to know something of this from the links which he continues to maintain with kinsmen in the village, and also on occasions when he revisits his ancestral home.

Economic relations cut across the boundary of the village in a variety of ways. Many landowners live outside the village. Agricultural surpluses are sold outside. Land has come into the market. Several villagers are engaged in white-collar jobs in the neighbouring towns. The village is becoming progressively a part of a wider economy. We get some indication of the working of this economy by trying to analyse the ways in which it affects the lives of the villagers.

The village is linked through the system of Panchayati Raj to other villages and larger organs of local government. Some villagers take part in the activities of political parties. Political networks of diverse kinds link the individual villager to people occupying a variety of social positions both within and outside the village. They interconnect village leaders, district leaders, party bosses, members of the Legislative Assembly, financiers, and government officials.

This, then, is the broad field we seek to illuminate, although we focus attention on a single village. What is the central theme of the study here presented? Broadly speaking, our concern is with the phenomena of caste, class, and power (mainly in its political aspects) and with their changing relations. We deal first with each of the three phenomena separately, and then examine their interrelations in the context of change. After presenting an account of the physical structure of the village in chapter ii, we deal in turn with caste, class, and power in the three succeeding chapters. The concluding chapter seeks to analyse the changing relations between the three.

In a sense the caste structure constituted the basis of traditional society. Tanjore District in particular has been known for the rigidity and complexity of its caste structure. In the village this structure not only divided the population into sections of unequal ritual status, but also dominated economic and political life. The fundamental importance of the caste structure to the social life of the village can be seen in its settlement pattern (chap. ii), which clearly segregates the three primary segments—Brahmins, Non-Brahmins, and Adi-Dravidas—from one another. Although many areas of social life are now becoming to some extent "caste-free," the settlement pattern of the village continues to reflect the basic cleavages of the traditional structure.

Up to a point the caste system is relatively easy to represent. It can be viewed as a system of enduring groups whose mutual relations are governed by certain broad principles. Castes as enduring groups can be located with relative ease, since they are named and have fairly well-defined boundaries. The principles which govern their mutual relations, however, are complex in nature; these are discussed in some detail in chapter iii.

In contrast to castes, which are communities (or approximate to them), classes are categories rather than groups. By class we mean a category of persons occupying a specific position in the system of production (see chap. iv). In the context of the agrarian economy of Sripuram the class system comprises landowners, tenants, agricultural labourers, and their relations. Relations between landowners, tenants, and agricultural labourers have a standardised character and are, to some extent, enduring in nature. Further, they are defined in legal or quasi-legal terms. Social and economic relations between persons depend a good deal upon their mutual positions in the class system. In Sripuram the class system overlaps to a considerable extent with the caste structure, but also cuts across it at a number of points.

It is far more difficult to define power in formal terms, or to relate it to enduring groups and categories comparable to castes or classes. Some power is, of course, located in formal structures such as *panchayats* and parties. In addition to these, there are informal groupings which are of great importance, although they are fluid in nature and do not have boundaries which are easy to define. Finally, an understanding of power also requires the analysis of networks of interpersonal relations which cut across the boundaries of caste, class, *panchayat,* and party.

Caste, class, and power relate in different ways to the broader phenomenon of social stratification. The caste system is clearly a hierarchical system, although the nature of this hierarchy may be difficult to ascertain beyond certain broad terms. Landowners, tenants, and agricultural labourers also constitute a hierarchy, although here again a big tenant may be economically more powerful than a very small landowner. The distribution of power, in its turn, creates a certain hierarchy in the village, although of a very fluid and amorphous character.

The hierarchies of caste, class, and power in the village overlap to some extent, but also cut across. It is the argument of this study that in the traditional structure the cleavages of caste, class, and power tended much more than today to run along the same grooves. The Brahmins were the landowners, and they also constituted the traditional elite. This is no longer the case at present. The social system has acquired a much more complex and dynamic character, and now there is a tendency for cleavages to cut across one another.

The sharpness of the traditional cleavages continues to be reflected in the settlement pattern of the village. In the past, when the division of the village into Brahmins, Non-Brahmins, and Adi-Dravidas dominated not only rituals, but also economic and political life, it must have seemed natural for the three communities to live apart. Today there are many areas of life which are becoming progressively "caste-free." Thus, landownership, occupation, and even education are not to the same extent dependent upon caste. Yet the physical structure of the village continues to be consistent with the cleavages in its traditional social structure. Not only is there even now a strong feeling of identity within each segment of the village—a legacy from the past—but certain political developments tend to heighten this feeling of identity.

In spite of this, there are powerful forces which tend to loosen the hold of caste in many areas of social life. Education is no longer a monopoly of a single group of castes. In the traditional system Sanskritic learning was monopolised by the Brahmins. When Western education first came at the turn of the century, that, too, became a virtual monopoly of the Brahmins. Today the educational system is far more open, both in principle and in practice. Many Non-Brahmin and even Untouchable boys now attend the schools at Sripuram and the adjacent town of Thiruvaiyar. Education not only enables the Non-Brahmins and Adi-Dravidas to compete on more equal terms with the Brahmins for white-collar jobs, but also provides them with more equal chances of political participation.

In the towns and cities white-collar jobs are relatively caste-free. Non-Brahmins from Sripuram can now work as clerks or accountants in offices at Thiruvaiyar and Tanjore along with Brahmins, although it is true that not many of them have seized the new opportunities. Within the village, land has come into the market. There are numerous factors which lead some of the Brahmins to sell their land, enabling Non-Brahmins and even a few Adi-Dravidas to buy it. As land comes into the market, the productive organisation tends to free itself from the structure of caste.

In a way changes in the distribution of power have been the most radical. The traditional elite of Sripuram, composed of Brahmin landowners, has lost its grip over the village. The new leaders of the village depend for their power on many factors in addition to caste. New organs and institutions have been created, and, with them, new bases of power. Most of these are at least formally independent of caste. And the formal structure of rules does tend to have some effect in altering, if not weakening, the role of caste in the field of politics.

The process of modernisation is a complex one. It is activated by a variety of social, economic, and political forces. Among other things, it tends to loosen the rigidity of the traditional structure and to provide greater choice to the individual in entering into interpersonal relations which cut across the boundaries of the old, established groups. This study tries to throw some light on the process of modernisation by examining how different areas of social life are being gradually detached from the traditional structure.

Changes in the social system of Sripuram can be viewed in several ways. Following the terminology of Dahl (1961), they can be viewed as changes from a system of cumulative inequalities to one of dispersed inequalities. Indeed, the social history of Sripuram shows many striking parallels with that of New Haven as this has been presented by Dahl. The parallels are all the more striking because the two communities would on the surface seem to differ in almost every important way. In Sripuram, as in New Haven, wealth, power, and social prestige were initially combined in the same set of individuals. In both communities economic advantages have been dispersed and new social strata have risen to power, although the stages through which these changes have come about and their causes are different in many respects.

Speaking in more general terms, one can say that in Sripuram a relatively closed social system is being transformed into one which is relatively open. A closed system is one in which different elements such as caste, class, and power are combined in broadly the same way. Of course, no social system is absolutely closed.

There is always some scope, however limited, for alternative combinations. But the choice allowed for different combinations varies greatly from one society to another and, in the same society, over a given period of time. Caste society has been viewed as a classic example of a closed system, and until recently Sripuram exemplified some of the most distinctive features of such a system. Till the end of the nineteenth century caste played a part in almost every important sphere, and the social, economic, and political life of the village was dominated by the superiority of the Brahmins. Today many spheres of life have become relatively independent of caste, and the authority of the Brahmins, who once enjoyed what may be called decisive dominance, is challenged at every point. This study seeks to examine how the transformation has come about, and to isolate some of the factors which have brought it about.

One important concomitant of the transformation from a closed to a relatively open system is the differentiation of institutional structures which had earlier been subsumed under a more comprehensive framework. In the traditional order of Sripuram both the class system and the distribution of power were to a large extent subsumed under caste. Both class and power positions have today a greater measure of autonomy in relation to caste. In other words, one encounters today a greater range of possibilities in the combination of caste, class, and power positions, although even in the past the combinations were not absolutely fixed.

One may question the legitimacy of applying concepts such as class to the study of societies in which economic relations have been governed by traditional obligations and inherited status. Weber (1948, p. 182) seems to argue that it is meaningful to talk of classes only in a market economy: ". . . always this is the generic connotation of the concept of class: that the kind of chance in the *market* is the decisive moment which presents a common condition for the individual's fate. 'Class situation' is, in this sense, ultimately 'market situation.' " While market forces seem to have played a relatively unimportant part in the traditional system of Sripuram, they cannot by any means be ignored today. The existence of such forces, which bring about changes in the distribution of property, makes it necessary to study the class system as a thing in itself, governed by properties which are in part independent of caste. And in order to see how the class system operates today it is important to understand how the relations between landowners, tenants, and agricultural labourers (or categories corresponding to them) were governed in the past. Nor would it be true to say that even in the past such categories were determined *entirely* by caste.

The differentiation of the class system has been brought about by the introduction of the cash nexus and the development of market mechanisms. When land comes into the market, its chances of remaining frozen within a particular caste are reduced. In chapters iv and vi the structure of agrarian relations in Sripuram and its gradual dissociation from caste are discussed. The processes discussed there seem to be of fairly general occurrence. Bailey (1957) has shown how, in an Orissa village, land which was formerly frozen within the Warrior caste has become gradually dispersed. Gough (1955, 1960) has indicated a similar tendency in a village very close to Sripuram.

Changes in the distribution of power in Sripuram can be seen as being broadly of two kinds. In the first place, power has shifted from one set of dominant castes (the Brahmins) to another (the Kalla and the Vellala groups of castes among the Non-Brahmins). In the second place, power has shifted from the caste structure itself and come to be located in more differentiated structures such as *panchayats* and political parties. The dominant caste was the principal locus of power in the traditional village. This is no longer the case today. The manner in which power is being dissociated from the structure of caste and is coming to be located in more differentiated structures is discussed in chapters v and vi.

The extent to which the distribution of power has differentiated itself from the caste structure seems to be more striking than corresponding changes in the class system. The transfer of land from the Brahmins to the Non-Brahmins has been insignificant in comparison with shifts in their political positions. That the changes in the distribution of power are particularly striking in Sripuram is partly owing to the unique position of the Brahmins in Tamil society. There can be no doubt, however, that elsewhere in the country, as in Sripuram, politics is being increasingly used as an avenue of social mobility, particularly by those sections of society which had been hitherto classified as "backward" (see Béteille, 1965).

II

The field work on which this study is based was conducted largely at Sripuram over a period of about ten months in 1961 and 1962. During my stay at Sripuram I had ample opportunity to visit neighbouring villages, and I also made a few brief visits to other districts in the company of some of the residents of the village.

I did my field work in Sripuram while living with the people as one among them. I was permitted to live in the *agraharam,* in a Brahmin house—a privilege, as I was often told, never before extended to an outsider and a Non-Brahmin. I dined with the Brahmins and had access to most of their houses. I was perhaps the only Non-Brahmin ever to have sat and eaten with the Brahmins in Sripuram on ceremonial occasions. I was identified with the Brahmins by my dress, my appearance, and the fact that I lived in one of their houses.

My identification with the Brahmins was, however, not an unmixed blessing. I soon discovered that it made me suspect in the eyes of the Non-Brahmins and Adi-Dravidas, who at first regarded me as just another Brahmin from North India. My access to these groups was, therefore, far more limited than to the Brahmins. I usually went to their streets to elicit answers to specific questions. I was not able to move with them as freely as with the Brahmins. Among the Adi-Dravidas there was an additional difficulty. No Brahmin normally goes to an Adi-Dravida street; if he does so, he is required by tradition to take a bath before he enters the *agraharam.* My visits to the Adi-Dravida streets had, as a consequence, to be made discreetly, although sometimes I was even accompanied there by one or two "progressive" Brahmins. Also, I had many opportunities to meet the Adi-Dravidas outside their streets, particularly in the back-yards of certain Brahmin houses, and in the fields during the agricultural season.

Consequently my data for the Adi-Dravidas and also, to some extent, for the Non-Brahmins are of a poorer quality than for the

Brahmins. But it has to be realised that there was, in fact, very little choice. Had I lived with the Non-Brahmins, the Brahmins would not have moved freely with me. Had I lived with the Adi-Dravidas, the *agraharam* would have been inaccessible. I chose to live with the Brahmins for practical reasons and also because this gave me an opportunity to gain some insight into the literate cultural tradition of the region.

Had I lived with the Adi-Dravidas this study would perhaps have had a different focus. A somewhat different picture of Sripuram—not necessarily contradictory to the present one—would perhaps be the outcome. I have tried at every stage to balance the views expressed by Brahmins with those of the other groups. But this has not been possible beyond a certain level. The only way to provide a corrective to this study at the present is to bear in mind these limitations.

I should like to emphasize that the study is qualitative in its character and emphasis. I have tried to understand Sripuram not in quantitative and statistical terms, but, to quote Professor Popper (1957, p. 24), "in terms of conflicting tendencies and aims." I have tried in some measure to understand its social life from within, in terms of the values and meanings attributed to it by the people themselves. I frequently discussed my interpretations of their society with the villagers. Sometimes they surprised me, not only by the range of their knowledge, but also by their power of analysis.

My status as a resident of the *agraharam* was a curiously ambiguous one. In many ways I was marked out as an outsider—by my name, my religion, and my very moderate linguistic equipment—and I shared the uncertain status of the outsider, particularly during the early part of my stay. Yet in many ways I was also an heir to the broad cultural tradition of which Sripuram formed a part, and I shared with the villagers many of their interests and concerns. I do not here wish to enter into a discussion on the relative advantages of the fieldworker as "outsider" and "insider." But it is evident that my ambiguous status gave me the scope at least to seize upon the crucial advantages of both.

My field work was not done in a very planned or organised manner. I did not enter the field "armed with a battery of hypotheses," and I have no doubt that, given my broad objective, such an equipment would have done more harm than good. My objective, at least to begin with, was indeed very broad. I wanted to understand, in the broadest sense of the term, the village and its social life. I hoped that by the end of my field work I would come to *know* the village, rather than merely *know about* it. To this end I set about observing an endless variety of phenomena and collecting information on temple rites, family disputes, agricultural techniques, and virtually everything I could lay my hands on. I realised, of course, that I would have to face the problem of selection sooner or later, but I wanted this to be done later rather than sooner. I also knew that in a more subtle manner the process of selection was working all the time, directing my enquiries one way rather than another and leading me to record certain facts and not others, often enough without my full awareness.

A comprehensive understanding of a society from within enables the sociologist to grasp directly its basic principles of organisation and to decide with some confidence which factors in a given context are more important and which are less. But the attainment of such a direct understanding is only one part of the task. The other and no less difficult task is to translate this understanding into the language of sociology.

The use of a certain framework for presenting the material here has meant, of course, that some facts have been highlighted at the expense of others. As one reads through this work, it is this selective presentation which will naturally dominate one's attention. But it should at once be pointed out that this presentation is based on an understanding to which facts of a much broader range have contributed. The exclusion of many of these facts of not to deny altogether their contribution to the development of the study which is presented here.

As more and more Indian sociologists take up field studies of sections of their own society, they will have to face certain problems which have not yet been posed in a very conscious or systematic manner. In a sense the British anthropologist doing field work in an African tribe is in a happier position. He does not have the same degree of concern, the same kind of involvement in the problems of the society which he studies. He comes to the field with a relatively open mind. This luxury is denied to the sociologist when he is studying his own society, particularly when that society is passing through a phase of active change.

It has by now become a truism that full objectivity in the social sciences is beyond attainment. As such, the sociologist has to examine critically at every stage the kind of concern which he carries into his research. There is no gainsaying the fact that most Indian intellectuals today are committed to social change, economic development, and political modernisation, and this commitment, no doubt, gives a particular focus to their enquiries.

If in this study of a Tanjore village there is very little preoccupation with purity, pollution, and rituals in general, this is perhaps a reflection of the way in which I perceive Indian society to be moving today. This perception is, no doubt, coloured by my own position in a particular sector of Indian society. Yet, as it has been put by Mannheim (1936, p. 111), "the fact that our thinking is determined by our social position is not necessarily a source of error. On the contrary, it is often the path to political insight."

III

Before entering into an analysis of the village it may be useful to introduce the reader briefly to the cultural area of which it forms a part. I do not propose to give here a lengthy or exhaustive account of the history and culture of Tanjore District. For a broad and general survey of the area I refer the reader to two books which have a fairly comprehensive coverage: *Madras District Gazetteers: Tanjore,* by F. R. Hemingway, and *Tanjore District Handbook,* by B. S. Baliga. The area has also been studied by professional anthropologists (in particular, Gough, 1955, 1960, and Sivertsen, 1963).

Sripuram is situated in the Tanjore taluk of Tanjore District, adjacent to Thiruvaiyar and at a distance of about eight miles from Tanjore town. The Panchanadeeshwara temple at Thiruvaiyar is famous throughout Tamilnad, and this area has been open to the traffic of pilgrims for well over a thousand years. Today bus routes connect Sripuram, by way of Thiruvaiyar, with Tanjore, Kumbakonam, and other important centres in the district. Thus, the location of Sripuram in the delta of the Kaveri and adjacent to Thiruvaiyar has kept it exposed to social and cultural influences from outside for a very long time.

The recorded history of the district goes back about two thousand years. The first dynasty of which we have authentic evidence, and the one which is in many ways the most remarkable, is the Chola dynasty. The extent and boundaries of the Chola kingdom varied greatly with the fortunes of its different kings, but the core of the empire—Chozanadu proper—was made up essentially of the delta of the Kaveri along with the eastern portion of Trichy District and the southern edge of South Arcot. At all times the western part of Tanjore District, particularly the Thiruvaiyar area, seems to have occupied a position of prominence in this empire.

The Cholas were well known as patrons of civilisation and the arts of life. They built irrigation works and temples extensively. Without going into the details of social life during the Chola period, one can say that the foundations of the type of village organisation which survived up to the period of British rule had already been laid. *Agraharams,* or Brahmin villages, of the type which was common in the area until recently, were established extensively during the rule of the Cholas. "Faith in the unique merit of the gift of land (*bhu-dana*) was very common and frequently acted on by those who could afford it. Thus it came about that new colonies of pious and learned Brahmins were settled in the different parts of the country and gained control of local affairs through the *Sabha* and its executive. [And sometimes] a new settlement of Brahmins was superimposed on a more ancient community by the constitution of a *mangalam.*" (See Sastri, 1955, pp. 492–493.)

The Cholas were succeeded after an interval by the Telugu Nayakas, and these in turn by the Marathas, whose rule lasted till the beginning of the British period. The rule of these two dynasties partly accounts for the linguistic and cultural diversity of Tanjore. Both the Nayakas and the Marathas were patrons of learning and the arts, and several *agraharams* were set up during their rule. The Telugu Nayakas in particular were patrons of the Vaishnava religion. The Marathas established *vedapathashalas,* or schools for training in the scriptures, and *chhattrams,* or hospices; some of these survive to the present day.

Tanjore District has a total area of 3,740 square miles and a total population of 3,245,927 persons. This gives it a population density of 868 per square mile which is considerably higher than the state average of 669, Tamilnad itself being one of the most densely populated states in the country (Census of India, 1962, p. 340). The high density of population in the district is largely due to the fertility of the soil and its high agricultural productivity; there are no large industrial or urban centres in the district which can be held to account for any high concentration of population.

Of the total population of the district, 79.6 per cent is classified as rural and the rest as urban (Census of India, 1962, p. 341). The urban sector is mainly made up of a number of small towns. Tanjore and Kumbakonam are the only towns of moderately large size, each having a population of around 100,000. On the other hand, there are several towns of smaller size in the district. Thiruvaiyar, which is typically one of them, has a population of 11,171. The villages of the district, particularly in the western part, are fairly large, and one frequently comes across villages having more than 2,500 persons.

It is necessary here to draw attention to one important typological feature of villages found in these parts. Villages containing "communities of learned Brahmins" seem to have existed, and to have constituted a distinctive type, from fairly early times. During the Chola period they were referred to as *mangalam* or *chaturvedi mangalam*. Later, the term *agraharam* came into use to refer to a community of Brahmins, to the street in which they lived, and sometimes to the entire village (there are villages in Tanjore district known as Ganapatiagraharam, Palliagraharam, and so on). Even today the distinction between villages with and without *agraharam* is of fundamental significance typologically. It should be made clear, however, that *agraharam* villages constitute only a small proportion of the total number of villages even in Tanjore District.

The vast majority of the population of the district consists of Tamil-speaking Hindus. There are, in addition, small minorities of Telugu- and Marathi-speaking people who have been established in the district for generations. There is also a small community of silk weavers speaking what is locally known as "Sourashtra," i.e., a dialect of Gujarati, in this case with an admixture of Tamil. Among religious minorities, Muslims and Christians are numerically the most important.

The division of the population into castes constitutes one of its most important sociological characteristics. We shall consider here the caste system only as it operates among the Hindus, although similar phenomena are found among Muslims and Christians. The numerous castes found in this area are grouped into three broad divisions: Brahmin, Non-Brahmin, and Adi-Dravida (the last being also referred to as Harijan or Untouchable). This threefold grouping of castes is characteristic of Tamilnad and, by and large, of South India as a whole. It does not seem to have the same significance in North India.

The term Brahmin is applied to a congeries of castes and subcastes which are socially quite distinct from each other. There can be said to be three main Brahmin categories: (1) those who officiate as priests for Non-Brahmins; (2) those who serve as temple priests; and (3) those who were traditionally devoted to learning and the study of the *shastras,* the scriptures of Hinduism. These categories are of unequal rank, the last being generally recognised as the highest. There is no intermarriage between them, and, in fact, each category is itself made up of a number of subcastes (see chap. iii).

Many of the Tanjore Brahmins are, or were until recently, fairly big landowners, or *mirasdars*. Since the beginning of the twentieth century absentee landlordism has become common among the Brahmin *mirasdars* of Tanjore. It must be noted, however, that although many of the big *mirasdars* of Tanjore have been Brahmins, several Non-Brahmins have owned as much land as they, if not more.

The Non-Brahmins as a category are more diverse and heterogeneous than the Brahmins. Sometimes even Christians and Muslims are included among them, but generally the Adi-Dravidas are excluded. The Non-Brahmins constitute the largest of the three main caste divisions. They are often collectively designated as Shudras by the Brahmins, but this is, at best, a loose characterisation. The Non-Brahmins have certain broad uniformities in their style of living, although there are very wide variations between the different Non-Brahmin castes. In general, they can be said to be less "Sanskritic" than the Brahmins.

The Non-Brahmins include mainly landowning castes, such as the Mudaliyars; landowning and cultivating castes, such as the Vellalas, Gaundas, and Padayachis; trading castes, such as the Chettiyars; artisan castes, such as the Kusavans (Potters), Tachchans (Carpenters), and Tattans (Goldsmiths); servicing castes, such as the Ambattans (Barbers) and Vannans (Washermen), as well as a large number of other specialist castes. One or more of these castes will be found to be particularly influential, or dominant, in every district. Thus, the Mudaliyars are dominant in Chingleput, the Padayachis in North Arcot and South Arcot, the Gaundas in Coimbatore, and so on. In Tanjore the Vellala and the Kalla groups of castes seem to be the most influential, the Kallas in spite of their somewhat low position in the traditional hierarchy. The political importance of the Kallas in the Thiruvaiyar area, particularly, is more or less indisputable.

The third tier in the caste structure is composed of the so-called Untouchables, usually referred to as Adi-Dravidas or Harijans. As Scheduled Castes they have a special position and status guaranteed to them by the Indian Constitution. They constitute about twenty-three per cent of the total population of the district. As a group of castes they are distinct and separate from the Non-Brahmins, with whom they should not be confused. The two main Adi-Dravida castes in Tanjore District are the Paraiyas and Pallas.[1]

The Adi-Dravidas have hitherto been both economically and socially depressed. They are in most cases agricultural labourers, as they were in the past; they also engage in other forms of labour, such as digging and road building. Very few of them own land. Socially they have been debarred by tradition from entering the Brahmin streets, temples, and other public places. These disabilities have been largely removed by law, but many of them continue to operate in practice. The new political climate, however, seems to be on the whole favourable to the Adi-Dravidas.

Most of Tanjore District is made up of the delta of the Kaveri. The climate is warm and moist and there are two yearly monsoons. Agriculture constitutes by far the most important

---

[1] To avoid variation and possible confusion, "Adi-Dravida" is used hereafter to designate the third tier in the caste structure.

source of livelihood for the people of the district. Tanjore is, in fact, known as the granary of South India. By contrast, industry is poorly developed. Tanjore owes its agricultural plenitude to a favorable combination of rainfall and artificial irrigation. Its irrigation system, dating back to the time of Karikala Chola in the first century A.D., is one of the chief glories of Tanjore District.

There are two classes of cultivable land in the district, *nanja* and *punja*. *Nanja* is wet or irrigated land and is greater in extent and importance than *punja*. Paddy is raised only on *nanja* land, which is occasionally used for raising other crops as well, either after the paddy harvest is over, as in the case of black gram and green gram, or in rotation with paddy, as in the case of banana or sugar cane. *Punja* is unirrigated or dry land, and is used for raising millets, oilseeds, and vegetables.

The principal crop cultivated in Tanjore District is paddy (i.e., rice). Generally, two paddy crops are grown, the first being a short-term crop known as *kuruvai,* and the second being of longer duration and known as *samba* or *thal adi*. A special class of land, the strip between the bed of the river and its embankment, is known as *paduhai*. It is very fertile and generally used for growing cash crops such as banana, betel vines, and sugar cane.

Along with high agricultural productivity, Tanjore District has been characterised by great polarity of agricultural incomes. It is difficult to give in brief an adequate account of the relations of production, particularly in view of certain basic changes which have been created, at least in law. Until recently Tanjore was well known for its *mirasdars,* large and small, many of whom had very little connection with the actual business of cultivation. With the recent enactment of laws fixing ceilings on agricultural holdings, large estates have begun to break up, although it is true than many ways have been devised to evade the law.

The estates, large and small, were often cultivated on lease, and the conditions of lease were generally exploitative in nature. The lessor in many cases demanded as much as 70 or 75 per cent of the produce even though the supplying of plough cattle, seeds, and manure was done by the lessee. With the passage of the Tanjore Tenants and Pannayal Protection Act in 1952, the legal position of the lessee became more secure. The lessee was given the right to retain 40 per cent of the produce, and this was later raised to 60 per cent. In many places these laws exist largely on paper although they have, certainly, brought about a change in the climate of landlord-tenant relations.

While on the one hand there has been a substantial class of rentiers, on the other hand there was and still is an even larger class of landless labourers. A large number of the latter belong to the two Untouchable castes of Paraiyas and Pallas. Their position up to the nineteenth century was more or less that of serfs tied to the soil. Legislative enactments over the last several decades have no doubt freed them in one sense, but often have also left them without employment because under the new conditions land-owners do not any more feel the obligation to support them.

Chapter II

The Village:

Its Physical Structure

This chapter is an account of the physical structure of Sripuram. It involves, first, a brief consideration of the location of Sripuram in relation to important geographical and cultural landmarks, and, second, a more detailed analysis of its internal arrangements—the settlement pattern, the disposition of streets with regard to one another, the situation of temples and other community centres, and so on.

It will be seen that the physical structure of the village is, in some measure, a reflection of its social structure. The distribution of population is not haphazard or random, but evinces a more or less conscious plan. This plan brings out in a graphic manner some of the basic unities and cleavages in the social structure of the village. People who are close to each other in the social system tend to live side-by-side; people whose social positions are widely different live apart. Other things being equal, physical distance can be seen as a function of structural distance.

The village has certain clear territorial divisions, and social values are attached to these. The *agraharam,* for instance, is not only a cluster of habitations, but also the centre of social life for the Brahmins. During marriages, and on the occasion of temple festivals arranged by the Brahmins, the customary processions go only through the *agraharam,* although it is generally said that such processions go around the village. To the Brahmins the *agraharam,* in more ways than one, *is* the village.

The Pallacheri, similarly, is not just another quarter of the village; it is a place which no Brahmin should enter. The concept of pollution attaches not only to groups and individuals, but also to places. The same is true of the concept of purity. The temple precincts are generally regarded as sacred. But not all of them have equal sanctity for every group in the village. Thus, for the Shri Vaishnava Brahmins, the venue for ceremonial gatherings during marriage or initiation is the Vishnu temple and not the Shiva temple, into which many of them will not even enter.

It will be noticed that the values represented in the distribution of space in Sripuram are largely those of its traditional order, in which positions in the class and power structures were on the whole governed by positions in the caste structure. Today, with the differentiation of the class system and the distribution of power, the social system of Sripuram has become too complex to be adequately contained within any single scheme of geographical representation. As will be seen later, there have been some minor changes in the plan of settlement, but these have not kept pace with the more fundamental changes which are coming about in the social system of the village. Rather, it seems that the settlement pattern has captured the traditional structure of the village, which was to a much greater extent closed than that of today. A study of this pattern thus provides a good point of entry into the understanding of the traditional structure, whose basic cleavages continue to play an important part in the contemporary life of the village.

II

Sripuram is situated on the north bank of the Kaveri, in the Tanjore taluk of Tanjore District. It is about eight miles north by northwest of Tanjore and is adjacent to Thiruvaiyar on the western side. This area, which constituted the heart of the Chola country, has been settled for at least two thousand years. Throughout the deltaic part of Tanjore District one encounters villages with ancient temples on either side of the Kaveri River and its branches. The Kaveri has a twofold significance in the lives of the villagers. It provides a copious supply of water for irrigation, and it is ranked high among the rivers held sacred by Hinduism. Brahmins, particularly, prefer to live close to the river

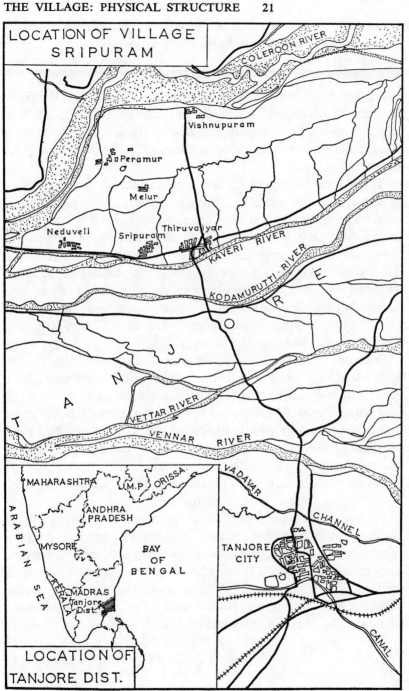

LOCATION OF VILLAGE SRIPURAM

LOCATION OF TANJORE DIST.

because religious merit is acquired by performing the daily *sandhya* rites on the waters of the Kaveri.

The river skirts the village on its southern side. Running parallel to the Kaveri, on its northern side, is a metalled road which separates the residential area of the village from the river. Between the river and the metalled road lies a belt of the land which is known in these parts as *paduhai*. Bananas and betel vines are usually grown here, and sometimes sugarcane and clumps of bamboo.

The metalled road, which is at a stone's throw from the centre of the residential area, has been in existence for about three decades. Even before it was metalled, this road served as an important artery. In fact, a regular traffic of pilgrims has passed along it for centuries. This road connects the village with Thiruvaiyar, which is adjacent to it on its eastern side. From Thiruvaiyar there are regular bus services to Tanjore and Kumbakonam. On the other side, to the west, the road leads to the Grand Anicut (the control works for the Mettur irrigation system, at the head of the delta).

Sripuram stands midway between the Grand Anicut and Kumbakonam, being at a distance of about twenty miles from each. Although the number of buses running directly between the two places is small, the traffic in lorries is considerable. These lorries carry mainly paddy, unrefined sugar, plantains and plantain leaves, betel, and other agricultural products. It should be noted, however, that although Sripuram is situated on the highway, people continue to transact their business through Thiruvaiyar, which is at a distance of less than a mile.

Sripuram owes many of its characteristics to its geographical position in the delta of the Kaveri. The delta is both fertile and of relatively easy access. Situation in such an area makes possible the expansion of social ties far beyond the individual village as well as the development of close interrelations with nearby villages. Villages in the Kaveri delta find themselves automatically on the cultural map of Tamilnad.

III

A village usually consists of settlements and the agricultural land around them. A distinction has been made by geographers and social anthropologists between nucleated villages, in which all the dwellings are clustered in one place, and dispersed villages, where each settlement stands apart and is surrounded by its own plot of land. According to this classification Sripuram would be regarded as a nucleated village. It should be pointed out, however, that even in such villages the dwellings are not always concentrated in one single area, but frequently in two or more distinct centres. This fact has a structural significance which will later be examined in some detail.

Sripuram by itself does not constitute a revenue village, but is grouped for revenue purposes along with another village, Melur, which is at a distance of about one mile to its north. Each village has its own separate social existence, although the two are interrelated in a number of ways. The interrelation makes itself most clearly felt in the sphere of land tenure, since there is no way of distinguishing between land belonging to Sripuram and that belonging to Melur. People from both Sripuram and Melur, as well as a large number of outsiders, own land in this one revenue village, which is named after Melur. Also, people from Sripuram own land in a number of other revenue villages, particularly in two of them which are close to Sripuram. It follows from this that the social identity of a village cannot be established simply on the basis of land tenure.

In fact, a close study of landowning shows some degree of connection between the three revenue villages of Melur (inclusive of Sripuram), Peramur, and Vishnupuram. Peramur is adjacent to Melur on its northwest, and Vishnupuram is about three miles away, to the northeast. The present connection between the three villages is explained by the fact that until about a hundred years ago they constituted a single revenue unit. The joint revenue records of these three villages are said to have been kept in the *paimash chitta,* the word *chitta* denoting the record of land titles maintained by the village accountant. The *paimash chitta* is, however, no longer available.

The connection between these three revenue villages, with their several clusters of habitations, highlights a certain feature in the settlement pattern of the area which deserves consideration. Till the end of the nineteenth century the ownership of most of the land in these three villages was shared between a community of Brahmins and a certain Maratha family related to the princely line of Tanjore. The Brahmin community had its earlier settlement at Melur, and shifted a little more than a hundred years ago to Sripuram. In addition to this community there were settlements of Non-Brahmins at Peramur and Vishnupuram, consisting mainly of families engaged in agriculture and associated occupations. These settlements of Non-Brahmins at Peramur and Vishnupuram continue to exist, but they have become progressively disengaged from the economic control exercised over them by the Brahmin landowners of Sripuram.

Thus, the word "village" has a number of different connotations. In the context of land tenure and with regard to revenue administration, Melur (including Sripuram), Peramur, and Vishnupuram constituted a single village till about a hundred years ago, and Melur and Sripuram still constitute a single village. In other regards these different settlements have each a distinct social identity. An *agraharam* village had invariably a number of Non-Brahmin and Adi-Dravida settlements attached to it. Its social connections with these, however, varied widely, depending in part upon physical distance.

Although Sripuram has lost most of its association with Peramur and Vishnupuram, it continues to be related to Melur in a number of important ways. Three aspects of its association with Melur may be indicated here: (1) since much of the land owned and cultivated by the residents of these two units happens to be in one and the same revenue village, landowners from Sripuram have tenants at Melur, and cultivators from Melur engage labourers from Sripuram; (2) the Iyengars of Sripuram, who constitute the majority of Brahmins there, have their ancient temple at Melur, where, among other things, a ten-day religious festival is held every year; and (3) Sripuram and Melur have a common village *panchayat*.

Sripuram proper, then, is essentially a cluster of habitations having a certain geographical and social identity. This identity, however, is something relative and not absolute. It has to be clearly understood that the word Sripuram means different things to different people, and under different circumstances.

For the Brahmins, Sripuram signifies generally the *agraharam*, the residential area and the community of Brahmins living within it. A stranger is likely to be surprised that Brahmin residents usually give as the strength of the village a figure around one hundred families. When told that the village must have at least three hundred families, they agree, saying that this must be so if one includes the families of Non-Brahmins and Adi-Dravidas. This experience is not particular to Sripuram, but is repeated in most *agraharam* villages, where Brahmins often give as the strength of the village the number of households in their own residential area and not the total number of houses. There is a similar tendency among Non-Brahmins to exclude Adi-Dravidas, though Brahmins are usually included by them.

A number of households in Sripuram which physically form a part of it are associated for revenue purposes with another unit situated about two miles to its east. This other unit, which we shall refer to as Mangudi, constitutes what is known as a *mukhasa* village. The term *mukhasa*, in general, refers to a village or piece of land enjoying a special position with regard to the payment of revenue. In Tanjore District "it is used to denote the private estate of the late Raja, being made up of lands which His Highness Sarabhoji retained at the cessation of the province" (Iyengar, 1933, p. 141). *Mukhasa* land may form part of an ordinary village, or an entire village may be classed as *mukhasa*. In the former case, for convenience of revenue administration the *mukhasa* land is grouped not with the village of which it is physically a part, but with a nearby *mukhasa* village, which may be separated from it by a couple of miles.

Physically Sripuram proper constitutes a more or less compact unit. The houses are clustered together within a small area, giving the village a fairly distinct physical entity. The total population of the village is 1,400 and is distributed in 349 households. The breakdown of households and population by caste group is given in table 1.

The village, which appears as a unit from outside, reveals fairly clear physical divisions when examined from within. It divides itself into three more or less well-defined physical segments, the *agraharam*, the *kudiana* (Non-Brahmin) streets, and the *cheri* (Adi-Dravida residential area). Of these, the first and the last are the most distinctive. The Non-Brahmin households in the *kudiana* streets are, by comparison, physically more dispersed and socially more heterogeneous.

TABLE 1

CASTE GROUPS IN SRIPURAM

Caste Group	Households	Population
Brahmin	92	341
Non-Brahmin	168	688
Adi-Dravida	89	371
Total	349	1400

The *agraharam* runs in an almost perfect straight line from east to west, parallel to and near the metalled road. It is separated from the metalled road by the backyards of the Brahmin houses and by a large coconut grove. The *cheri* is farther back from the metalled road and also parallel to it. The houses of the Adi-Dravidas, or Untouchables, are symmetrically arranged on either side of their street, just as the Brahmin houses are arranged on either side of the Brahmin street. In between the *agraharam* and the *cheri* are the Non-Brahmin houses, arranged in a number of streets which lack the symmetry of either the *agraharam* or the *cheri*. Some Non-Brahmin houses are also to be found along the metalled road and in front of the Shiva temple at the western extremity of the village. Across from the temple is a solitary Thotti Untouchable hut, clearly separated from the Non-Brahmin houses.

These territorial divisions are of great importance because social values are attached to them. For instance, the *agraharam,* where the Brahmins' houses are located, is the centre of Brahmin social life. There are in all 98 separate dwellings in the agraharam, including a few which are unoccupied. Besides the dwellings, there are a few buildings used for other purposes, such as the shrine attached to the Ahobila *madam* (or *mutt*) at the western end, and the school buildings at the eastern end.

The houses in the *agraharam* are packed close to each other, and there is very little room for expansion. Frequently, they are connected with each other internally through small openings, usually having grilles, which facilitate ventilation and the easy exchange of oil, spices, and sundry items of domestic consumption between womenfolk living in adjoining houses. Practically every Brahmin house has on the outer side a kind of open

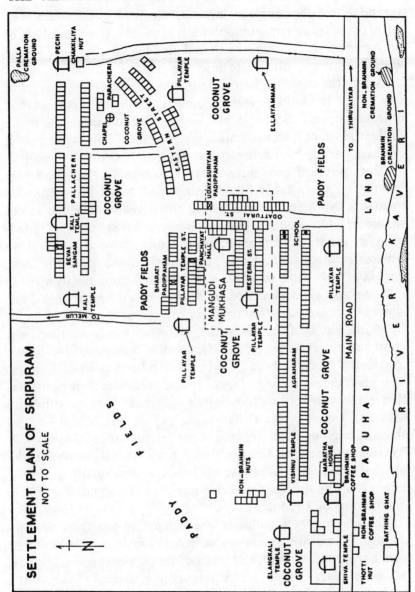

SETTLEMENT PLAN OF SRIPURAM

NOT TO SCALE

verandah, locally known as a *payal,* which faces the street. The *payal* occupies an important position in the everyday social life of the *agraharam*. The menfolk sit and chat here during the daytime and, in summer, often late into the night.

Within the *agraharam* anyone may go and sit on the *payal* of any house. It would be a gross breach of etiquette to voice any objection openly. Some people, however, resent use being made of their *payal* as a sort of public gossip centre. This is prevented, at least partly, by having one's *payal* enclosed by a wall.

Close physical proximity between houses in the *agraharam* makes possible a fairly intense quality of social life among its members. Nothing happens within the *agraharam* which is not sooner or later—sooner rather than later—brought to the knowledge of the entire community. There are two ways in which news travels: externally, from one *payal* to another among the men, and, internally, from one house to another among the women.

The physical proximity of houses in the *agraharam* should not simply be regarded as the cause of the intimate nature of social life within it. In fact, the social life is as much a cause as a consequence. Brahmins come from other places to live in the *agraharam* precisely because they wish to be close to each other. This gives them a feeling of security and facilitates their participation in the numerous socio-religious activities which constitute an essential feature of the Brahminical way of life. It also enables them to bring up their children in the "right sort of atmosphere." There are many new families which have recently settled in the *agraharam* at Sripuram. One of the reasons normally given for this is that the *agraharam* here contains a large and respectable community of Brahmins.

The *agraharam* is, thus, in every sense of the term, a community. There are numerous occasions, mainly of a ritual or ceremonial nature, on which most of its members come together at some place within it. A common occasion is when the bridegroom is received on the evening before the day of marriage; at that time practically every adult Brahmin comes to the Vishnu temple situated at the head of the *agraharam*. In a marriage house, or in a house where some other important ceremony is taking place, one usually finds a large and representative section of the *agraharam,* both men and women.

Just as the physical proximity of the Brahmin houses creates conditions for the *agraharam's* being a community, so also the physical separation from the rest of the village makes it possible for this community to be a more or less exclusive one. Here again one has to see the physical separation between the *agraharam* and the rest of the village as both a cause and a consequence of the social separation of the Brahmins from the rest of the population.

No Non-Brahmin has ever lived in the *agraharam* at Sripuram. In certain villages not very far away a few Non-Brahmins have purchased houses in the *agraharam* and have even started living there. This is an entirely new phenomenon, at least in Tanjore District, and it is a cause of consternation among the Brahmins. In one or two villages it has led the Brahmin residents to move out. Sripuram has so far managed to maintain the exclusiveness of its *agraharam*, although this too has been assailed once or twice.

Brahmins object to Non-Brahmins' staying in the *agraharam* on a number of grounds. The reason which they most frequently give to outsiders is that Non-Brahmins eat meat, fish, and other unclean things. If these were cooked in the *agraharam,* the odours emitted would create intolerable conditions for the Brahmins. Besides, bones and scales in the form of refuse would be strewn all about. The Brahmins have an overweening consciousness of their own cleanliness, which they contrast with the dirty habits of other people. At the level of the village this is partly justified, since the typical Non-Brahmin—who is, as often as not, a peasant—is usually less clean in his personal habits than the typical Brahmin *mirasdar*.

But the objection to Non-Brahmins on the ground that they eat unclean things is hardly the only or the most significant one. There are Shaivite Non-Brahmins whose entry into the *agraharam* as residents has been opposed although they are vegetarians just like the Brahmins. The resistance to Non-Brahmins has, in fact, far deeper roots. Their entry into the *agraharam* would upset a pattern of life which has been established over centuries. To the Brahmins such a contingency bears the appearance of a threat to their tradition and their cultural heritage. For them the *agraharam* is not only a physical unit; it is a community and a way of life.

While, on the one hand, the *agraharam* is closed to Non-Brahmins from the village or the region, it is, on the other hand, open to Brahmins from any part of the country. The present population includes people affiliated to three language areas, Tamilnad, Andhra Pradesh, and Mysore. Some fifty years ago a Brahmin mendicant from North India used to live in a house in the middle of the *agraharam*. This house is still referred to as the *gosaimanai* ("mendicant's abode").

Though the Brahmins live within the *agraharam*, and there is much flow of people from one part of it to another, the houses are not distributed in a haphazard way. Notwithstanding the corporate character of the community of Brahmins, there are subdivisions among them, and these subdivisions are represented, although not very clearly, in the physical plan of the *agraharam*. Other things being equal, persons belonging to the same subcaste, or to the same lineage within a subcaste, tend to live in adjacent houses. But there has been much movement of people to and from the *agraharam*, and this has altered greatly the disposition of population within it.

Many of the older families have left the village, and their houses are now occupied by newcomers, among whom are those who have come to the village as sons-in-law and those who have simply bought or rented houses at Sripuram for one practical reason or another, though even persons in the latter category usually have some distant relatives in the village. Today only a minority of dwellers in the *agraharam* can be said to be living in their ancestral homes. More than a dozen families live in rented houses, and this has led persons who are in no way related to become next-door neighbours, or even to share the same house. There is one house in the *agraharam* which is shared by a Smartha and a Shri Vaishnava, both of them newcomers. Fifty to sixty years ago the settlement pattern of the *agraharam* was more consistent with the cleavages between castes.

It seems likely that the eastern part of the *agraharam* was settled first. The ancestral houses of most of the people belonging to the Periam and Dikshitar lines are in this part, and these lines are the two oldest ones among the Vadagalai Iyengars of Sripuram. At present there is only one Periam family belonging to the direct line. The other Periam houses in the eastern end are now occupied by their sons-in-law or have been sold or rented to other people.

Similarly, the present families in the direct male line of the Dikshitar group also inhabit the eastern end of the *agraharam*. There are four houses, on either side of the street, occupied by families which are closely interrelated. The other Dikshitar houses, again mostly at the eastern end of the *agraharam*, are, as in the case of the Periam, occupied by sons-in-law, cognates, or newcomers to the village.

The old Smartha houses stand in a block in the centre of the *agraharam*. On the southern side are four houses adjacent to each other which are occupied even today by Smartha families. Facing these are four houses also occupied by Smarthas. Some of the others have changed hands, and several of the present occupants are tenants and not owners.

The western half of the *agraharam* is comparatively new. The houses belonging to the Mysore group are all situated here. The Mysore group consists of families which are not all agnatically related. They are Vadagalai Iyengars, but their roots in the village do not seem to be as deep as those of the two other Vadagalai Iyengar lines. Today, however, they form a comparatively important section, being represented in Sripuram by half a dozen households, all inhabiting the western part of the *agraharam*.

The distribution of the other households in the *agraharam* seems to be more or less haphazard and not to bear witness to any conscious plan. As has been indicated earlier, the different subcastes, and the different lines within a subcaste, were localised to a greater extent two generations ago. Today the older distribution of population has been disturbed, largely because of the movement of people to and from the village. Smartha and Shri Vaishnava houses are juxtaposed much more often than in the past, when they were spatially more discrete. Perhaps this is also a reflection of the fact that socially these two communities have come closer together.

The physical separation between Smartha and Shri Vaishnava houses is, and has been, different in important ways from the separation between the *agraharam* and the Non-Brahmin streets. Even in the past it was never rigidly enforced. It came about in a more or less spontaneous manner, as a result of kinsmen's constructing their houses next to each other. The movement of a Non-Brahmin into the *agraharam* would cause apprehension among the Brahmins and would, to some extent, disturb the social order. On the other hand, the movement of a Smartha family into a house once occupied by Shri Vaishnavas would not. Clearly, this is a reflection of the fact that the structural distance between Smarthas and Shri Vaishnavas is much smaller than that between Brahmins and Non-Brahmins (see chap. iii).

IV

The Non-Brahmins, unlike the Brahmins, do not live in one single street, but are distributed in a number of streets. The Non-Brahmin population is both larger and socially more diverse than the Brahmin. The number of castes and subcastes among them is greater and the structural space over which they extend is also wider. The Non-Brahmin community does not have the same kind of corporate life which is present among the Brahmins. There are fewer occasions on which they all come together at one place. This corresponds to some extent to the comparative lack of spatial compactness among them and to their being socially more heterogeneous.

The architecture of Non-Brahmin houses shows a wider range of diversity than is found in the houses of the *agraharam*. In spite of differences in size and other details, the Brahmin houses are basically alike in construction. They are all made of brick and mortar, and the roofs are, at least partly, made of concrete or tiles. Some of the Non-Brahmin houses also are of this kind. There are others, however, which are more appropriately described as huts, being made primarily of mud and thatch. Huts of this kind are completely absent in the *agraharam*.

The distribution of castes and subcastes in the Non-Brahmin streets is basically similar to what one finds in the *agraharam*. There is no single street, or part of a street, which is exclusively inhabited by a particular caste. Streets here are not named after castes as is the practice in certain villages (cf. Gough, 1955, 1960). But castes and subcastes do tend to live in compact blocks. Here again the former distribution of population has, to some extent, been disturbed, although movements to and from the

Non-Brahmin streets have not been as extensive as in the case of the *agraharam*.

There are four principal streets in the Non-Brahmin quarters. These are Odatturai Street, Western Street, Pillayar Temple Street, and Eastern Street. The houses on these streets are all situated on the northern side of the *agraharam*. In addition there are certain clusters of houses situated around the western end of the *agraharam*, extending to the south as well as the north. There are also some shacks along the main road, which, as we have seen, runs parallel to the *agraharam* on its southern side.

Odatturai Street meets the *agraharam* at right angles, at its eastern end. Proceeding northwards along it from the point of intersection, one finds Non-Brahmin houses on either side; proceeding southwards, the same street meets the main road, again at right angles. Odatturai Street was at one time the place where boats used for crossing the Kaveri were kept. In those days neither this street nor the *agraharam* was inhabited as they are today. The first Brahmin house at the eastern end is really on Odatturai Street. The *agraharam* proper begins on the other side of this street and runs from east to west.

Proceeding along Odatturai Street, one comes to Western Street, which runs westward at right angles to it. All the houses on this street, as well as some on Odatturai Street around the point where the two meet, are affiliated to the *mukhasa* village of Mangudi to which reference has already been made. In all, there are 62 households belonging to Mangudi. These households constitute a compact block.

Proceeding further along Odatturai Street, one comes to a tri-junction. This is the point at which Odatturai Street, Pillayar Temple Street and Eastern Street converge. Pillayar Temple Street runs westward, almost in a straight line. Eastern Street runs in the opposite direction, but not in a straight line. It is the longest of the Non-Brahmin streets, but, nevertheless, is less than half the length of the *agraharam*. The houses of most of the important Non-Brahmins, including that of the *panchayat* president, are situated in Eastern Street.

The string of Non-Brahmin houses near the Perumal temple bears, on the whole, a shabbier appearance than the four streets referred to above. This is a less respectable part of the Non-

Brahmin quarters, and the people living here are mainly menials and domestic servants employed in the *agraharam*. The huts around the Shiva temple and the shacks on the main road have a similar character. In fact, the people of this area have a certain notoriety for rowdyism, thievery, and immoral traffic. Several of them are alleged to be the offspring of mixed and irregular unions. Broadly speaking, they represent the lowest strata of the Non-Brahmin population in the village. It should be noted that physically they are clearly separated from the main block of the Non-Brahmin population, which is concentrated in the four streets described above.

There is one Non-Brahmin house which requires special notice since it occupies a rather distinctive position physically as well as socially. This is the largest and in some ways the most conspicuous house in the village. It stands on the main road and has a fairly extensive garden, enclosed by walls, and is the only house in the village to have a front garden. This house is the seat of a Maratha family which has distant connections with the princely line of Tanjore. It is quite distinct in its appearance as well as its situation from both the Brahmin and the other Non-Brahmin houses. Today it has a rather dilapidated and unkempt appearance, although the spacious garden and the approach lined with crotons seem to bear witness to a more expansive past. The family is said to have owned at one time a little less than half the land in the village, almost all of which it has now lost. Socially the distance of this Maratha "Kshatriya" family from the local Non-Brahmin peasantry was and still is as great as, if not greater than, its distance from the Brahmins.

Attached to the outer compound wall are what seem to have been a number of outhouses. They are now occupied by some Non-Brahmin families, and the village post office is also located in one of them. These structures were formerly used as a kitchen and resthouse for pilgrims passing along the road. In fact, a substantial endowment, consisting of the house and land, was made by the Tanjore prince for religious and charitable purposes, and the Maratha family was placed here to exercise management and supervision.

It is probable that the Maratha house, along with its *chhattram*, or hospice, was in existence here even before the *agraharam* came into being. One finds such families stationed in several villages hereabout, occupying a more or less similar position in their social life. They were established largely during the latter half of Maratha rule in Tanjore. The *chhattram* at Sripuram ceased functioning many years ago, but the owner of the house is still referred to as *chhattrattappa* (*chhattram* and *appa*, "father").

V

The Adi-Dravida *cheris* have both physically and socially a distinct character of their own. The Adi-Dravidas are often regarded—particularly by Brahmins learned in the *shastras*—as being outside the pale of Hindu society. Judged in terms of the traditional *chaturvarna* scheme, they do in fact constitute what Hutton (1961) has designated as "exterior" communities. This is consistent with the fact that they are not permitted to reside in the heart of the village but only on its fringes, or far away from the Brahmin and Non-Brahmin streets.

The word *cheri* has a specific physical, social, and ritual connotation. It signifies a residential area, inhabited by Adi-Dravidas, entry into which causes pollution to the Brahmin. Even today no orthodox Brahmin would consider entering a *cheri*. Most of the Brahmin residents of Sripuram have never seen the inside of their *cheri,* although they have lived in the village all their life and the *cheri* is at a distance of only about a hundred yards from their street.

The prejudice against Brahmins' entering the *cheri* is, to some extent, reciprocal. There is a traditional belief among Adi-Dravidas that the entry of a Brahmin into the *cheri* will lead to ill luck. It is said that about fifty years ago if a Brahmin entered a *cheri,* the inhabitants would break their cooking pots (which in those days were exclusively earthenware). There is also a vague belief that such a visit causes sterility. Today, however, these ideas have lost their force, and there is at least one Brahmin in Sripuram who visits the *cheri* more or less regularly.

In all, there are six Adi-Dravida streets, or *cheris,* attached to Melur-Sripuram. These are not all in one place, but in three different places separated from each other by distances of half a mile to a mile. Only one of the six *cheris* is in Sripuram proper, in the sense that it is physically contiguous to the Non-Brahmin settlement there. The other settlements are in the midst of paddy fields, separated clearly from the main villages to which they are attached. The *cheris*, more often than not, are situated in a manner which emphasizes their social exclusion from the village, rather than their social identity with it.

The disposition of Adi-Dravida *cheris* differs in many ways from that of the main villages to which they are attached. Two *cheris* which physically are contiguous with each other and socially form a single unit may be attached to two revenue villages which are widely separated. For instance, about six furlongs to the west of Sripuram there are several *cheris*, some inhabited by Pallas and others by Paraiyas, and all these *cheris*, except one, belong to Neduveli village, which is associated for revenue purposes with one half of Peramur. The one exception, known as Kudidangi Pallacheri, is attached to Melur-Sripuram.

So distinct and separate are these *cheris* that sometimes a Brahmin resident of a village may not be clear as to which *cheris* are attached to his village, or to which village a particular *cheri* is attached. This lack of knowledge or awareness on the part of the Brahmin reflects an important social reality: that one's social perception is limited by the nature and intensity of one's social interactions. Once again the conclusion emerges that "the village" is socially not a clear-cut unit with well-defined boundaries, but that it means different things to different people.

Of the six Adi-Dravida streets referred to above, one is in Sripuram proper, one is adjacent to Neduveli, and the other four are found in a cluster not far away from the main settlement at Melur. It should be remembered that when a Brahmin or a Non-Brahmin speaks of Melur or Sripuram he normally excludes the two latter settlements and only occasionally includes the former. For the present we shall consider only the *cheri* at Sripuram, although in many important ways it is connected more closely with the other *cheris* than with the rest of Sripuram.

The Pallacheri at Sripuram runs in a straight line from east to west, with houses on either side of the street. It is situated on the northern fringe of the village, and is reached by a path which emerges at right angles from Eastern Street and meets it, also at right angles. At the eastern end of the *cheri* there is a road running southward and connecting with the main road, which runs from east to west, about a furlong to the south. Thus, one can reach the main road from the *cheri* directly without going through the Non-Brahmin streets, although the Pallas do use these streets according to their convenience. They are debarred only from passing through the *agraharam.*

The houses in the *cheri* evince homogeneity of physical character, like those in the *agraharam;* only, they represent the other end of the scale. They are built wholly or partly of mud and thatch and bear a general appearance of squalor. The surface of the street is uneven and full of puddles. Whereas in the *agraharam* one house follows another in an ordered sequence from east to west, here two or three huts are often huddled together, one behind the other.

There is a great shortage of houses and building space in the *cheri.* Not infrequently two or three families live in a single hut. There is constant complaint from the Pallas that a certain Brahmin *mirasdar* who owns a grove there does not dispose of it and enable them to build additional homes. There has been some organised attempt on their part to raise funds in order to expand the existing facilities for housing. Although Government has provisions for giving certain benefits in this regard, nothing concrete has so far been achieved. Some local leaders, in addition to the *panchayat* president, have been approached, and when the Minister for Co-operation recently visited the village, the matter was placed before him.

Socially also the Pallacheri has a homogeneous and corporate character such as, to some extent, is present in the *agraharam.* In fact, the social composition of the Pallacheri is even more homogeneous than that of the Brahmin street. Within the *cheri* people move about freely from one house to another and form the kind of informal groups which are common in the *agraharam.* There are numerous occasions on which all the members of the Pallacheri come together, as at the time of marriages or during temple festivals. Whereas the exclusiveness of the *agraharam* is somewhat tempered by the continual presence in it of Non-Brahmin servants, farm hands, and cartmen, the Pallas are more or less left to themselves in their *cheri.* Almost their only visitors are castemen from the other *cheris* in the village, or from other villages. There seems to be a greater measure of unity and solidarity in the Pallacheri than in any other quarter of the village.

There are, however, divisions even among the Adi-Dravidas, and these divisions are, in turn, reflected in the disposition of houses. The two main groups hereabout are the Pallas and the Paraiyas. The two communities almost always live in separate streets, and in this sense their social separation may be said to be greater than the social separation between the different Brahmin castes. In Sripuram and the villages around, this separation is further heightened by the fact that the Paraiyas are Christians.

In addition to the Pallacheri described above, there is a small and separate cluster of Paraiya huts. These are situated near a grove which stands towards the east between the Pallacheri and Eastern Street. There are only five households of Paraiyas here, leading a separate existence in their own settlement, with their own well and their own place of worship. In the *cheris* at Neduveli the Pallas and Paraiyas do not take water from each other's wells even in times of acute water shortage. This separation between the Pallas and Paraiyas, of which the Brahmins are well aware, is often quoted by the latter as a justification for keeping the Pallas in their place.

The Pallas are fairly unanimous in their view that no Paraiya can or should be allowed to live in their *cheri*. Within the Pallacheri, again, there are certain houses which stand somewhat apart from the main line of huts. These belong to the Pariyari, or barber, and the Vettiyar, or person who looks after the cremation ground. Both these occupations are considered degrading and a certain stigma is attached to them. In the eastern end of the Pallacheri, clearly separated from the main line of houses, is a hut which is inhabited by the solitary Chakkiliya family in the village. The Chakkiliyas as a caste are uncommon in these parts, and this hut is conspicuous even in the *cheri* by its shabby appearance and its clear separation from the Palla habitations.

In the discussion above an attempt has been made to give an account of the disposition of the different communities inhabiting Sripuram. We have tried to show that Sripuram is a unity in only a limited sense of the term. The manner in which the different houses are distributed reveals the existence of cleavages as well as unities. Three conclusions emerge from the facts which have been presented so far: (1) Sripuram as a whole constitutes a unit in a physical sense and, to a much lesser extent, in the social sense; (2) the primary cleavages within this unit subdivide it into the three more or less well-defined communities of Brahmins, Non-Brahmins, and Adi-Dravidas; and (3) each of these subdivisions, particularly the first and the last, is a unit in a much more fundamental sense than the village as a whole.

VI

It remains for us now to consider certain important public places in the village, such as the temples, reading rooms, and *panchayat* hall. These will have to be considered both from the point of view of their physical location and that of their social significance. Certain temples are—and, in the logic of things, can only be— situated in certain streets. Other public places, such as the *panchayat* hall, cannot be situated in the *cheri,* for instance, because this would automatically exclude the Brahmins from participation at meetings there.

There are about a dozen temples and shrines in the village. The principal ones are devoted to Vishnu, Shiva, Vinayakar, and Kali in various forms. Some of the temples are used almost exclusively by certain communities in the village. Some others serve a wider public, but are, nonetheless, associated specifically with one or another group of castes. No temple has the same meaning or serves the same purpose for all the castes in the village.

The Vishnu temple ministers to the needs of the *agraharam.* To a great extent the religious life of the Brahmins revolves around it. It has to be remembered that the majority of Brahmins in Sripuram are Shri Vaishnavas and that the Smartha Brahmins also generally worship Vishnu. Non-Brahmins do not come to the Vishnu temple, except for a few menials who carry the deity during processions, and the pipers and drummers. It is situated, appropriately, inside the *agraharam,* at its western end, where it dominates the entire Brahmin street.

The Shiva temple occupies a different position both physically and in the socio-religious life of the village. It is situated on the main road, away from the *agraharam,* to the west of the village site and slightly to its south. No Shiva temple would be situated inside an *agraharam,* far less an *agraharam* dominated by Shri Vaishnavas. In a sense the Shiva temple dominates the entire village. It is by far the tallest and most impressive structure in Sripuram. It is also the principal link between the old Sripuram and the new one. Its detached physical position makes it accessible to everyone, although Adi-Dravidas would not be welcome and would not normally go there. Very orthodox Iyengars do not enter the Shiva temple; in comparison with the Vishnu temple, it is neglected by the Brahmins. The Non-Brahmins, however, go to it freely and take part in its rituals.

The Elangkali temple also stands more or less detached from the village settlement. It is adjacent to and on the northeast of the Shiva temple. Elangkali is what is usually referred to as a "village deity" (see Gough, 1955, p. 47). Her temple, more than any other in the village, is open to every inhabitant. Even the Pallas are now admitted, although only into the outer compound. The Elangkali temple is typically the centre of Non-Brahmin religious activities, although Brahmins also worship here, and Non-Brahmins in their turn take part in organising worship at the Shiva temple.

In addition to the Elangkali temple, there are two other Kali temples in the village. Both are situated in the Pallacheri and consequently have a much more restricted congregation. The smaller of the two Kali temples stands at the western end of the *cheri* and faces the entire street. The larger one, which is also the older, is situated about twenty yards in front, and also faces eastward. Closely related to each other, these two temples together constitute the pivot around which public worship in the *cheri* revolves.

At the eastern end of the village, beyond the Non-Brahmin streets, there is a small shrine situated in a grove. This is devoted to Ellaiamman, a female deity guarding the boundaries of the village. Shrines to boundary deities, who are usually personified as women, are common in this area and are associated less with Brahmins than with Non-Brahmins. They are usually small and inconspicuous, and offerings are made to them only periodically. Neither physically nor socially do they occupy the same prominent position as the Shiva and Vishnu temples.

Temples to Vinayakar are usually small and inconspicuous, although they are very common, both in the villages and on the roadside. Vinayakar, or Pillayar, is worshipped alike by Shaivites and Vaishnavites, and by Brahmins and Non-Brahmins. There are half a dozen Vinayakar temples in the village, one or two of which are unused and in ruins. Two of them are situated on the main road, one near the eastern approach to the village, and the other to the west, facing the Shiva temple. The rest are situated in the Non-Brahmin streets.

In addition to Ellaiamman, there is a boundary deity specifically associated with the Pallacheri. This deity, known as Pechi, is placed in a small shrine at the eastern end of the *cheri*, whence it keeps watch over any malignant agency which may try to enter the street. This shrine and the two Kali temples are among the few structures in the *cheri* constructed mainly or wholly of brick and mortar.

The small cluster of Paraiya huts is dominated by a chapel which was built there some thirty years ago. The chapel is under the jurisdiction of the Roman Catholic parish priest at Thiruvaiyar. It is a simple structure, practically bare inside but for a crucifix and a lamp which is lighted every evening. The chapel is quite a common feature of Paracheris in this area where the Paraiyas are mostly Christians.

The three communities—Brahmin, Non-Brahmin, and Adi-Dravida—have separate places for the disposal of the dead. The Brahmins cremate their dead, and the entire *agraharam* is served by a single cremation ground, on the river bank and opposite the eastern end of the *agraharam*. The Non-Brahmins also cremate, but use a separate place, situated a little to the east of the Brahmin one and also on the river bank. The Pallas have recently taken up the practice of cremation instead of burial. Their cremation ground, however, is not on the river bank, but inland and near a pool of water. The Paraiyas bury their dead in a cemetery which is within the boundary of Thiruvaiyar.

Among other places of importance in the village is the *panchayat* room. The location of this centre, or rather, the recent change in its location is of particular importance. Until the 1940's the *panchayat* held its sittings in a makeshift structure adjacent to the Vishnu temple, at the western end of the *agraharam*. Up to this period the *panchayat* was dominated by the Brahmins, and political power in the village was concentrated in their hands. There were some Non-Brahmins members, but they were clearly of lesser importance, and Adi-Dravidas were excluded. Thus it was fitting that the *panchayat* should conduct its deliberations in the *agraharam*.

In the 1940's a profound change came about in the political structure of the village. Non-Brahmins came to dominate the *panchayat*, and since Independence the *panchayat* presidents have been Non-Brahmins. Power shifted from the *agraharam* to the Non-Brahmin streets (see chaps. v and vi). Along with this the location of the *panchayat* hall also shifted. Today the *panchayat* hall is a permanent structure located in Pillayar Temple Street in the Non-Brahmin quarters. Social life in the Brahmin and Non-Brahmin streets, as we have seen, tends to be autonomous to some extent. When important social or political meetings are held in the new *panchayat* hall, the majority of Brahmins find themselves automatically excluded.

Conspicuous among the mud huts in the Pallacheri is a comparatively new brick and mortar structure situated a little behind the bigger of the two Kali temples. It was built around 1952 and is the centre of the *sevai sangam* ("service society"), a newly created organisation among the Pallas which acts as a kind of *panchayat* (see chap. v). The hall of the *sevai sangam* is used for holding meetings of the *cheri panchayat* (which is different from the village *panchayat*) and also as a sort of clubhouse and gossip centre. Its use is confined to Pallas alone. Young men come and sleep here in the afternoons, as it is the only commodious hall in the *cheri*. It is here that important visitors to the *cheri* are entertained, if for no other reason that the shortage of space elsewhere.

Reading rooms (*padippaham*) are becoming an increasingly important feature of villages in this area. Their place in the social and political life of Sripuram will be examined in chapter v. Here it will suffice to describe their location in the village, and to mention that they serve as centres not only of "cultural" activities, but also of party political organisation. There are two reading rooms in the village, the Bharati *padippaham* and the Udayasuriyan *padippaham*. The former has loyalties to the Congress party, the latter, as its name indicates,[1] is a D.M.K. organisation. Both are situated, characteristically, in the Non-Brahmin streets, the D.M.K. centre in Odatturai Street and the other in Pillayar Temple Street.

The village school, by contrast, is situated in the *agraharam*. It was started in 1926, mainly through the initiative of a Brahmin resident of Sripuram, and it is still largely dominated by the Brahmins, although there are many Non-Brahmin and Adi-Dravida students. The school has three separate buildings, all at the eastern end of the *agraharam*. Two of these are used for holding classes; the other is used for the preparation of midday meals and as a hostel for a number of boarders. The location of the school in the *agraharam* enables boys of the lower castes to have access there, and this, as we shall see later, has the effect of partly lowering the physical barrier between Brahmins, Non-Brahmins, and Adi-Dravidas of the younger generation.

VII

In the preceding discussion some emphasis has been placed on internal divisions in the village as these are reflected in its physical structure. The cleavages most clearly represented are those of caste rather than of the economic or political systems. People belonging to the same group of castes (e.g., Brahmins) live together, but not necessarily people belonging to the same class (e.g., landowners). This is understandable because, at least in the village, a caste or group of castes constitutes a community, whereas this is rarely, if ever, true of a class. There is another point which has to be kept in mind. In the past the hierarchies of class and power were much more consistent with the cleavages of caste than they are today. (For example, the Brahmins constituted both the landowners and the traditional elite of the village; see chap. vi.) Such being the case, the settlement pattern then was consistent not only with the cleavages of caste, but also with those of class and power. Over the last several decades the class system and the distribution of power have acquired a more fluid charac-

---

[1] *Udayasuriyan,* or the rising sun, is the party emblem of the Dravida Munnetra Kazhagham (D.M.K.).

ter and have become, to some extent, dissociated from the structure of caste. The physical structure of the village has not meanwhile undergone any substantial change; it continues to reflect the primary cleavages of its traditional social structure.[2]

---

[2] In certain other villages, however, Non-Brahmin landowners have started buying houses in the *agraharam*. This has not happened yet in Sripuram.

Chapter III

The Caste Structure

It has been shown that the division of the village into a number of castes constitutes one of the most fundamental features of its social structure. In Hindu society, caste divisions play a part both in actual social interactions and in the ideal scheme of values. Members of different castes are, up to a point, expected to behave differently and to have different values and ideals. These differences are sanctioned by Hindu religion.

While some areas of social life in Sripuram have become relatively "caste-free," there are many others which continue to be governed by caste. The individual's position in the caste structure is fixed by birth and is, to this extent, immutable. Formerly birth in a particular caste fixed not only one's ritual status, but, by and large, also one's economic and political positions. Today it is possible to achieve a variety of economic and political positions in spite of one's birth in a particular caste, although the latter is still very important in setting limits within which choice in the former is possible.

The term "caste" itself requires some discussion. It has been used to mean different things by different people in a variety of situations. Indeed, it is doubtful whether much will be gained in clarity by giving to the word a single rigorous meaning at the outset. What people mean by caste in day-to-day life is different from the meaning it has in the traditional literature, or from what people consider to be its traditional and orthodox meaning. Sometimes by "caste" people mean a small and more or less localised group; at other times the same word is used to refer to a collection of such groups. Here we will see that this ambiguity in the use of the term reflects one of the basic features of the caste structure.

The English word "caste" corresponds more or less closely to what is locally referred to as *jati* or *kulam*. In addition to *jati* and *kulam,* many of the villagers, particularly the Brahmins, are familiar with the concept of *varna*. Although the terms *jati* and *varna* refer normally to different things, the distinction is not consistently maintained. *Varna* refers to one of the four main categories into which Hindu society is traditionally divided; *jati* refers generally to a much smaller group (see Srinivas, 1962, pp. 63–69). The English word "caste" is used to denote both, not only by foreigners but also by villagers who are familiar with English. It will be shown that there is no real contradiction in this, for the word *jati* has a series of meanings, and by extension it is applied to what, according to traditional usage, should be designated as *varna*. Thus, it is quite common for a person to say that such and such an individual is a Brahmin, or even a Kshatriya, by *jati*. Within a given context such usage is intelligible, and does not generally lead to ambiguity (see Béteille, 1964).

Some have tried to solve the problem by using the terms "caste" and "subcaste" to refer to primary divisions and their subdivisions. This is not altogether satisfactory, because the caste system is characterised by segmentation of several orders. Thus, if the Tamil Brahmins are referred to as a caste, then the Smarthas will be a subcaste, the Vadamas a sub-subcaste thereof, and the Vadadesha Vadamas a sub-sub-subcaste. To apply this usage consistently would be both difficult and tedious.

To begin with, caste may be defined as a small and named group of persons characterised by endogamy, hereditary membership, and a specific style of life which sometimes includes the pursuit by tradition of a particular occupation and is usually associated with a more or less distinct ritual status in a hierarchical system. These terms will be discussed at some length later because a certain measure of ambiguity is attached to the definition of each.

The caste system gives to Hindu society a segmentary character.[1] The population of Sripuram is divided into a large number of castes or *jatis*, each having a certain measure of autonomy. A caste may be seen as a segment occupying a more or less specific position in a system of segments (see Evans-Pritchard, 1940). The structural distance of one caste from another may be great or small, depending upon their mutual positions, which are fixed within broad limits. Thus, the structural distance of Vadama from Brihacharanam is smaller than its structural distance from Shri Vaishnava, which is smaller than its structural distance from any Non-Brahmin caste. This way of looking at the mutual positions of castes is fruitful only up to a point; beyond this, such positions are both ambiguous and subject to change over time.

It will be seen that just as the total system can be broken down into a large number of castes, these in turn can be grouped together into a few broad divisions. These primary divisions are of great sociological significance, and a consideration of their nature provides a good starting point for our analysis.

II

It has been pointed out earlier that Brahmins, Non-Brahmins, and Adi-Dravidas not only live in different parts of Sripuram, but also in some measure regard themselves as having separate identities. Historically they have occupied different positions in the economic structure of the village, and these differences continue to exist, although a certain amount of levelling down has taken place in the last three decades. Politically there is some identification between these sections and the ideologies of certain parties (see chap. vi). To the extent that traditional values continue to operate, the three sections occupy different positions in the ritual hierarchy, the Brahmins at the top and the Adi-Dravidas at the bottom.

Apart from occupying rather different positions in the economic, political, and ritual systems, the three groups of castes are in the popular mind associated with different qualities and attri-

---

[1] Cf. Dumont (1957*b*, p. 3): "a caste group cannot be considered as a self-contained whole—as a society in itself—but only as a segmentary, or structural, group in the entire system."

butes. These differences are sharpest between Brahmins and Adi-
Dravidas, while the Non-Brahmins occupy an intermediate
sphere which overlaps considerably with each of the other two.

In some ways the most striking difference between Brahmins
on the one hand, and Non-Brahmins and Adi-Dravidas on the
other, is in their physical appearance. This difference is summed
up in various popular sayings, one of which runs as follows:
Parppan karuppum paraiyan sehappum ahadu ("Dark Brahmins
and light Paraiyas are not proper"). In the popular image the
Brahmin is regarded not only as fair, but also sharp-nosed, and
as possessing, in general, more refined features. Although some
Non-Brahmins also have features of this kind, they are rare
among the cultivating and artisan castes who constitute the bulk
of Non-Brahmins in Sripuram. Among Adi-Dravidas fair skin-
colour is so conspicuous by its absence that normally a Brahmin
would not be mistaken for a Palla or a Paraiya.

These differences are of significance because fair skin-colour
and features of a certain type have a high social value not only in
Sripuram, but in Tamil society in general, as indeed in the whole
of India. The Brahmins are extremely conscious of their fair
appearance and often contrast it with the "black" skin colour of
the Kallas, or the Adi-Dravidas. A dark-skinned Brahmin girl is
often a burden to the family because it is difficult to get a husband for her.

Traditionally, fair skin-colour has been associated with the
"Aryans" from whom the Brahmins claim descent and with whom
they are now identified by leaders of certain separatist political
parties. The *gotra* system, which is an essential feature of Brahmin social structure, links each one of them by putative ties of
descent to one or another sage after whom the *gotra* is named.
(The *gotra* is an exogamous division whose members are believed, particularly among the Brahmins, to be agnatically descended from a saint or seer.) It is commonly believed that the
Brahmins of an earlier generation, like the sages who were their
forebears, were often endowed with *brahmatejas,* a quality which
gave to their appearance a peculiar glow and serenity. This is
frequently contrasted with the coarse and undistinguished features of the Non-Brahmins.

Among the Shri Vaishnavas, who constitute the majority of

Brahmins in Sripuram, the Vadagalai section is generally believed to be fairer than the Thengalai. It is often pointed out that a large number of Shri Vaishnavas have Non-Brahmin origins and were brought into the Brahmin fold through conversion by Ramanuja. Smarthas and Shri Vaishnavas frequently twit each other about the purity of their Brahmin blood. These claims and counter-claims are evidence of the high value placed on purity of blood and affiliation to a particular stock in the context of caste endogamy and ranking among the Brahmins.

Among the Non-Brahmins also certain castes have specific physical traits. In Sripuram, for instance, the Kallas are quite distinctive in appearance. They are tall, dark, and well built and are known (and feared) throughout the area for their physical prowess. It is not only his appearance, but also his carriage and bearing, which give a distinctive stamp to the typical Kalla in the village. One has to bear in mind that carriage, bearing, and facial expression often contribute as much to the physical identity of an individual or a group as do measurable somatic traits.

It seems probable that a particular upbringing and style of life leaves some impress on the appearance of people. A college-educated and urbanised Kalla, following a sedentary occupation such as the practice of law, has a different bearing and appears different from the generality of Kallas who are peasants and cultivators. He looks more "refined" and "cultivated." And refinement of a particular kind, both in appearance and behaviour, has a high social value among Brahmins. One of the Shri Vaishnavas in Sripuram often pointed out that a certain Kalla friend of his who is an advocate at Tanjore "looks different" from the Kallas in the village.

No doubt the popular belief that the Brahmins constitute a separate race is fallacious and will not bear examination from the anthropological point of view. But social movements and political ideologies are often based not on technically correct, but on popular conceptions, and to that extent the latter are real and require to be understood. The real physical differences of the Brahmins, and the popular belief that they constitute a separate race, have led to their being isolated socially and politically to a much greater extent in Tamilnad and South India as a whole than in the north.

There are also typical differences in physical appearance between Non-Brahmins and Adi-Dravidas, as, indeed, there are between the different Non-Brahmin castes. On the whole the Pallas and Paraiyas appear to be darker, shorter, and more broad-nosed than the Non-Brahmins, who, it must be remembered, constitute a very heterogeneous category both physically and culturally. These differences do not, however, have the same social significance as in the case of the Brahmins, for they have not generally been posed in racial terms or made the basis of any political ideology.

Dress also is in some ways distinctive of caste in the broader sense of the term. Among Brahmins, men are required by tradition to wear the eight-cubit piece of cloth or *veshti* after initiation. The traditional style of wearing the *veshti* by having the ends tucked at five places (*panchakachcham*) carries a ritual sanction among all Tamil Brahmins. Non-Brahmins or Adi-Dravidas, at least at Sripuram, do not wear the *veshti* in this way.

The Brahmins are rapidly giving up their traditional mode of dress. They now wear the four-cubit *veshti* by simply wrapping it around the waist, or they wear the eight-cubit *veshti* in this way without any *kachcham*. On ritual occasions such as marriage and *upanayanam* (initiation), however, they are required to wear the *veshti* in the traditional style. Temple priests also, at least while they are officiating, are required to wear the *panchakachcham*, as are priests who officiate at domestic ceremonies. In Sripuram there are about a dozen men, mostly past the age of fifty years, who normally dress in the traditional Brahminical style.

Differences between castes are carried further in the matter of women's dress. The principal garment used by all is a long piece of unsewn cloth known as the *podavai*, but there are important differences in the length of the cloth and in the manner in which it is worn. Among orthodox married Tamil Brahmin women the *podavai* is eighteen cubits in length and is worn with the *kachcham*, the ends being tucked in various ways. Non-Brahmin women do not usually have the *kachcham*, and among them the length varies between ten and twelve cubits, the garment generally reaching down to the ankles as with the Brahmins. Among the generality of Adi-Dravida women the *podavai* is considerably smaller in size and reaches just below the knee, leaving the legs uncovered.

Among Brahmin women especially, wearing the *podavai* in a specific way symbolises a particular culture or style of life. Minor distinctions of dress have been preserved with care and kept alive for generations, although, even in this, recent trends have been favouring a levelling down of differences. Tamil-, Telugu-, and Kannada-speaking Brahmin women have each their distinctive style of dress, and all these differences are in evidence even in a small village like Sripuram. Among Tamil Brahmins, again, a Shri Vaishnava woman will never wear her dress in the Smartha style, nor will a Smartha woman adopt the Shri Vaishnava mode.

Among Non-Brahmins also one finds in certain cases peculiarities of dress expressing the distinctive style of life of a particular caste. Thus, according to traditional usage, the Kalla women in Sripuram avoid wearing garments of dark blue or similar colours since this is thought to give offence to Karuppan, a deity who is worshipped particularly by members of this caste.

Today, however, there is a trend towards greater standardisation of dress among women. Styles which were distinctive of particular castes are ceasing to be so, or are disappearing entirely. Married Brahmin women are slowly giving up their traditional mode of dress and beginning to take to the twelve-cubit *podavai* worn without a *kachcham,* as is common among Non-Brahmin women. It is true that in Sripuram such women constitute a small minority, but it is a minority which is increasing. The new style of dress blurs distinctions not only between Smarthas and Shri Vaishnavas, but also between Brahmins and Non-Brahmins. Yet even when married Brahmin women take to wearing the shorter, twelve-cubit garment, on ritual occasions they dress in the manner traditional to their caste. The more elaborate dress is called *madi saru* ("pure garment").

Among Adi-Dravida women there seems to be a movement upwards, towards wearing longer garments like those worn by the Non-Brahmins. This is particularly true of the younger generation of Palla women in Sripuram. The older women continue to wear the shorter piece of cloth, especially while they work in the fields. The younger Adi-Dravida women have also started wearing blouses, whereas a generation ago the universal practice seems to have been to wear no separate upper garment. Thus in dress, and hence to some extent in outward appearance, differences between Non-Brahmin and Adi-Dravida women are tending to become smaller.

Whereas among Brahmin women the style of dress proclaims whether one is a Smartha or a Shri Vaishnava, the same purpose is served among men by the caste mark. Smartha men apply the *vibhuti,* which consists of three horizontal stripes made with consecrated ash, across the forehead and sometimes on other parts of the body as well. The *vibhuti* is an emblem of Shiva and its application has ritual significance. Similar ritual significance attaches among Shri Vaishnavas to the *namam,* which consists of a red (sometimes yellow) vertical stripe at the centre of the forehead, encased in a white U-shaped mark among the Vadagalai section and a Y-shaped mark among the Thengalai.

The *vibhuti* or the *namam* is also worn by certain Non-Brahmins according as they are Shaivites or Vaishnavites. In Sripuram there are several Shaivite Vellalas who apply the *vibhuti* more or less regularly. Hence the caste mark cannot serve as a satisfactory differentium, since it cuts across the Brahmin–Non-Brahmin division. Further, among Brahmins of the younger generation the wearing of the caste mark on ordinary occasions is falling into disuse.

It is clear that, although up to a point each subcaste, or caste, or group of castes maintains its distinctive identity, forces have been operating towards an ironing out of differences in dress and general appearance. In a large city like Madras it may be difficult to distinguish between a Brahmin and a Non-Brahmin, particularly if both are engaged in the same kind of occupation. But in a village such as Sripuram, in spite of the forces of secularisation and the general influence of mass-produced consumers' goods, broad distinctions are still maintained.

III

It would perhaps be an exaggeration to say that Brahmins, on the one hand, and Non-Brahmins and Adi-Dravidas, on the other, represent two cultures. Nonetheless one cannot but be impressed by the differences between them while examining their speech and language. In Tanjore District, particularly, Sanskrit has been a major influence on the Brahmins, both by way of enriching their thought and learning and by giving to their speech a particular character. It is well known that throughout Tamilnad Sanskritic scholarship has been a near monopoly of the Brahmins, while Non-Brahmins have specialised in Tamil studies (see Gough, 1955, pp. 38–39).

The Brahmins of Sripuram are heirs to a long tradition of Sanskritic learning, whereas among the Non-Brahmins no such tradition has existed. Among the Adi-Dravidas literacy itself is a new phenomenon and is as yet confined to only a few persons. Some of the Vellalas, at least, have been familiar for generations with the devotional literature in Tamil, and perhaps it is no accident that the only professional Tamil *pundit* or teacher in Sripuram is a Vellala. It should, of course, be pointed out that virtually all adult Brahmins are literate in Tamil, which is, in fact, the language of their speech. The important point, however, is that even today they seem to attach greater value to Sanskrit, although only a few of them have more than a smattering of it.

In Sripuram the Brahmins are alive to the fact that the flow of events renders it increasingly difficult to transmit through the family their tradition of Sanskritic learning, and that ultimately it may become extinct. They require their sons and daughters to take up the study of Sanskrit in school, although it may be an optional subject. One of their principal grievances against the present educational system is that Sanskrit does not occupy within it the position of eminence which, according to them, it should.

A few years ago an informal school was started in the *agraha-ram* with a view to imparting some elementary knowledge of Sanskrit to the children and thereby keeping alive an ancient heritage. The school sits in the evening for about an hour on the *payal* of one of the Brahmin residents who is a teacher in the Sanskrit College at Thiruvaiyar. He runs the school himself and charges only a nominal fee for the maintenance of petromax lanterns. The school is generally known as the *sahashranamam* class, but in addition to the *sahashranamam* (thousand names) of Vishnu, Lakshmi, and so on, other *slokas* or verses in Sanskrit are taught. Both boys and girls between the ages of four and fourteen years attend the school, but it is open only to the Brahmin children of the *agraharam*.

Brahmins themselves regard their familiarity with Sanskrit as a sign of refinement, and a very high social value is attached to it. It sometimes enables them to engage in subtle arguments about abstract matters, since Sanskrit has a rich philosophical idiom. Moreover, the language of ritual among the Brahmins is almost entirely Sanskrit. This ritual is extremely elaborate in nature, even if one ignores entirely the complex temple rites and takes into account only those rites which the individual Brahmin is required to perform daily, monthly, annually, and at various points in his life cycle.

There are minor distinctions of speech among Brahmins which the outsider, not familiar with the niceties of caste specialisation, is likely to miss. Thus, the Iyers normally say *rasam* for pepper-water, whereas the Iyengars have a special word, *sattumadu*. The Iyengars address the father's younger brother as *chittiya*, whereas among the Iyers he is called *chittappa*. The ceremony of washing the idol is known among Iyers as *abhishekham,* and among Iyengars as *thirumanjanam*. These distinctions, however slight they may appear, have been kept alive for generations, particularly in the vocabularies of kinship and ritual. Today there seems to be a tendency for words to be interchanged a little more freely and easily.

The Tamil which is spoken by the Non-Brahmin peasants of Sripuram is different both in vocabulary and accent from the speech of the Brahmins. This difference is much wider than the difference between Smarthas and Shri Vaishnavas. Adi-Dravidas in their turn have their own forms of intonation, and it is not difficult even for a Brahmin to distinguish an Adi-Dravida from a Non-Brahmin by his speech. As more and more Adi-Dravida children go to school and come into contact with both Non-Brahmin and Brahmin boys and girls, differences in speech tend to be levelled out, at least to some extent.

As against the comparatively simple and unsophisticated Tamil used by the Non-Brahmin peasantry, there is the trend towards a revival of Tamil in its pure or classical form. This trend has been associated with the Non-Brahmin movement, and today it is kept alive by the D.M.K., the Tamil Arasu Kazhagam, the Nam Tamizhar, and other parties and associations. Tamil of this variety is consciously de-Sanskritised, and it is often abstruse and difficult to comprehend. It has been given vitality through the speeches of the many eloquent D.M.K. leaders, and also in part through the films. The impact of this style on the Non-Brahmins of Sripuram has not been very significant, although the majority of them have been exposed to the influence of D.M.K. speeches as well as Tamil films.

The differential importance of the two languages, Sanskrit and Tamil, with regard to the styles of living of the Brahmins and Non-Brahmins, can be seen in the choice of personal names. Brahmins almost always have Sanskritic personal names. In a sense this is inevitable because names of men and women are chosen from among names of deities, and the major deities of the Brahmins, particularly the Shri Vaishnavas, are all Sanskritic. Non-Brahmins take their names from Tamil saints, local deities, and local heroes, as well as from certain popular Sanskritic deities. Among Brahmins, Shri Vaishnavas are more exclusive in their choice of personal names than Smarthas.

IV

Many of the important differences between Brahmins, on the one hand, and Non-Brahmins and Adi-Dravidas, on the other, are expressed in the sphere of rituals. Up to a point rituals can be regarded as standardised ways of expressing distinctive aspects of the style of life of a group or a category. Rituals serve to express in dramatic form not only the unity within a group, but also the cleavages between different sections of it. High points in the style of life of a particular community are often kept alive through ritual sanctions. Normally one group does not discard its particular rituals in favour of those of another unless it considers the style of life of the latter to be in some ways superior to its own.

Among the rituals which a Brahmin is regularly required to perform is one associated with the daily meal. This ritual, known as *pariseshanam*, should be performed both before and after the meal by every Brahmin male who has been initiated. It is a brief and simple rite involving the recitation mentally of certain Sanskrit verses and the movement of the right hand in a prescribed manner. Non-Brahmins do not perform this ritual and are, in general, not conversant with it.

A story which is often related by the Brahmins in Sripuram tells how a Non-Brahmin who was trying to masquerade as a Brahmin was found out. The Non-Brahmin had sat down to eat a ceremonial meal along with the Brahmins, a thing which would never be permitted unless he were to conceal his identity. Before commencing the meal, the Non-Brahmin, in imitation of the Brahmins, began performing the *pariseshanam*. But instead of moving his right hand in the clockwise direction as should be done, he moved it counterclockwise. His identity was immediately revealed, and he was beaten and thrown out of the gathering.

The common meal has an extremely important social and ritual significance in Hinduism. When a large number of people gather together for a meal, ritual undertones are invariably associated with it. The common meal expresses symbolically both the unity of those who eat together and the cleavages between those who are required to eat separately. Ritual separation, having been elaborated to a high degree in Hindu society, serves to maintain the cleavages within the caste system. Generally two castes will not interdine unless the structural distance between them is small. Some castes are more exclusive in their commensal restrictions than others.

Broadly speaking, the higher the status of a caste, the more rigid it is in the matter of accepting food from the others. Thus, Brahmins do not accept cooked food from Non-Brahmins or Adi-Dravidas, although both of the latter accept such food from the Brahmins. Again, Non-Brahmins do not accept cooked food from Adi-Dravidas, although the latter accept it from them. This principle, however, is by no means a universal measure for the assessment of caste rank. Thus, orthodox Shri Vaishnavas do not accept food from Smarthas, or even sit for meals along with them, but the Smarthas are far less rigid in the matter of accepting food from the Shri Vaishnavas; yet it must not be inferred from this that Smartha Brahmins are lower in rank.

An examination of the manner in which the rules of commensality operate among the Brahmins of Sripuram will help us to gain some understanding of the nature of structural distance between different segments in the caste system. Since similar principles are operative in the case of Non-Brahmins and Adi-Dravidas, their part in the two latter cases will be indicated only briefly.

The Iyengars, who constitute the majority of Brahmins in Sripuram, are admitted to be the most exclusive in the matter of commensality. When a feast takes place in the *agraharam* on account of birth, marriage, death, or some other occasion for ceremony, normally only Brahmins are invited to the meal. A few Non-Brahmins may be called, particularly if they are related to the family as servants or tenants, but they are given food separately in the backyard after the Brahmin guests have been served. Otherwise, particularly during marriage, a few influential Non-Brahmins may come to see the girl, and they are given betel leaves, areca nuts, bananas, and coconuts, but not food in the proper sense of the term which includes cooked rice in one form or the other. Generally speaking, a Brahmin wedding at Sripuram, and the attendant feast, is a Brahmin affair; Non-Brahmins have very little to do with it, and still less Adi-Dravidas.

Although Non-Brahmins are not generally invited to participate in feasts held in the *agraharam,* they may be invited under certain circumstances. Even in such cases there is no question of their eating along with the Brahmins; separate arrangements have to be made for them and they are served after the Brahmins, including the cooks, have been fed. Recently a marriage took place at Sripuram of a girl of that village. The groom's father had written in advance from Pudukkottai to the bride's people, saying that he would bring some Non-Brahmins with his party and that arrangements were to be made for their being fed. Normally, of course, such intimation would not be necessary, because the groom's party in the case of Brahmins is generally made up only of Brahmins.

Brahmins, on their part, do not dine at Non-Brahmin weddings. Generally they do not even attend, although the wedding may be taking place in the next street. If they go, they are given betel leaves, areca nuts, and fruits—things which are not regarded as having any element of pollution attached to them. Orthodox Brahmins, particularly among Shri Vaishnavas, do not accept cooked food of any kind, including coffee, from Non-

Brahmins. Some of the more "progressive" and younger Brahmins, however, accept coffee and snacks when they visit their Non-Brahmin friends at Tanjore and elsewhere. For one thing, such Non-Brahmins, being town bred, are closer to them in their style of living than the peasants of Sripuram, and for another, social restrictions are more stringently observed in one's own village than outside.

When an important ceremony such as marriage takes place in the *agraharam,* it is obligatory on the part of the host to invite every family in the *agraharam* to the feast which forms a part of the occasion. Today, most of the Brahmins sit together and generally no distinction is made in the matter of serving. A generation or so ago, however, at wedding and other feasts Smarthas and Sri Vaishnavas sat in separate rows, although they were served at the same time. The fact that Smarthas and Shri Vaishnavas of the younger generation freely interdine is another indication of the lessening of structural distance between the two communities to which reference was made in the preceding chapter.

Orthodox Shri Vaishnavas, particularly of the older generation, still do not sit along with Smarthas on such occasions, nor do they accept cooked food of any kind, or even water, from the hands of Smartha Brahmins. Such people are known usually as *vaidic* (orthodox) in contrast to the ordinary people who are called *laukic* (lay or secular). The *vaidic* Shri Vaishnavas perform all the ritual duties of the Brahmin strictly according to tradition; their daily life is a continuous round of rituals. They wear the *veshti* with *panchakachcham,* keep the tuft or *kudumi,* and, among the Vadagalai section, usually wear a yellow *namam* instead of the red one worn by *laukic* people. The distinction between *vaidic* and *laukic* does not, however, correspond to distinctions specific to the caste system, because in the same family one brother may be *vaidic* while another is *laukic.*

Although the two categories are not endogamous, and although one's status as *vaidic* or *laukic* is not entirely ascribed by birth but depends to some extent on personal choice, the distinction has one aspect which is usually associated with the caste system. Generally *vaidic* Iyengars do not eat in public or with *laukic* people, even though the latter may be of their own caste. They do not normally eat food cooked by anyone but their own close relatives, and if one has undergone the important *baranya-sam* rite, he usually refuses food cooked by anyone but himself or his wife.

In examining the rules of commensality we find that the whole of society is broken up into segments, each segment forming a unit within which commensality is more or less freely allowed. In the broadest sense, the Brahmins together constitute such a segment, since commensality is by and large confined within it so far as the individual member is concerned. The broad Brahmin category is further segmented into Smarthas and Shri Vaishnavas, and for the orthodox, and for a considerable number of people in the older generation, the bonds of commensality often stop short at the boundary of each of these subdivisions. The Smarthas are further segmented into Vadama, Brihacharanam, and so on, but segmentation at this level does not seem, at least in the recent past, to have been associated with commensal restrictions.

Commensal restrictions go hand in hand with a certain speciali-sation of food habits which has been carried to a high degree by the Brahmins. Shri Vaishnavas, for instance, make use of silver utensils to a much greater extent than the others. In the Hindu scheme of values silver is considered to be, relatively speaking, "pollutionproof"; in other words, the pollution attached to a utensil by another person eating or drinking out of it can be more easily removed if it is made of silver rather than bell metal, aluminium, or stainless stell. Orthodox Shri Vaishnavas offer water to their Smartha guests in silver tumblers and food in silver plates. Smarthas are generally less particular about the rigidities of pollution.

In the kind of food eaten also there is a good deal of variation. All Tamil Brahmins are vegetarians, and the eating of meat, fish, or eggs is considered polluting. The Adi-Dravidas eat meat of various kinds and also fish and eggs. Non-Brahmins show a wide range of variation. Most of them in Sripuram eat meat of certain kinds, although not regularly. A few of the Shaivite Vellalas do not eat meat at all, and some avoid eating it on particular days. The eating of meat or otherwise among the Vellalas of Sripuram cannot be exactly identified with caste since it is largely a matter of personal choice, although there are some Vellalas who refrain from eating meat as a group.

Differences in food habits, which are so clear between the broad Brahmin, Non-Brahmin, and Adi-Dravida divisions, are also perceptible, although on a reduced scale, between the smaller subdivisions. Thus, among Adi-Dravidas, the Paraiyas eat beef, or did so until recently, whereas the Pallas refrain from beef, but eat pork. In Sripuram the Pallas not only do not interdine with the Paraiyas, but do not take water from the Paraiyas' wells or allow the Paraiyas to use theirs; this seems to be the general practice in the area as a whole.

The avoidance of meat by Brahmins, of pork by Vellalas, and of beef by Pallas has ritual sanctions. Sometimes, however, food habits are specialised along caste lines without any apparent ritual basis. Vegetarian food among Non-Brahmins has a different taste from that of the Brahmins, being generally more heavily spiced and hotter. Coffee is the most popular beverage among Brahmins, but Non-Brahmins, both in their homes and in restaurants, show a preference for tea. This is only partly explained by the fact that tea is less expensive.

V

We have seen that differentiation in styles of living has been developed to a very high degree within the caste system. Not only are there differences separating Brahmins from Non-Brahmins, but differences among Brahmins separate Shri Vaishnavas from Smarthas and, among Shri Vaishnavas, Vadagalai from Thengalai. The entire social world of Sripuram is thus divided and subdivided so as to constitute a segmentary structure in which each segment is differentiated from the other in terms of a number of criteria, major and minor. Further, in this structure the segments are not all equally separated from each other, but some are closer together and others further apart. For instance, the distance between Vadagalai and Thengalai Iyengar is smaller than the distance between either of them and any Non-Brahmin segment.

It is beyond the scope of the present study to give an exhaustive account of all the ways in which the different castes differ from each other, or to consider in any detail all the different segments which constitute the social system of Sripuram. We have attempted to give, therefore, only a broad survey of general differences in styles of living, and to pursue the account in some detail only with regard to one group of castes, the Brahmins. Differentiation among Non-Brahmins and Adi-Dravidas follows a similar pattern which it would be tedious and repetitious to work out in their case also.

In the agrarian economy of Sripuram the three categories— Brahmin, Non-Brahmin, and Adi-Dravida—have occupied rather different positions traditionally and are continuing to do so, by and large, even now. Very broadly speaking, one can characterise the Brahmins as landowners, the Non-Brahmins as cultivating tenants, and the Adi-Dravidas as agricultural labourers. This characterisation highlights only the typical positions. It holds true particularly with regard to Brahmins and Adi-Dravidas. Among the Non-Brahmins it admits of numerous exceptions since there are both landowners and agricultural labourers among them, and also there are Non-Brahmins of artisan and servicing castes who do not directly engage in agriculture.

Not all Brahmins are landowners, nor are all landowners Brahmins. The typical Brahmin in Sripuram is, nonetheless, a *mirasdar,* and it is he who sets the pattern for others to follow. In addition to landownership, Brahmins traditionally have engaged in various priestly functions, either as domestic priests or as temple priests. In Sripuram, however, the majority of Brahmins have been *mirasdars* devoted to the pursuit of learning and have not engaged in priesthood as a profession or a means of livelihood. There are today only three families in the *agraharam* which have priesthood as the principal source of livelihood.

Brahmins in general can be classified into three broad categories according to their calling and social position. The first category includes those who have been traditionally associated with the pursuit of learning and have lived on grants made by princes and patrons. These include the Smarthas proper and the

Shri Vaishnavas. The term "Vedic Brahmin" will be applied to this category, although the choice is not altogether a happy one.[2] The second category is made up of those who act as domestic priests for the Non-Brahmins; they are known as Panchangakkarans. The Panchangakkaran Brahmins in this area are Telugu-speaking. It should be emphasized that the Vedic Brahmins (the Shri Vaishnavas and the Smarthas proper) do not act as domestic priests for Non-Brahmins—at least, not in this area. The third category comprises temple priests or Archakars; it is made up of Kurukkals, or priests who officiate at Shiva temples, and Bhattachars, or those who officiate at Vishnu temples.

These three categories of Brahmins constitute three endogamous divisions, each with further subdivisions. It is important to recognise the differences in status and position between them. The Vedic Brahmins are more or less unanimously acknowledged as being higher in rank than the two other categories of Brahmins. They are not dependent for their livelihood on the good will of the Non-Brahmin peasantry in the same way as the Panchangakkarans and, to some extent, the Kurukkals and Bhattachars. Their economic position, derived as it often is from the prince, or the state, gives them a certain independence and enables them to be more or less detached from the social and ceremonial world of the Non-Brahmins.

When a Shri Vaishnava or Smartha *mirasdar* attends a Non-Brahmin wedding in the village, if he does so at all, he goes as a superior and as an honoured guest. The Panchangakkaran, on the other hand, is at least partly in a position of dependence; he has to earn his livelihood by attending to Non-Brahmins on occasions of birth, marriage, and death. No wonder he is looked down upon by the Shri Vaishnavas and Smarthas! The temple priests, or Archakars, are also in a position of dependence, although not as much as the Panchangakkarans. Their earnings come in some part from the offerings of Brahmin as well as Non-Brahmin devotees.

The overwhelming majority of Brahmins in Sripuram belong to the "Vedic" category. There are only two families of temple priests, one serving the Vishnu temple in the *agraharam* and the

---

[2] As an alternative I have thought of the term *"mirasdar* Brahmin," which seems to be equally unsatisfactory.

other serving the Shiva temple at Melur as well as the Kali temple at Sripuram. (The worship of the Shiva temple at Sripuram was traditionally vested in the second family, but the office was transferred to one of the priests of the Thiruvaiyar temple owing to certain irregularities on the part of the previous incumbent.) There are no Panchangakkarans residing at Sripuram. The Non-Brahmins of the village get the services of *purohits,* or domestic priests, from Thiruvaiyar. Further, the Bhattachar at Sripuram has very little direct connection with the Non-Brahmins, since the Vishnu temple where he serves caters almost exclusively to the *agraharam.* Only the Kurukkal is, to some extent, tied up with the religious life of the Non-Brahmins, and this by virtue of his office as priest of the Kali temple, where Non-Brahmins come to offer worship more often than Brahmins.

The Brahmin has by tradition and scriptural injunction a number of roles: pursuit of learning; acceptance of alms; ministration to the spiritual needs of the populace. Although these roles may be combined in a single person, this is not always the case. The image of the Brahmin in the popular mind is of a person who lives by ministering to the religious needs of people. This image, as we have seen, is rather divorced from the real position of the Brahmins in Sripuram. In this village today there is only one Brahmin who acts as a *purohit.* But he ministers only to the religious needs of the *agraharam,* and only to the majority of Shri Vaishnavas, not to all the members of the *agraharam.* The Smarthas as well as certain other Shri Vaishnavas have *purohits* from among their own subcaste living at Thiruvaiyar and Tanjore.

The Vedic Brahmins of Sripuram do not today live by scholarship, although many of them can trace their descent from persons who did so in the past and were endowed with property for the purpose. Once a Brahmin scholar acquired property, it was handed down from generation to generation and the descendants became *mirasdars* by inheritance of ancestral property. It was not strictly obligatory on their part to keep up the family tradition, although many of them did so in practice. Thus, at the beginning of this century the Brahmins of Sripuram included a number of Sanskrit scholars pursuing their family traditions, and most of them owned at least a few acres of land. In course of the last sixty years the movement of population in and out of the *agraharam* and the sale of land by many Brahmins have reduced the number of *mirasdars* among them and, to some extent, disturbed the occupational homogeneity of the *agraharam*.

Today many Brahmins in the *agraharam* have taken up what may be considered new occupations. There are several clerks and schoolteachers among them. But one can easily see that in the choice of new occupations they have retained a certain continuity with the past and have not departed significantly from it. By and large, the most important element in their style of living has been preserved in their new occupations. No Brahmin has taken to any manual work in the real sense of the term. There is one person who has taken a job as a mechanic in a transport undertaking, but this is a recent occurrence and is regarded as exceptional.

Non-Brahmins, on the other hand, engage in various kinds of manual work. In Sripuram there are no big Non-Brahmin landowners, although there are absentee landlords among the Non-Brahmins living at Thiruvaiyar and Tanjore. The principal cultivating castes among the Non-Brahmins are the Vellalas, Padayachis, and Kallas. Most of them are directly engaged in cultivation in one form or another. There is no ritual rule which prohibits the use of the plough by them as in the case of Brahmins; in fact, using the plough is their traditional occupation. There are some fairly prosperous Vellala and Kalla landowners who do not themselves till the soil, but supervise the work of agriculture. This practice, however, is exceptional rather than general; the Non-Brahmin cultivator in Sripuram adopts it only when he has acquired a good bit of land, and generally after he has passed a certain age.

In addition to these moderately well-to-do Vellala owner-cultivators, there are a few others who have taken to nonmanual occupations. These include the Tamil *pundit* referred to earlier, and a few shopkeepers and clerks. Up to now the adoption of these occupations has been exceptional among the Non-Brahmins of Sripuram, and it does not appear to have significantly affected their styles of living. There is only one Non-Brahmin family which is significantly different from the others in this regard. This is the Maratha family which owned at one time a good proportion of the land in Sripuram and whose members in their ways and habits are clearly *mirasdars* rather than peasants.

The Non-Brahmins of Sripuram also include artisan castes such as Potters and Carpenters, and servicing castes such as Barbers and Washermen. The artisan castes do not all perform their traditional occupation today. But manual work enters as an important component in their style of living in the large majority of cases. Finally, there are many Non-Brahmins who are engaged as cartmen, masons, and labourers of one kind or another within and outside the village.

If manual labour plays an important part in the lives of Non-Brahmins, it does so to an even greater extent among the Adi-Dravidas. The Pallas not only engage in manual work, but their work in general is nonspecialised and unskilled, and less prestige is attached to it than to the work of the Non-Brahmin artisans. Occupations are graded by people in a more or less conscious manner, and the more degrading tasks such as hoeing, digging, and carrying earth are reserved for Adi-Dravidas. Although there is a good deal of overlap between the work of Non-Brahmins and Adi-Dravidas, one can say, with some simplification, that the typical Non-Brahmin peasant in Sripuram is a sharecropper or a cultivator, whereas the typical Adi-Dravida is an agricultural labourer.

Occupation, however, is only one component, although an important one, in the style of life of a people. It has to be remembered that apart from the two families of temple priests there are no significant differences in traditional occupation among the Brahmins of Sripuram. Further, the new occupations adopted by them maintain a certain continuity with the past and, seem to be more or less equally accessible to all varieties of Brahmins in the village. In spite of this, there are many differences among them, reflected particularly in their religious culture.

It should be made clear that social differentiation among Brahmins has been largely a feature of the traditional structure, and that these differences in Tamilnad were intimately associated with sectarian affiliation. Recent currents of westernisation and secularisation are partly breaking down these traditional differences, and sectarian loyalties tend to become weaker and be subsumed under loyalties of a wider kind. The Shri Vaishnava of the present generation is no longer, like his ancestor, a strict follower of the rules of his sect to the exclusion of all other principles of worship.

The Brahmins of Sripuram represent three language groups: Kannada, Telugu, and Tamil. The Kannada and Telugu Brahmins use somewhat corrupt forms of their respective languages when speaking at home; for other purposes they use Tamil. It is important to emphasize the linguistic and cultural diversity of the Brahmins, because it highlights an important aspect of their position in the social structure. The Brahmins as a group have been far more mobile than other groups, and a Brahmin caste has generally a much wider territorial extension than a Non-Brahmin caste. In the traditional system the Brahmins often moved from one region to another to settle on land granted to them by a particular king or prince. Connections were often maintained across very wide distances. Thus, some of the Tamil Brahmins of Sripuram have kinsmen in Mysore who settled there many generations ago on land given to them by the Mysore king. Some Telugu Brahmins who were granted land in Sripuram have relatives in Andhra Pradesh whom they visit to this day.

There is only one household of Kannada-speaking Madhva Brahmins in Sripuram. This household settled in Sripuram only about fifteen years ago, although the ancestors of the present head of the household had lived in Tanjore District for a number of generations. There are fourteen households of Telugu Brahmins, belonging to several subdivisions. The Telugu Brahmins are all Smarthas and have many things in common with the Tamil Smarthas, although there are minor differences in their social and ceremonial life. In addition, they have separate *purohits* or domestic priests to serve their religious needs.

The Tamil Brahmins of Sripuram are divided into two main groups: Smarthas and Shri Vaishnavas. Sometimes the Kurukkals are included in the broad category of Smarthas, although there are important differences between them and the Smarthas properly so called. Similarly, the Bhattachar may, for certain purposes, be included in the broad category of Shri Vaishnavas. Having given earlier some account of the occupational and other characteristics of the Kurukkals and Bhattachars, we shall not say anything further about them for the time being, particularly in view of the fact that there is only one family of each in the village.

Some indications have already been given of differentiation between Smarthas and Shri Vaishnavas. It seems clear that in its origin the difference was essentially doctrinal and sectarian. Other important differences developed, however, in the course of time. Today sectarianism among the Brahmins is decidedly on the wane. Intellectually there is a greater emphasis on the unity of Hinduism and the Brahminical way of life. Side-by-side with this, social differentiation between Smarthas and Shri Vaishnavas, and the structural distance between them, has been lessening.

The Smarthas, or those who follow the *smritis*, are affiliated to the eighth-century monistic philosopher Shankaracharya. Doctrinally they assert the unity of the individual soul (*jivatman*) and the cosmic soul (*paramatman*). In their worship they give a place to both Shiva and Vishnu, as well as to other deities in the Hindu pantheon. In addition to various Sanskrit religious texts, particularly those of Shankaracharya, they accept the authority of the Thevaram and the Thiruvachagam, the works of the Tamil *nayanmar* saints. The general term "Iyer" is usually applied to Smartha Brahmins as against the Shri Vaishnavas, who are referred to as Iyengars.

In Tamilnad the Smarthas greatly outnumber the Shri Vaishnavas. The Shri Vaishnava are not only a much smaller community, but they also seem to have come into existence at a later date. Doctrinally the religion of the Shri Vaishnavas is nourished by two different streams. On the one hand are the philosophical writings in Sanskrit of Ramanuja, the twelfth-century protagonist of "qualified" monism, and his followers; on the other are the devotional songs or Prabandhams, in Tamil, of the various *azhwars* or devotees of Vishnu.

The range of deities worshipped by Shri Vaishnavas is much more limited than that of the Smarthas. Vishnu is the role deity in the Hindu pantheon to whom they offer their total allegiance. Along with Vishnu, of course, goes the worship of his consort Lakshmi. Vishnu is worshipped in various forms; among his many *avatars,* or incarnations, the most popular are Rama and

Krishna, and also, to some extent, Narasimhan. An important place in the cycle of Vishnu cults is occupied by Garuda, the mythical bird-carrier of Vishnu. Hanuman occupies a niche in many Vishnu temples as a model of pure devotion to his master Rama.

In addition to Vishnu, his consort Lakshmi, and his mythical devotees Garuda and Hanuman, Shri Vaishnavas also offer worship to the different *azhwars* who were devotees of Vishnu in this world. Images of one or more *azhwars* are often found in Vishnu temples, and the birthdays of *azhwars* are ritual occasions among Shri Vaishnavas, both in the temple and in the home. The importance of the *azhwars,* however, is not equally great among all sections of Shri Vaishnavas, more emphasis being placed on their worship by the Thengalai section than the Vadagalai.

It is necessary to highlight the exclusive nature of Shri Vaishnava religion because it has important structural implications. It had in the past built a wall between them and the Smarthas and, to some extent, all other Brahmins. Not long ago there used to be bitter conflicts between Smarthas and Shri Vaishnavas, not only in the village, but in the region as a whole. These conflicts were often doctrinal in their basis, but numerous other factors also crept in. Their memory, although somewhat blurred today, continues to keep alive the separation between the two communities.

In traditional society the cycle of ceremonial activities played a very important part in the social life of the Brahmins. The temple was the pivot around which many of the ceremonials revolved. This position, largely, it still holds. A Shri Vaishnava keeps himself away from all temples other than those devoted to Vishnu. An orthodox Shri Vaishnava of an earlier generation would, on no account, enter a Shiva temple, where many of the important religious and ceremonial activities of the Smarthas (and also the Non-Brahmins) are held. There is a saying among the Shri Vaishnavas that one should not enter a Shiva temple even when pursued by an enraged elephant.

Shri Vaishnavas of the younger generation are increasingly growing alive to the fact that the rigid sectarianism of their forefathers is no longer in keeping with the atmosphere of the time. There seem to be two factors which work towards a lessening of exclusiveness on their part. First, the recent trend in Hinduism has been towards a synthesis of the different doctrines at the ideological level. This has been partly due to the influence of the West, which has also ushered in a certain measure of secularisation. The second unifying force has been the Non-Brahmin movement, which has created in many Brahmins the feeling that unity among them is a necessary condition for their survival.

Today in Sripuram it is no longer unthinkable for an Iyengar to enter the Shiva temple, although the younger people go there only occasionally and the older and orthodox never. History was created in the village a few years ago when a much respected Iyengar agreed to be on the committee for renovating the Shiva temple. This person, who has had college education at Madras and has been considerably influenced by Western thought, decided to make a break with the past in spite of the warnings of his more orthodox kinsmen. Characteristically, he justified his action by saying that divisions between Vaishnavas and Shaivas are of comparatively recent origin and therefore do not form a part of Hinduism in its pristine form.

Smarthas are by principle more liberal in their worship than Shri Vaishnavas. They venerate both Shiva and Vishnu, although Shiva is perhaps given greater importance. There is no rule among Smarthas against the worship of Vishnu. In fact, Shankaracharya himself is credited with having composed a hymn in praise of Govindan, who represents an aspect of Vishnu. Among Western-educated people there is a tendency to characterise Iyengars as Vaishnavas and Iyers as Shaivas. This is incorrect in the case of the Iyers, whose allegiance to Shiva is not in principle of the same kind as the allegiance of the Iyengars to Vishnu.

Although it can be said that Smarthas venerate Shiva and Vishnu in almost equal degree, this may not be true in a given structural situation. In Sripuram, Smarthas and Shri Vaishnavas have lived together for generations, and it has not always been a case of peaceful coexistence. The numerically preponderant Shri Vaishnavas have tended to run things their own way, particularly in the management of the Vishnu temple, which is the temple of the *agraharam* as a whole. In the 1880's there was a dispute over this temple between Smarthas and Shri Vaishnavas, and the dispute was taken to the courts. Even today the charge is made sometimes by Smarthas that the attitude of Shri Vaishnavas is arrogant and overbearing.

Until fairly recently several Smarthas refused to participate in the activities of the Vishnu temple as a retaliation for like behaviour on the part of Shri Vaishnavas with regard to the Shiva temple. One prominent member of the Smartha community, who died recently, is said to have spent his leisure hours in lengthy tirades against the Shri Vaishnavas. Since he was learned in three languages—Tamil, Sanskrit, and English—he could more than hold his own against the Shri Vaishnava elders in asserting that Shankaracharya was superior to Ramanuja, and Shiva to Vishnu.

Today the process of mutual separation has been reversed, and Smarthas and Shri Vaishnavas have come closer together. But although the element of intolerance has been reduced, there are still important differences of emphasis which affect differentially their styles of living.

The Shri Vaishnavas are themselves divided into two more or less endogamous subdivisions, the Vadagalai and the Thengalai sections. Members of these sections generally marry among themselves, although within the last two generations there have been intermarriages between them in Sripuram. Today, however, the Thengalai section is a very small minority in the village, being represented by only two households in addition to that of the Bhattachar, or temple priest, who also belongs to this section. In the previous century there were considerably more Thengalai people in Sripuram. Many have moved out since then.

Doctrinal and ritual differences between Vadagalai and Thengalai are smaller than those between Smartha and Shri Vaishnava. This enables social relations to develop more easily between them. Thus, marriages between Vadagalai and Thengalai, although infrequent, have taken place in Sripuram. No marriage has taken place in the village between a Smartha and a Shri Vaishnava. The idea of such a union would, certainly, meet with great disfavour on both sides. In contrast, at Sripuram a Thengalai priest officiates at the Vadagalai temple and a Thengalai youth who is being trained to officiate as family priest in the village already assists at marriage and other ceremonies in Vadagalai households. No Smartha priest could conceivably be called to officiate at a Shri Vaishnava wedding.

As a group, the Vadagalai Shri Vaishnavas of Sripuram are further segmented in terms of affiliation to one or another *jiyar,* or preceptor. There are certain important rites such as *samasaranai* and *mantropadesham* which have to be undergone by every true Shri Vaishnava, and which are required to be administered by a particular preceptor, who is usually at the head of a regional organisation known as *madam* or *ashramam.* Affiliation to one or another of these organisations creates bonds between people, and such affiliation is usually transmitted through the family. Most of the Vadagalai Iyengars of Sripuram are affiliated to the Ahobila *madam,* although some are affiliated to the Andavan *ashramam* and some are Swayamacharya (i.e., they have their own preceptors within the family and are not affiliated to any organisation).

The affiliations just described do not have much structural significance, at least not today. Intermarriage and commensality are freely allowed between members having different affiliations, although preferential kin marriage tends to restrict such unions in actual practice. Sometimes an individual may change his affiliation to a particular organisation on his own initiative. Thus, some of the Swayamacharya people, not having anyone in their family qualified or willing to act as a preceptor, have affiliated themselves to the Ahobila *madam.*

Divisions among the Smartha Brahmins are more numerous and elaborate. This is partly because the Smarthas as a whole constitute a much larger unit than the Shri Vaishnavas. There is, however, some ambiguity about the use of the term "Smartha." Kurukkals, or Shaivite temple priests, are included among them by some (see Thurston, 1909, I, 334), but in Tanjore District it is customary to regard the Kurukkals—and also the Panchangakkarans—as being different from the Smarthas proper. The latter are subdivided into four principal sections, although certain other sections are also included elsewhere. The four principal sections are Vadama, Brihacharanam, Astasahashram, and Vattiman (see Gough, 1960, p. 16).

The Tamil Smarthas of Sripuram belong mostly to the Brihacharanam section. Of the eighteen Smartha households enumerated in the village in 1961, fourteen were Brihacharanam, three were Vadama, and one was Astasahashram. Sometime towards the end of 1961 a Vattiman family also moved into the village.

Thus today all the principal sections of the Smarthas are represented in Sripuram, although in unequal strength.

These four Smartha sections are endogamous, although among Western-educated people in the cities intermarriages between them do take place from time to time. No such intermarriages have taken place in Sripuram within memory. There are minor differences in styles of living between these four communities, but these differences are today of so little importance as to be almost nonexistent. The people of the Brihacharanam section are said to have been more strongly Shaivite than the Vadamas, who gave almost equal importance to Shiva and Vishnu. Again, in these parts the Vadamas are generally the biggest *mirasdars* among the Smarthas; hence their weddings and other ceremonies are generally performed on a more lavish scale. The Vattiman, on the other hand, have a reputation for being very frugal. They frequently engage in moneylending and are notorious for the high rates of interest which they charge.

The two primary sections, Brihacharanam and Vadama, are further segmented. Thus, the Brihacharanam group in Sripuram is divided into Mazhanattu Brihacharanam and Kandramanickya Brihacharanam. Similarly, the Vadamas include Vadadesha Vadama and Chozhadesha Vadama, of which only the latter are represented in Sripuram. Some of these subdivisions appear by their names to be territorial in origin. In traditional society, when geographical mobility was considerably more restricted, they had perhaps greater significance than today. At present their main role is to delimit the sphere of marital ties, which do not generally go beyond the boundaries of these subdivisions. In a few instances girls from Sripuram belonging to the Mazhanattu Brihacharanam subsection have been given in marriage outside the village to men of the Kandramanickya subsection.

VI

Thus we see that the Brahmins who are a segment of the rural society of Sripuram themselves constitute a segmentary system. There are divisions within them which are subdivided, and some of these subdivisions are themselves further subdivided. These divisions and subdivisions—segments of different orders—are relevant for different purposes and assume importance under different social situations. Before entering into a discussion on the social significance of the different orders, we present a summary picture of this segmentation as it exists in Sripuram (table 2). It should be emphasized that this gives only a general idea of the nature of segmentation among the Brahmins of Tamilnad and is not arranged with hierarchy in mind. It is not an exhaustive summary, owing to the exclusion of several groups, such as the

TABLE 2

SOCIAL SEGMENTATION AMONG BRAHMINS IN SRIPURAM

Category	Number of Households	Number of Persons
Kannada-speaking Madhva	1	4
Telugu-speaking Smartha		
Konaseemadravida	7	19
Velnadu	4	18
Mulahanadu	3	10
Tamil-speaking Smartha		
Brihacharnam		
Mazhanattu Brihacharanam	9	42
Kandramanickya Brihacharanam	5	13
Vadama: Chozhadesha	3	20
Astasahashram	1	2
Tamil-speaking Shri Vaishnava		
Vadagalai	55	197
Thengalai	2	9
Temple Priests		
Bhattachar (Thengalai)	1	2
Kurukkal	1	5
Total	92	341

Panchangakkarans, because they are not represented in Sripuram.

Thus, in a single *agraharam,* consisting of ninety-two households of Brahmins, we find twelve named endogamous divisions. Each of these may be referred to as a caste or *jati.* These castes or *jatis* are grouped together according to prescribed ways into larger divisions which are also called castes or *jatis.* We note the two characteristic features associated with segmentary systems: (1) larger divisions are subdivided into smaller ones which are further subdivided into still smaller ones, and (2) smaller units are grouped together into larger ones which are themselves grouped together into still larger ones. The processes of fission and fusion are not arbitrary, but follow prescribed patterns and are dependent upon context and situation.

If we begin with a small segment, such as Mazhanattu Brihacharanam, we find that this is the unit which is particularly relevant for the purpose of marriage. In choosing one's marriage partner, broader affiliations are largely irrelevant because, in spite of many things which are shared in common, marital ties are not extended beyond a certain point. The fact that marriages are generally limited by the boundaries of this group also means that it is the widest kinship unit. Taking the case of Sripuram, we find that all those who belong to the group of Mazhanattu Brihacharanam are related to each other by numerous ties of kinship and affinity. The same is true of other units such as Konaseemadravida among the Telugu Brahmins and Vadagalai Iyengars among the Shri Vaishnavas.

The Mazhanattu and Kandramanickya subsections together form the Brihacharanam section in the village. There are free commensal relations between them, and today marriages also sometimes take place. They are characterised by a common style of life in which the worship of Shiva plays a somewhat more important part than the worship of Vishnu. As far as the other Tamil Smarthas (e.g., the Vadama) are concerned, the Brihacharanam constitute an undifferentiated unit.

Although distinct in relation to the Vadama as far as marriage and other minor aspects of ritual life are concerned, the Brihacharanam form a single unit along with them in relation to the Shri Vaishnavas. These two, together with the Astasahashram (and the one Vattiman family recently settled), constitute the Tamil Smartha group in the village. They are distinct in many ways both from the Shri Vaishnavas and from the Telugu Smarthas. They have their own style of dress for women, their own manner of serving food, their own set of rites and ceremonies. In relation to the Shri Vaishnavas they constitute a single undifferentiated unit, with a distinctive style of living. There is full commensality within the group.

Up to this level, the relations between the units considered can be defined in more or less simple terms: the higher the order of segmentation, the smaller the structural distance between two adjacent segments. Thus, the structural distance between Kandramanickya and Mazhanattu Brihacharanam is smaller than the structural distance between Brihacharanam and Vadama, which is smaller than the structural distance between Tamil Smartha and Shri Vaishnava. But what about the structural distance between Tamil Smartha and Shri Vaishnava, on the one hand, and Tamil Smartha and Telugu Smartha, on the other?

In certain regards the Tamil Smarthas are closer to the Shri Vaishnavas. They speak the same language and are heirs to the same broad cultural heritage. They are both indigenous to the area, and this is particularly important today in view of the resurgence of regional loyalties associated with the formation of linguistic states.

On the other hand, doctrinally the Tamil Smarthas are very much closer to their Telugu counterparts. Both are followers of the same general doctrines and affiliated to the same broad sectarian organisation, although there are minor variations of custom between them. In the actual practice of religion also both groups pay homage to Vishnu as well as Shiva and hence differ from the Shri Vaishnavas in like manner. In Sripuram the Tamil Smarthas seem in general to have been closer to the Telugu Smarthas than to the Shri Vaishnavas, particularly in the recent past. This has been so partly because both reacted in the same way to the aggressive sectarianism of the Iyengars and perhaps also because both have been in a minority in relation to the latter. It is difficult to say what the alignment would have been like if the Telugu Smarthas had been numerically preponderant and the Tamil Smarthas and Shri Vaishnavas together constituted a minority.

Whatever the differences between them, the Tamil and Telugu Smarthas, the Shri Vaishnavas, the Madhvas, and the temple priests together constitute a more or less undifferentiated unit in relation to the Non-Brahmins and Adi-Dravidas. As far as the latter are concerned, differences of doctrine or sect affiliation between Brahmins are of little consequence. To the Non-Brahmins and Adi-Dravidas the Brahmin represents a generalised type, associated with a style of life which is distinct in relation to their own and within which minor variations are inconsequential.

Thus, although among Brahmins the terms "Iyer" and "Iyengar" are specifically associated with Smartha and Shri Vaishnava respectively, the Pallas of Sripuram generally refer to their Iyengar *mirasdars* as Iyer.

The nature of the caste system is such that every Brahmin individual has multiple affiliation. He is at the same time a Kandramanickyam, a Brihacharanam, a Smartha, and a Brahmin. There is no contradiction in this, because affiliations at different levels have relevance to different social facts. Since caste refers to a multiplicity of things, and not to one single thing to the exclusion of others, it is legitimate to use the word "caste" or *"jati"* for each order of segmentation.

In the context of marriage it is usually the last order of segmentation which is relevant. A man who is approached with an offer of marriage is likely to declare that his caste or *jati* is Mazhanattu Brihacharanam, or Konaseemadravida, or Vadagalai Iyengar, because this is what is important in regard to the selection of a spouse. To declare oneself as Brihacharanam, or simply as Smartha, would be too vague. On the other hand, in the context of doctrinal or sectarian affiliation the relevant order of segmentation is Smartha. It is enough for a person to say that his caste is Smartha for others to know which gods he worships and which set of doctrines he follows. Vis-à-vis a Shri Vaishnava a man usually speaks of himself as a Smartha. To say that he is Mazhanattu Brihacharanam or Chozhadesha Vadama would be superfluous in such a context.

Smarthas and Shri Vaishnavas, who are differentiated with regard to one another, are together viewed as a unit by Non-Brahmins and Adi-Dravidas. To a Non-Brahmin it is generally irrelevant whether a man is a Brihacharanam or a Vadama, a Smartha or a Shri Vaishnava; by and large it suffices for him to know that he is a Brahmin. A Brahmin, when asked the name of his caste by a Non-Brahmin, usually says that he is a Brahmin; if he were to refer to himself as a Kandramanickya Brihacharanam, he would perhaps be unintelligible.

A Non-Brahmin is not generally aware of all the niceties of segmentation among the Brahmins. To him these are largely irrelevant. When, during the 1962 elections, some members of the Dravida Kazhagam came to campaign in Sripuram, they made attacks against the Brahmins as a group and not against particular sections of it. To them the Brahmins are a caste, not a group of castes. The fact that the Brahmin category includes hetero-geneous elements is often unimportant in the context of political life in Tamilnad today.

The entire history of the Non-Brahmin movement in Tamilnad shows that in political contexts the Brahmins have been treated as an undifferentiated category—a single caste. The leaders of this movement set themselves in opposition against Brahmins as a whole—rich and poor, Smartha and Shri Vaishnava, temple priest and Vedic scholar. Perhaps one consequence of this long and bitter political conflict has been that Brahmins as a category have acquired a new identity and a new consciousness of unity. When C. R. Pattabhiraman stood for election from the Kum-bakonam parliamentary constituency, the *agraharam* people in Sripuram voted for him because he was a Brahmin; his being a Smartha Brahmin was of secondary importance.

The administration has long regarded Brahmins as a single caste and has not taken account of differences among them. Jobs in government offices and seats in technical institutions have been denied to persons on the ground that they were Brahmins, never explicitly because they were Vadamas or Smarthas.

The same principles apply to the Adi-Dravidas. Although there are divisions and subdivisions among them, in the context of state politics or administration the caste of a person is not Devendra Palla or Kizhakkatti Paraiya, but simply Adi-Dravida. Brahmin *mirasdars,* by and large, refer to their Adi-Dravida *pannaiyals* as Harijans and not by the name of their specific subdivision, which is not always known to them. The Adi-Dravidas and, to a lesser extent, the Non-Brahmins in spite of their many subdivisions are often regarded as undifferentiated units by the Brahmins.

Thus we see that caste is a segmentary system. One level of segmentation is relevant for purposes of marriage, another for general religious and sectarian affiliation, and a third for political purposes. It must not be thought, however, that this pattern of segmentation is a rigid one and that it applies uniformly to all categories. For one thing, the extent of segmentation may vary from one caste to another; e.g., the Smarthas are segmented to a higher degree than the Shri Vaishnavas.

Again, although it is generally true that Kandramanickya sees itself as a separate unit only in relation to Mazhanattu, and merges into a wider unit, Brihacharanam, in relation to Vadama, and into a still wider unit, Smartha, in relation to Shri Vaishnava, in actual life this process does not by any means operate with clockwork precision. In certain regards—e.g., the manner of serving food—the Thengalai are closer to the Smarthas than to the other major section of the Shri Vaishnavas. And, of course, there is the question of territorial loyalties cutting across cleavages in the caste structure.

Divisions and subdivisions within a caste are based upon a plurality of factors. Thus, the ultimate divisions among the Telugu Smarthas—Konaseemadravida, Velnadu and so on—seem to be territorial in origin, as do the divisions Chozhadesha and Vadadesha among the Vadamas. At other levels the division is based upon doctrinal affiliation, as in the division between Smarthas and Shri Vaishnavas. Sometimes the basis is linguistic, as between Tamil and Telugu Smarthas. Frequently a number of factors play a part at the same level, as in the division between Thengalai and Vadagalai, which not only restricts choice of mates, but also has doctrinal and ritual significance.

Being segmentary in nature, the caste system evinces the two characteristic processes associated with such systems: fission and fusion. A small segment merges or fuses with an adjacent segment in relation to a segment of a higher order. Thus, there is fusion of Brihacharanam and Vadama in relation to Shri Vaishnava. On the other hand, in the context of internal relations the cleavages within a wider unit become clear and sharply focussed. Thus, the Shri Vaishnavas, who constitute a single unit in relation to Smarthas, divide themselves into Vadagalai and Thengalai in relation to each other.

Historically the process of fission seems to have been a fairly general and widespread feature of Hindu society. Hutton (1961, pp. 50–51), for instance, refers to the fissiparous tendency as an inherent feature of the caste system. In the past, perhaps, the number of orders of segmentation, as well as the number of segments, tended to increase progressively. Today greater importance seems to attach to the opposite process of fusion. Thus, in the sphere of marriage, unions between Mazhanattu and Kan-

dramanickya Brihacharanam, and between Thengalai and Vadagalai Shri Vaishnavas, are becoming increasingly common. In
the matter of commensality Smarthas and Shri Vaishnavas are
rapidly becoming a single unit. In their general styles of living the
different categories of Brahmins have more in common today
than they had in the past.

VII

So far the Non-Brahmins have by and large been considered as a
homogeneous and undifferentiated category. There is some
reason for doing this when one sees them in relation to the
Brahmins, for Non-Brahmins, in general, share certain common
elements which give to their style of life a distinctive character in
contrast to that of Brahmins. This is particularly true in a village
such as Sripuram where the bulk of the Non-Brahmins are
peasants in the widest sense of the term.

It is common for Brahmins to refer to Non-Brahmins collectively as Shudras. This is not a very precise term of reference and
even Brahmins would generally exclude Chettiyars and the
so-called Maratha Kshatriyas from its purview. It is, however,
used fairly widely to designate the generality of cultivating,
artisan, and servicing communities who constitute the overwhelming majority of Non-Brahmins. In Sripuram, with the sole
exception of the single Maratha family, the Non-Brahmin population as a whole is regarded by the Brahmins as forming a single
broad category, the Shudras.

The term "Shudra" has a more or less specific meaning in the
fourfold hierarchy of traditional Hinduism. It is associated not
only with a specific rank in this ideal hierarchy, but also with
specific occupations, a specific style of life, and specific liabilities.
Although regarded collectively as Shudras by the Brahmins, the
Non-Brahmins themselves are by no means unanimous in accepting this appellation. Many of them, such as the Padayachis, claim
to be Kshatriyas. The Vellalas have, likewise, claimed to be
Vaishyas.

Claims by Non-Brahmin castes to Kshatriya or Vaishya status
seem in many instances to be of recent origin. It is a well-
known fact that the decennial censuses provided opportunities for

such claims to be made with some purpose and effect. What is of interest is that in earlier censuses all Non-Brahmin castes had in many cases been grouped together as Shudras. Thus, a census conducted in Trichy District in 1831 classified the entire population into "Brahmins, Muslims and Soodras" in addition to having a separate category for Untouchables (see Kumar, 1962, p. 354).

Although the term "Shudra" has fallen into comparative disuse in recent years, the English term "Non-Brahmin" has gained currency, particularly owing to its association with certain political movements and parties. It is essentially in the political context that the Brahmins regard the Non-Brahmins as a single unit in opposition to themselves, and now occupying a dominant position in the state.

The Non-Brahmins, who constitute a unit in relation to the Brahmins, are, however, even more heterogeneous than the latter. There is the same kind of segmentation among them and the multiplicity of segments is greater. In Sripuram alone there are twenty-four major segments, some of which are further sub-divided. It is not possible here to go into all the details of caste segmentation among the Non-Brahmins, and attention will be drawn only to the major segments and briefly to some of their subdivisions.

One major obstacle to a brief and clear discussion of Non-Brahmin castes lies in the confusion of terminology. Caste names among Non-Brahmins have been undergoing transformation by a process which seems to be fairly widespread. Members of a certain caste A begin to adopt a particular title or surname B and soon they return B as their caste name. As a consequence, members of the same caste may return different caste names, and sometimes members of different castes adopt the same title or caste name.

The Kallas of Sripuram have adopted the title "Servai," and most of them give Servai as the name of their caste, although some retain the old caste name, Kalla. Servai, or "Servaikkaran," is again a title adopted by members of other castes as well (e.g., Ahamudiya and Marava). Similarly, the term "Muppan," or "Muppanar," figures as a title among people with diverse caste affiliations (e.g., Odaiyars and Maravas), and some people also declare Muppan to be the name of their caste. Again, "Pandaram" represents an occupation, a title, and also the name of a caste or subcaste.

The phenomenon of "passing" seems to have become fairly widespread among Non-Brahmin castes in recent years. Castes which traditionally occupied a low position often adopt individually, or in groups, names associated with higher social strata. Concerning the Ahamudiyas in Chinglepet, North Arcot, Salem, Coimbatore, and Trichy, W. Francis wrote in 1901 (quoted in Thurston, 1909, I, 5): ". . . they are much less numerous than they were thirty years ago. The reason probably is that they have risen in the social scale, and have returned themselves as Vellalas. Within the same period, their strength has nearly doubled in Tanjore, perhaps owing to the assumption of the name by other castes like the Maravans and Kallans." Sometimes it is impossible to verify such claims.

Increased geographical mobility and a general loosening of the ritual restrictions associated with caste have made it possible for claims to higher social status to be put forward and even accepted in a number of cases. An instance of this, having a somewhat dramatic character, took place in Sripuram about a decade ago. A person by the name of Raman came to the village and started living in one of the Non-Brahmin streets, saying that he was a Padayachi by caste. He worked as a mason and, as such, had free access to the Brahmin houses in the village.

Raman lived in this manner for three to four years. Then one day, while he was standing outside the coffee shop on the main road and exchanging betel leaves and lime with some Non-Brahmins, a passer-by approached him and began to speak to him. The stranger expressed surprise at finding the Non-Brahmins accepting betel leaves and lime from the mason and wondered how they could be so liberal. It was then revealed that Raman the mason was not a Padayachi at all, but a Palla and a caste-fellow of the stranger. Needless to say, he was beaten by the Non-Brahmins and had to flee the village, leaving most of his belongings there.

If it has been possible for a Palla to pass as a Padayachi, a Padayachi can with much greater ease pass as a Vellala. In fact, there are certain doubts about the caste affiliation of some of the persons living on the main road, particularly those among them who are newcomers to the village. Since intermarriage with close relatives is frequently practised by many Non-Brahmins, a section of people, by confining marital relations among themselves, can claim to be Vellalas, Ahamudiyas, or Padayachis. Generally speaking, commensality is no longer a serious bar, so that if the "genuine" Padayachis in the village have some doubts about the validity of a newcomer's claim as a Padayachi, they can satisfy themselves by refusing to offer their daughters to him in marriage. The newcomer would not necessarily find much difficulty in getting a girl from among his relatives, who, like him, might have also styled themselves as Padayachis.

Thus, the caste structure among Non-Brahmins has acquired a somewhat flexible character over the last fifty years. The arrangement of the different segments with regard to each other, instead of remaining static, has shown a tendency to change, and this change has sometimes been rather rapid in nature. A few of the old boundaries between segments have disappeared; some others have become less rigid. By and large, there has been a tendency towards an expansion of units and for smaller units to group themselves into larger aggregates.

As among the Brahmins, here also the structural distance between segments is variable. Some segments are more closely related to each other than to the others. But the diversity among Non-Brahmins seems to be greater, partly because they comprise the bulk of the population of the state.

Although the entire Non-Brahmin population of Sripuram is Tamil-speaking, not all the castes are of local origin. There are Marathi-speaking people like the Maratha Kshatriyas and Telugu-speaking people like the Nayudus and the Reddiyars.

The Tamil-speaking Non-Brahmin castes can themselves be classified into different groups. Any such classification is, of course, bound to be arbitrary to some extent because it can hardly take into account all the different features which characterise a group of castes. But, broadly speaking, the majority of Non-Brahmin castes of Sripuram fall into one of three main categories of cultivating castes, artisan castes, and servicing castes. In some instances it may be difficult to decide into which of the three main divisions a particular caste should be placed, the reasons for which will be explained below.

One word of caution should be introduced at this point. It has to be recognised that the classification proposed is a functional one, in terms of traditional occupation. Now, the relationship between traditional and actual occupation has always been of a somewhat uncertain nature, and this is particularly so today. Agriculture has perhaps always attracted a number of people from the artisan and servicing castes. Today, with the disintegration of village handicrafts, many specialised castes have almost entirely lost their traditional occupation. Sometimes it happens that a community is a specialised caste only in its name, which is not infrequently that of some occupation historically associated with it, whereas in reality it can hardly be distinguished from the generality of cultivating castes.

The bulk of the Non-Brahmin population of Sripuram belongs to what may be very broadly described as cultivating castes. Not all cultivating castes, however, are of the same kind, nor are they related to each other equally closely. Some are closer to each other than to the others. Here also the same pattern of segmentation is discernible as among the Brahmins, although the contours are somewhat more blurred.

Among the cultivating castes of Sripuram there are two more or less clearly defined groups, the Vellala group and the Kalla group.[3] These two groups, although fairly clearly defined in relation to each other, are further differentiated internally. In addition to these, there is a third group, less homogeneous than the first two and comprising those cultivating castes which do not belong either to the Vellala group or to the Kalla group. The Padayachis constitute the most important caste in this group from the point of view of numbers.

The Kalla, Marava, and Ahamudiya castes constitute a distinct

---

[3] My classification of Non-Brahmin castes is somewhat different from that of Kathleen Gough (1960, pp. 16–17). The difference may be due to local factors. At any rate, I have thought it advisable to group together Kallas, Maravas, and Ahamudiyas, as they are frequently viewed as a unity not only in my area, but also elsewhere (see Dumont, 1957a, 1957b).

category (see Dumont, 1957*a*). They can be distinguished particularly from the Vellala group by their close-knit organisation (their "tribal" character, as some call it), the comparative unimportance of Sanskritic elements in their culture, and their tradition of lawless and violent life which still makes them feared by the generality of people. The Kallas also seem to be distinctive in their physical features, being larger in build than other Non-Brahmins and characterised by a domineering appearance.

Kalla, Marava, and Ahamudiya constitute what is generally called the Mukkulattor ("people of the three castes"), or the Muvendrakkulam ("the triple line of Indra"). They are closely related to each other by their myth of origin, which represents them as being descended from the three natural sons of Indra by Ahalya, the wife of the *rishi* Gautama. Although the three castes have differences among themselves, they are often treated as a unit not only by the Brahmins, but also by other Non-Brahmins. In and around Sripuram, where the Kallas are numerically and otherwise preponderant, the word "Kalla" is often used as a generic term to include Maravas and Ahamudiyas as well.

It has been recorded that Kallas give Marava and Ahamudiya as names of subcastes among them, and that likewise Maravas return Ahamudiya as one of their subcastes (see Thurston, 1909, I, 8). In Sripuram there are no Maravas, but there are Kallas and a few Ahamudiyas. They do not intermarry, but otherwise have similar customs. Further, both Kallas and Ahamudiyas in Sripuram adopt the title of Servai, or Servaikkaran. Political loyalties are very strong within the "three castes," and, other things being equal, a Kalla will support an Ahamudiya against a Vellala.

The Kallas constitute a significant bloc in Sripuram. Although fewer in number than the Vellalas, they are better organised and are politically very important. Their political importance derives from the fact that they are the dominant caste in the region. In the General Elections held in 1952, 1957, and 1962, the majority of candidates put up by the different parties for the Thiruvaiyar Assembly Constituency were Kallas. The Kallas are said to constitute about thirty per cent of the total population of the constituency. The president of the village *panchayat* of Melur-Sripuram is a Kalla.

The Kallas themselves do not constitute a homogeneous or

undifferentiated unit. They are subdivided internally, the basis of subdivision being often territorial in nature. Dumont (1957a) has shown in detail the nature of segmentation within the caste as it obtains in the southern districts of Tamilnad. The subdivisions in the Sripuram area seem to follow a slightly different pattern.

The Ambalakkara have often been classified as a subdivision of the Kallas (see Dumont, 1957b, p. 8). Thurston (1909, I, 26) writes: "Till recently the term Ambalakkaran was considered to be a title of the Kallans, but further enquiries have shown that it is the name of a distinct caste, found chiefly in the Trichinopoloy district." In Sripuram the Ambalakkaras are generally regarded as distinct from the Kallas, although closely related to them. Intermarriage between them is not practised. The Kallas proper, however, freely intermarry with each other, and in Sripuram they constitute a more or less homogeneous unit.

Similarly, the Muttiriyas are closely related to the Ambalakkaras and the Kallas, although distinct from both. The distinction is enforced primarily in the field of marriage. Needless to say, under present conditions Kallas, Ambalakkaras, Muttiriyas, and Ahamudiyas freely interdine with each other. So far as Sripuram is concerned, the Kalla group of castes consists of four endogamous units: Kalla, Ambalakkara, Muttiriya, and Ahamudiya. Closely related in habit and custom, they are often regarded generically as Kallas by the other Non-Brahmins, in relation to whom they have a fairly strong sense of internal solidarity.

The Vellala group of castes is, in general, more "Sanskritic" in its style of life than the Kalla group. In Sripuram, for instance, many of the Vellalas are Shaivites, and they follow a somewhat stricter ritual code than the Kallas or Ahamudiyas. These ritual rules, however, seem to be losing their force among the younger generation of Vellalas, and the difference between Vellalas and Kallas in regard to their general style of life seems to be smaller today than it was in the past. The Kallas of Tanjore were known even sixty years ago to have been influenced considerably by the Vellalas among whom they lived.

The Vellalas constitute the largest Non-Brahmin caste in Sripuram and also in Tanjore District as a whole. They are the cultivating caste *par excellence* of Tamilnad. Yet the term

"Vellala" is rather confusing, because of its comprehensive use. Many castes of different origins have sought inclusion in this wide category and are calling themselves Vellalas or Pillais. Sometimes, on the other hand, an offshoot of the Vellalas adopts a specific title and comes to be regarded as a separate caste.

Even the Vellalas proper—those who are of Vellala origin and go universally by the name of Vellala—are not a homogeneous unit, but are subdivided into smaller sections. Without going into details, it must suffice to say that in Sripuram the Vellalas proper are segmented into three endogamous units: Chozhia Vellala, Karaikkattu Vellala, and Kodikkal Vellala.

The Chozhia Vellalas are the largest caste—or subcaste—in Sripuram. They are believed to constitute the truly indigenous peasantry of the Chola country. They have deep roots in the village, unlike the Kallas, many of whom have been settled there for not more than three or four generations. Cultivation is the traditional occupation of these Vellalas, although several of them now pursue various other occupations.

The Karaikkattu Vellalas are very similar to the Chozhia Vellalas in habits and customs, but the two do not generally intermarry. They are said to have had their traditional home in the Pandya country further south. They constitute a very small minority in Sripuram. The Kodikkal Vellalas are also very similar to the Chozhia Vellalas and are in all probability an offshoot of them. They derive their name from an occupational specialisation, the cultivation of betel vines. The cultivation of betel vines, it may be mentioned, is a difficult and highly specialised occupation requiring great skill in protecting the growing vines from excess of sun, rain, and wind. (The Muslims also are said to be experts in this art in the Thiruvaiyar area.) In Sripuram there are only four households of Kodikkal Vellalas, and not all of them pursue their traditional calling.

In addition to the Vellalas proper, there are a few households of Gaundas, or Konga Vellalas as they are sometimes called. The relationship between Vellalas and Gaundas is close, but difficult to specify in exact terms. The distinction seems to be basically territorial in origin. The Gaundas occupy in the Konga country (the districts of Coimbatore, Salem, etc.) more or less the same position which the Chozhia Vellalas do in the Chola country.

Intermarriage between Vellalas and Gaundas is not practised, but in other regards they pursue a more or less common style of life.

The Mudaliyars, also apparently very closely related to the Vellalas and perhaps an offshoot of them, are found mainly in Chingleput District. There are only three Mudaliyar households in Sripuram. Mudaliyar, in addition to being a caste name, seems to be used as a title by certain Vellalas. In Sripuram, however, the Mudaliyars form a distinct unit and do not intermarry with the Vellalas proper.

Finally, there is a single household belonging to the Nayanar caste, which is probably an offshoot of the Vellalas. The Nayanars are a small group. Besides agriculture, many of them are engaged in clerical and related occupations. The name "Nayanar" has religious connotations, being associated with the sixty-three Tamil Shaivite saints.

In addition to the Kalla and the Vellala groups of castes, there are certain other cultivating castes among the Non-Brahmins. Foremost among these, in numbers, are the Padayachis, or Vanniyas. The Padayachis claim to be Kshatriya and often style themselves as Vanniyakkula Kshatriya, but from the viewpoint of social esteem their position, at least in Tanjore, is lower than that of the Vellalas. The Padayachis of Sripuram are rated rather low in the social scale by both Brahmins and Non-Brahmins. They are, on the whole, less rigorous both with regard to ritual observances and in the matter of sex relations. Economically also they are in a somewhat lower position than the Vellalas and the Kallas.

Finally, there are a few households belonging to the Muppanar, Odaiya, and Naicker groups. These names appear to have been in their origin titles rather than caste names, but today they also refer to endogamous units comparable to the castes discussed above. By tradition these castes have been associated with cultivation. The Muppanars and Odaiyas are closely related in their styles of life.

The artisan castes form a somewhat distinct unit vis-à-vis the cultivating castes. Among them a special position is occupied by the group of five castes known collectively as Kammalan or Panchala. They comprise five occupational sections: Tattan

(Goldsmith), Kannan (Brass-smith), Tachchan (Carpenter), Kal-Tachchan (Stonemason), and Kollan (Blacksmith). In Sripuram this group is represented by five households of Tattans and one of Tachchans.

Tattans and Tachchans have much in common in their style of life. Sanskritic elements play an important part in their ritual and social life. They generally wear the sacred thread and claim to be Brahmins, having adopted Brahminical *gotras*. The Tachchans of Sripuram, as elsewhere, adopt "Asari" as their title. The two castes, although very similar in their social customs, do not intermarry. Both enjoy fairly high social esteem among the Non-Brahmins.

The third artisan caste in Sripuram consists of the Kusavans or Velans, who are potters by traditional occupation. The two Kusavan households in the village both pursue their traditional craft. The Kusavans seem to occupy a lower position in the scale of social esteem than the Tattans and, perhaps, the Tachchans.

The servicing castes among the Non-Brahmins of Sripuram are four in number. They are Pandaram, Melakkaran, Ambattan, and Vannan. Of these the first two are ranked fairly high, and the first, particularly, enjoys high social esteem. The last two occupy a rather low social position; the Vannans, particularly, are ranked lower than the generality of Non-Brahmin castes in the village.

The Pandarams are by traditional occupation a priestly caste. It seems probable that they are an offshoot of the Vellalas, whom they resemble fairly closely in their style of life, although the two do not intermarry. The Pandaram acts in a priestly capacity in various contexts. Generally he officiates as priest in temples dedicated to deities other than Vishnu and Shiva. In certain places he is in charge of temples devoted to Kaliamman, Mariamman, and other major female deities. In Sripuram, however, the principal Kali temple has a Brahmin priest, while certain lesser deities in the same temple (Karuppan, Maduraiveeran, etc.) are ministered to by a Pandaram. The same Pandaram officiates as priest for the boundary deities of the village and for the Kali temples in the Pallacheri.

The Melakkarans also are by tradition and actual occupation associated with temple functions. They supply pipers and drummers who provide the necessary music for important festivals in the Vishnu, Shiva, and Kali temples. Besides, their services are requisitioned, particularly by Brahmins, for important domestic functions such as marriage, *seemantham* (a pregnancy ceremony), and *upanayanam*. The Melakkarans in Sripuram claim the status of Vellalas and, like them, adopt Pillai as their title or surname.

The Ambattans are a caste of barbers. They are ranked fairly low in the ritual and social hierarchy. Their touch is considered polluting by Brahmins and orthodox Shaivite Vellalas, who are required to take a bath after being served by them. The Ambattan has other functions in addition to those associated with tonsure. He is also a physician, and one of the members of this caste in Sripuram, known for his skill in the arts of healing, used to be consulted by Brahmins as well as Non-Brahmins. Those of them who thus specialise are usually accorded higher social esteem. All members of the Ambattan caste in Sripuram adopt the title of Vaidyar, which means physician.

The Vannans, or Washermen, occupy a lower social position than the other servicing castes. Their occupation, the cleaning of soiled clothes, is considered polluting in the Hindu scheme of values. There is only one family belonging to this caste in the village.

In addition to the castes already noted, there are certain others which do not exactly fall under any of the three broad divisions considered. These include the Konans, who are cattle herders, and the Nadars, who are toddy tappers by traditional occupation. Both these castes are largely engaged in cultivation, since Sripuram does not provide suitable pastures for cattle herding to be a full-time occupation and the law of the state disallows the production of liquor.[4]

Finally, there are the non-Tamil speaking castes among the Non-Brahmins. These include one household of Reddiyars, an influential Telugu-speaking caste of cultivators, comparable in social position to the Vellalas; one household of Nayudus, an

---

[4] I have not discussed the grouping of Non-Brahmin and Adi-Dravida castes into the Left Hand and Right Hand subdivisions. This grouping does not play any significant part in the contemporary social structure of Sripuram. General discussions of the subject are given by Thurston (1909, V, 474 ff.) and Hutton (1961, pp. 67–70).

TABLE 3

SOCIAL SEGMENTATION AMONG NON-BRAHMINS IN SRIPURAM

Category	Number of Households	Number of Persons
CULTIVATING CASTES		
The Kalla group:		
Kalla	24	110
Ambalakkara	3	15
Muttiriya	6	20
Ahamudiya	6	33
The Vellala group:		
Vellalas proper		
Chozhia Vellala	49	198
Karaikkattu Vellala	1	8
Kodikkal Vellala	4	17
Gaunda or Konga Vellala	4	10
Nayanar	1	6
Mudaliyar	3	12
Other cultivating castes:		
Padayachi	27	81
Muppanar	5	15
Odaiyar	3	11
Naicker	2	9
ARTISAN CASTES		
Tattan	5	23
Tachchan	1	4
Kusavan	2	7
SERVICING CASTES		
Pandaram	4	17
Melakkaran	3	9
Ambattan	3	15
Vannan	1	5
OTHERS		
Konan	5	23
Nadar	1	7
NON-TAMIL CASTES		
Maratha	1	9
Reddiyar	1	2
Nayudu	1	11
Total	168	677

influential literate agricultural and mercantile caste of Telugu-speaking people; and the Marathas. The last have certain distinctive features in their style of life which makes them stand out from all the other Non-Brahmin castes in the village. The Marathas in Sripuram claim to be Suryavansi Kshatriyas and belong to the line of the former rulers of Tanjore. They constitute a group of aristocratic landowners whose social and economic position has now undergone some decline.

To sum up, we present a list of the Non-Brahmin castes inhabiting Sripuram (table 3). Some idea has been given of the nature of grouping and segmentation among the Non-Brahmins, without as much detail as was given concerning the Brahmins. As in the table of Brahmin castes, no attempt has been made to arrange the segments in a hierarchical order. (The nature of hierarchy among both Brahmins and Non-Brahmins is extremely complex, and to attempt to represent it in a single table would merely lead to confusion. A brief discussion of it will be presented in section ix.)

VIII

The Adi-Dravidas constitute a group which stands apart from the society of Brahmins and Non-Brahmins both by traditional law and in many features of social practice. We have seen how in Sripuram they live on the fringe of the village settlement, or far away from it. In appearance they are of darker colour and have coarser features than either the Brahmins or the generality of Non-Brahmins. Quite aside from that of the Brahmins, their speech is different in vocabulary and accent from that of the Non-Brahmins, although this difference is less noticeable in the younger generation; in their dress and their general style of life they are still conspicuously different from the Non-Brahmins of Sripuram.

The Adi-Dravidas also occupy a special position in regard to the law. The Constitution of India guarantees to them certain specific privileges in the matter of education as well as administrative appointments. In the politics of contemporary Tamilnad they are gradually beginning to organise themselves as an important power. There is some feeling among the Non-Brahmins that in the years to come the Adi-Dravidas may pose a serious threat to their position of political strength.

But although the Adi-Dravidas are often regarded as one single unit by the Brahmins and Non-Brahmins, and also by Government, there are divisions and subdivisions among them as in the case of the two other categories. Most of the Adi-Dravidas in Tanjore District belong to either of the two broad subdivisions, Palla and Paraiya. In Sripuram the Pallas, with eighty-two households, are in an overwhelming majority. There are five households of Christian Paraiyas, one household of Thottis, and one of Chakkiliyas.

The Pallas regard themselves as socially superior to the others and are so regarded by the Non-Brahmins and Brahmins. This is

TABLE 4

SOCIAL SEGMENTATION AMONG ADI-DRAVIDAS IN SRIPURAM

Category	Number of Households	Number of Persons
Palla	82	332
Paraiya	5	28
Thotti	1	8
Chakkiliya	1	3
Total	89	371

partly due to the fact that they have not been associated with the stigma of beef eating. Also, their traditional occupation, agricultural labour, is regarded as less degrading than that of the Paraiyas and Chakkiliyas. The Pallas in Sripuram have, in addition, adopted a number of Sanskritic practices. The Pallas are known to have several endogamous subdivisions, those of Sripuram all belonging to the Devendra section.

The Paraiyas of Sripuram are Christians, but conversion does not seem to have made any substantial difference in their style of life. They do not eat beef today, but are known to have done so in the recent past. Their traditional occupation includes the removal of dead cattle and the playing of tom-toms on certain ceremonial occasions, the former particularly being regarded as highly polluting.

The Thottis may be an offshoot of the Paraiyas. They are similar to them in social custom, but do not intermarry with them. The single Thotti household in Sripuram engages in its traditional occupation of scavenging. They speak Telugu, although they have been settled in the area for several generations.

The Chakkiliyas are by tradition associated with leather work and are generally believed to have been beef eaters. The Chakkiliyas of Sripuram do not engage in their traditional occupation, but work as agricultural labourers; they are not beef eaters today.

A summary listing of the Adi-Dravida castes in Sripuram (table 4) shows that segmentation among them is far less complex than among Brahmins and Non-Brahmins.

IX

Two further points regarding the caste system in general and its particular form in the village community of Sripuram concern (1) the hierarchical aspect of the system, i.e., the principles on which social rank is based and the extent to which they operate in practice—and (2) the nature of vertical solidarity, or intercaste relationships, within the village. Both points will be briefly discussed here. Caste hierarchy will be taken up again in the general context of social stratification, of which caste will be seen as representing only one aspect (chap. vi), and intercaste relations, with regard to both coöperation and conflict, will be discussed further in the sections dealing with the economic and political organisation of the village (chaps. iv and v).

It must first be recognised that principles of caste rank rest essentially on conceptions of social honour or esteem. Social esteem is attached to particular styles of life, and groups are ranked as high or low according to how or whether they pursue such styles. What is highly esteemed varies from one society to another and depends ultimately on the value-system of the society. In India ritual elements have historically occupied an important place in styles of life which have enjoyed high social esteem.

Status honour in a caste hierarchy is based partly upon wealth, but not entirely. It is based upon wealth to the extent that the possession of a certain minimum of wealth is a necessary condition to the pursuit of a certain style of life. Beyond this minimum, however, it is not true that any caste which is in possession of more wealth is by this fact in a position of superior social rank.

Status honour, in addition to being associated with specific styles of life, has in every society a strong traditional bias. Hence it is not enough for a certain caste to adopt a particular style of life in order to achieve higher social rank. It has to legitimise its position by working this style of life into a tradition; it has to establish its association with the style over a number of generations.

Although it may be possible to list the different attributes which enter into styles of life that are highly esteemed, such listing would be of limited value. In the first place, people do not rank different castes in terms of a rational application of particular standards. Second, the standards themselves are ambiguous, variable, and subject to change over time.

Thus, although hierarchy is an important feature of the caste system, we must not assume that wherever there is segmentation we can rank the segments as higher or lower. There are conflicting claims to superior rank, and often it is impossible to speak of a consensus. It frequently happens that two castes put forward rival claims to superiority with regard to which members of other castes may be indifferent or may not regard themselves as competent to decide either way.

The important point to bear in mind about the hierarchy of the caste system is its ambiguities beyond a certain level. These ambiguities are essential in a system which seems always to have permitted a certain degree of mobility. They are further increased by the fact that the basis of social honour or esteem, the entire value system on which the ranking of castes depends, has in recent times been undergoing important changes.

Ambiguities notwithstanding, one can say that the broad divisions, Brahmin, Non-Brahmin, and Adi-Dravida, are associated with different degrees of social honour or esteem. In the context of Sripuram, and perhaps of Tamilnad as a whole, there would be a wide measure of consensus that Brahmins rank higher socially than Non-Brahmins, who in turn rank higher than Adi-Dravidas. There are, no doubt, some Non-Brahmins who would challenge the relevance of such a system of grading; but most of them would accept it, and few would suggest a different order. Even though some Non-Brahmins may challenge the claim by Brahmins that they are superior in rank, this claim would certainly be acknowledged by the third party, the Adi-Dravidas. Thus, at the broadest level there is little ambiguity about social rank or the nature of the hierarchy.

Coming to subdivisions among the Brahmins, there would be fairly general agreement that the Smarthas and Shri Vaishnavas proper rank higher than the Panchangakkarans and the Kuruk-kals and Bhattachars. As between Panchangakkarans, on the one hand, and Kurukkals and Bhattachars, on the other, it is difficult to assign social precedence. The issue cannot in any case be decided with reference to Sripuram, since there are no Pan-changakkaran Brahmins in the village.

The position of comparative inferiority of the Panchangak-karans and Archakars may be partly explained by the fact that their occupation makes them dependent for their livelihood on services rendered to Non-Brahmins. Services to Non-Brahmins in a specific way do not enter into the style of life of the Smarthas and Shri Vaishnavas proper. Rather, their style of life revolves around the cultivation of scriptural knowledge and the perform-ance of individual and family rites, both of which are associated with high social esteem.

Shri Vaishnavas and Smarthas make competing claims to the highest social rank. The claims cannot be judged in terms of any fixed or objective standards. Shri Vaishnavas tend to be more orthodox and exclusive, and they may even refuse to take water from the hands of Smarthas. But this is not necessarily accepted as a sign of superiority, since Smarthas as well as other Brahmins regard it as an extreme example of bigotry and sometimes hold it up to ridicule. Shri Vaishnavas claim superiority on the ground that they are more rigorous and orthodox in their ritual observ-ances and that they do not worship non-Sanskritic deities as the Smarthas do. Smarthas maintain that Shri Vaishnavas are not Brahmins at all, but descendants of assorted people converted by Ramanuja.

It should be mentioned that questions of mutual rank today do not intrude into Smartha–Shri Vaishnava relationships except occasionally. It would be very far from the truth to think that Smarthas and Shri Vaishnavas spend most of their time, or even any significant part of it, trying to decide who ranks higher and who ranks lower. The most bitter and acrimonious disputes between them about mutual rank seem now to belong to the past. Brahmins of the present generation sometimes look back on this past with a certain amusement.

It should be recognised that the actual position of a caste in the village is not based merely upon certain absolute standards of social estimation, but depends also upon local factors. In Sripuram the Shri Vaishnavas are in a dominant position by virtue of their strength of numbers and their control over various aspects of social life in the *agraharam,* including control of the Vishnu temple. The Smarthas are in a position of relative weakness. But there are other villages where Smarthas are in a position of strength and the presence of Shri Vaishnavas in the *agraharam* is accepted only on sufferance.

Similarly, the question of relative superiority or inferiority between Vadagalai and Thengalai cannot be decided once and for all. Today the Sripuram *agraharam* is dominated by the Vadagalai Iyengars; but this has not always been the case. Less than a hundred years ago there were bitter disputes between the two sections over matters of social precedence.

In a narrow sense the question of social precedence between castes can sometimes be settled, but only in a limited way. In most big temples there is a more or less fixed order of distribution of *prasadam,* or consecrated food. This distribution sometimes, though not always, follows the lines of caste. Thus, Brahmins, when they are present, generally get the offerings first and then the distribution is made to Non-Brahmins. In the Vishnu temple at Sripuram the elders among the Vadagalai Iyengar get the *prasadam* first and then the others. This order, however, is not fixed for every village or every temple. There are many temples in which *prasadam* is distributed first to the Thengalai elders and then to the Vadagalai.

Thus, it is seen that social rank among the Brahmins is based upon a plurality of factors. Sometimes these factors are so heavily weighted in favour of a certain section that one can say with some measure of confidence that it ranks superior to some other section. In Sripuram, certainly, the Smarthas enjoy higher social esteem than the Kurukkals. But the weightage of these factors is by no means so unambiguous in every case. Very often it is difficult, if not impossible, to decide whether one subsection ranks higher or lower than another.

Determination of caste rank among the Non-Brahmins suffers similarly from ambiguity and the absence of universally accepted criteria. Conflicting claims to higher social rank are often expressed among the Non-Brahmins in the idiom of the *varna* scheme. Thus, some of them claim to be Brahmins, some claim to be Kshatriyas, and some claim to be Vaishyas. But the presentation of a claim does not necessarily, or even generally, lead to its acceptance. Thus, although the Padayachis claim to be Kshatriyas, and the Vellalas do not generally go above the Vaishya level in their claims, it is the Vellalas rather than the Padayachis who are, by and large, accepted as superior.

Claims to Vaishya status were put forward in an organised manner by the Vellalas at the time of the 1871 census. They made a petition to the municipal commissioners of Madras, protesting against their being classed as Shudras. In the petition the authority of Manu was cited to point out that "the Vellalas do come exactly within the most authoritative definition given of Vysias [and] do *not* come within the like definition of Sudras" (quoted in Thurston, 1909, VII, 366).

The Padayachis in like manner claim to be Kshatriyas, assuming the title of Vanniyakkula (i.e., of the fire race). "At the time of the census, 1871, a petition was submitted to Government by representatives of the caste, praying that they might be classified as Kshatriyas, and twenty years later, in connection with the census, 1891, a book entitled 'Vannikula Vilakkam: a treatise on the Vanniya caste,' was compiled by Mr. T. Aiyakannu Nayakar, in support of the caste claim to be returned as Kshatriyas" (*ibid.*, VI, 1).

Similarly, the Tachchans and Tattans claim to be Brahmins descended from Vishwakarma, the architect of the universe, and call themselves Vishwa Brahmins. They have adopted caste names such as Asari, Brahminical *gotras,* and other practices followed by the Brahmins.

Such claims to Brahmin, Kshatriya, and Vaishya status cannot be used as a basis for deciding questions of rank among the Non-Brahmins, because they are rarely, if ever, fully accepted. In the absence of a uniform set of principles for ranking castes it would perhaps be more meaningful to give some idea of the actual rank order as it exists among the Non-Brahmins in Sripuram.

There is a popular saying in Tamil: *Kallan, Maravan, Aha-mudiyan, mella mella wandu Vellalar anar. Vellalar ahi, Mudali-yar shonnar.* ("Kallan, Maravan, and Ahamudiyan by slow degrees became Vellala. Having become Vellala, they called themselves Mudaliyar.") This saying illustrates two important features of the system: (1) that there is a hierarchical order which can be ascertained in broad terms for any given area, and (2) that it is possible for individual castes to move up this order with some success.

Mobility in the caste system may be sought either through the *varna* idiom, which has an all-India spread, or through the idiom of the local system of *jatis.* When the Padayachis claim to be Kshatriyas, they try to make use of the *varna* idiom. When, on the other hand, the Ahamudiyas claim to be Vellalas, they make use of an idiom which has a more local character. Both kinds of idiom have been extensively used over the last several decades.

In the context of Sripuram the hierarchy of castes among the Non-Brahmins is clear up to a point; beyond this point there is a good deal of ambiguity. One can roughly determine the upper and the lower rungs, but in the middle regions ranking is uncertain. Thus, it would be generally admitted that the Vellala group of castes occupies a high position, and that the Vannans and Ambattans rank rather low. The Tattans and Tachchans also occupy high positions, while the Nadars would be ranked near the bottom. The Maratha family, of course, occupies a somewhat unique position. The bulk of the cultivating castes rank somewhat lower than the Vellalas. Beyond this, very little can be said with any measure of certainty.

The position with regard to the Adi-Dravidas is somewhat similar in Sripuram. The Pallas, who constitute the bulk of them, are regarded by reason of their occupation and their food habits to be less degraded than the Paraiyas, Thottis, and Chakkiliyas. Conversion to Christianity does not seem to make a real difference as far as the social rank of the Paraiyas is concerned. What is important is the style of life with which they have been traditionally associated and which still persists among them without very serious modifications.

X

Very little has been said so far about the nature of intercaste relationships in the village. The caste system is not only a hierarchical system, but it is also the basis of an elaborate division of labour. Every caste or *jati,* however broadly or narrowly one may define it, evinces two characteristics: (1) autonomy in certain spheres, such as marriage and kinship; and (2) dependence upon other castes in other spheres, such as economic and ritual services.

The discussion so far has tended to highlight the cleavages between castes, the fact that each caste has a certain identity of its own, however broadly or narrowly this identity may be expressed. But the division of a social system into groups or segments is only one aspect of it. The other aspect consists in the interactions— whether of coöperation, competition, or conflict—between these different units. We now turn to a brief summary of the interrelations between the different castes in Sripuram.

Interaction between castes is in evidence most clearly in the sphere of economic activities. The Hindu scriptures, in fact, assign different activities to the different sections of society— prayer, worship, and religious instruction to the Brahmin; warfare to the Kshatriya; commerce and husbandry to the Vaishya; and service to the Shudra. The harmonious working of the social system is made dependent on each order's coöperating with the others in the performance of its appropriate activities.

The real working of a social system, however, is often far removed from the ideal. The generality of Brahmins in Sripuram do very little by way of answering directly to the religious needs of the Non-Brahmins and Adi-Dravidas. With the exception of the families of temple priests, the Brahmins do not today and did not in the past offer services to the lower orders of their own society. One may argue that by their pursuit of knowledge and learning they have helped to keep alive the Great Tradition of Indian culture which provides a basis for unity over a much broader social sphere. But these activities have not required them to enter into social relations with the Non-Brahmins or Adi-Dravidas of their village in the ritual or ceremonial sphere. Such relations their forefathers perhaps had with Non-Brahmins of an entirely different kind, namely, the kings and princes whose social world was far removed from that of the village.

In the economic sphere the Brahmins of Sripuram do enter into relations with the Non-Brahmins and Adi-Dravidas. A large number of them are landowners, dependent upon the services of Non-Brahmins and Adi-Dravidas as tenants and agricultural labourers. Relationships in agricultural production will be discussed later (chap. iv), but we may note here that the ideology of caste itself forces Brahmin *mirasdars* to enter into economic relations with Non-Brahmins by forbidding to them the use of the plough.

Brahmin landowners engage tenants from among Non-Brahmins as well as Adi-Dravidas. In rare cases, where they have their land cultivated directly, they engage agricultural labourers usually from among the Adi-Dravidas. Often the Non-Brahmin tenant of a Brahmin landowner engages Adi-Dravida labourers to cultivate the land he has taken on lease. A complex set of ties thus binds together the Brahmins, Non-Brahmins, and Adi-Dravidas of the village in a web of economic interdependence.

Outside the sphere of agriculture there are the artisan and servicing castes which provide further links between Brahmins and Non-Brahmins. The disintegration of village handicrafts, however, has broken to some extent the chain of interdependence between the castes of Sripuram. For example, the Potter continues to supply pots to Brahmins, Non-Brahmins, and Adi-Dravidas, but on a reduced scale, since earthenware utensils have been largely replaced by metal utensils which come from outside.

Barbers and Washermen continue to serve the Brahmins and Non-Brahmins as before, but now they are paid in cash by the majority of the Brahmins and many of the Non-Brahmins. Their traditional bonds of service have been weakened, particularly with the Brahmins, as the relationships have acquired a contractual character. The Barbers and Washermen still come to the threshing floor of Brahmin *mirasdars* during the harvests and get a certain share of paddy, but this has become a token payment rather than a substantive one.

In the political sphere also there is interaction between the different castes, although these interactions do not always lead to a harmonious adjustment of interests. The village *panchayat* includes Brahmins, Non-Brahmins, and Adi-Dravidas among its members. In the *panchayat* decisions are taken which affect not only the interests of particular castes, but also the village as a whole. The nature of coöperation and conflict within the village polity, and the role of caste in it, will be examined in detail later. It is sufficient to note here that the village provides at least one framework within which different castes interact in various political processes.

Finally, religious festivals provide occasions for the coming together of different castes in the village. Worship in the Shiva temple and the Kali temple draws both Brahmins and Non-Brahmins, although most of the Shri Vaishnavas do not take a very active part in such worship. Once a year when the deity of the main Kali temple is taken around the village, even Adi-Dravidas join the procession.

Chapter IV

*Economic Organisation
and Social Class*

This chapter is devoted principally to a discussion of the organisation of production in Sripuram. This involves, first, a brief consideration of the nature of production in the physical sense of the term; what is produced, how it is produced, and the techniques which are employed in the process. It also involves an analysis in somewhat greater detail of the relations which are entered into by the members of the village, among themselves and with outsiders, for the purpose of production. Further, some brief observations are made on the mechanisms of distribution and exchange.

Chiefly we are concerned here with the class system as a system of social relations. To this end, the nature and composition of the different classes must be examined, and the rights, duties, and obligations which bind them to one another. Since these latter are defined in legal or quasi-legal terms, the relations between rules and their observance are also considered.

Because the concern here is with the broad relationships between the different social classes, we do not enter into a consideration of the details of income, expenditure, and the like. For one thing, such data are notoriously difficult to collect in an agrarian economy; for another, they would lead away from our principal concern. Since we attempt to treat caste, class, and power in terms which are more or less comparable, to provide detailed quantitative data for the economic system without being in a position to do the same for the caste or the power system would detract considerably from the unity of the study.

The economy of the village is based primarily upon agriculture, and hence the relations of production consist essentially of relations between categories of persons contributing in different ways to the process of agriculture. Such categories include landowners, tenants, and agricultural labourers. These, together with their interrelations, constitute the agrarian class structure of the village.

The traditional economy of land and grain embraced certain village crafts and services. Some of these still function in Sripuram, although the relations between artisan and servicing groups, on the one hand, and the agricultural classes, on the other, have become somewhat attenuated. Not only have such relations weakened over the last several decades, but they have tended to acquire a new and rather more contractual character.

In addition to the traditional occupations, many new ones have emerged in recent years. Some of these occupations take individuals outside the ambient of the village. Thus, a number of villagers are engaged in teaching and clerical occupations in towns such as Thiruvaiyar and Tanjore. The expansion of new occupations and certain changes in the relations between preëxisting ones perhaps make it necessary to speak of a traditional and a modern sector in the economy of the village. Yet it should be realised that occupations as well as economic relations intertwine with one another, and that the traditional and nontraditional elements in a village economy cannot be put into watertight compartments.

The economic structure of Sripuram does not have an autonomous existence, but is related to the economy of the wider region, and also to the other institutional spheres of rural society. The village is linked by complex distributive mechanisms to neighbouring marketing centres. What is produced in Sripuram is not all consumed there, and many of the things which are consumed in the village are acquired from outside. In addition, the process of agricultural production is itself dependent on relationships which frequently cut across the boundaries of the village.

The agrarian class structure of Sripuram reflects the class structure of the region and is to some extent conditioned by it. Relations between landowners, tenants, and agricultural labourers in the village correspond to such relations in the region as a whole, although each village is bound to have certain distinctive features. An important aspect of such relations over the last few decades has been their changing character. Recent changes in the class structure of Sripuram are fully intelligible only in terms of state-wide movements and shifts in position brought about by state legislation.

The productive organisation of the village has become more differentiated and complex than it was in the past. The mutual relations of landowners, tenants, and agricultural labourers are today governed by a variety of legal rules and market forces in addition to traditional norms. We will, therefore, consider the present nature of the productive organisation first, and then examine in chapter vi how in the past it was subsumed under the caste structure and the way in which the relationship between the two has acquired its present form.

II

The organisation of agriculture in Sripuram is such that most of the villagers are in one way or another dependent on it for their livelihood. To some extent, the agricultural season sets the pace of social life, although, characteristically, its influence on the culti-vating castes is much more pervasive than on the Brahmins. The annual cycle of ceremonies follows, in part, the rhythm of agriculture, and important agricultural operations are attended by religious rites.

Certain broad figures can be given for the different crops which are grown in the village. These are based on averages for the agricultural seasons of 1958/59, 1959/60, and 1960/61. The extent of the total cultivable land in the revenue village Melur-Sripuram is 801.76 acres; this consists of 105.32 acres of dry land and 696.44 acres of wet land (under river irrigation). On the average, 792.34 acres of the total were actually under cultivation in the seasons considered.

Practically all the wet land in the village is used for raising paddy. Dry land also is sometimes used in paddy cultivation for the preparation of what are called dry nurseries. In the average season 666.76 acres out of the total 792.34 acres were used for raising paddy. Of these, all but 58.87 acres were used for raising two paddy crops consecutively. The remainder of the wet land was devoted to the growing of sugar cane, bananas, and vegetables.

Crops grown in any considerable scale in addition to paddy are coconuts, bananas, sugar cane, and betel vine. These are generally grown on dry land, although sugar cane is grown also on wet land. Bananas are grown almost wholly on the class of dry land known as *paduhai,* and this is largely true of betel vines also. The acreages devoted to these crops for the seasons considered are: 36.23 for coconuts, 31.67 for bananas, 23.72 for sugar cane, and 15.72 for betel vines. This leaves only 18.24 acres for a wide variety of other crops ranging from vegetables and millets to bamboos and oilseeds.

Most of the cultivable land in the village is irrigated and is used for the raising of paddy. The agricultural season proper begins around the time when water is let into the Kaveri, although work on banana and betel-vine gardens goes on all through the year. Between harvesting the second paddy crop around mid-February and making preparations for the new seedbeds in early June is the slack season for agriculturists.

The principal stages of paddy cultivation are: preparation of nurseries; preparation of the field by ploughing and manuring; transplantation; weeding; and harvesting. From the very beginning these activities have to be geared to the point in time at which water is let into the Kaveri at the Grand Anicut. A difference of even a few days may affect the entire sequence, since the operations are coördinated fairly closely. Water is let in at the Grand Anicut sometime around the third week of June on a date which is earlier announced.

The preparation of nurseries is by two methods: dry nurseries (*puzhudi-kal*) and wet nurseries (*neer nattu*). Dry nurseries can be prepared even before water is let into the river, whereas wet nurseries are prepared only after this has been done. It is a little more expensive to prepare dry nurseries, and therefore most of the people in Sripuram depend upon the wet kind.

The great advantage in preparing dry nurseries is that one has the upper hand with regard to time. If one must wait till water is let in, it may become a little difficult to hire agricultural labourers, whose services are greatly in demand at this time. Brahmins and well-to-do Non-Brahmins depend largely on the labour of Adi-Dravidas for most of the physical work associated with tillage, and it may be difficult to get such people when they are most needed. This leads to delays which make it difficult to catch up with the normal schedule of operations right on to the end of the second harvest. The important part played in the processes of agriculture by "free" or "unattached" labour is a feature of the agrarian class structure to which we shall return later (cf. Gough 1955, 1960).

A few prosperous farmers and cultivators prefer to prepare dry nurseries. Work on these begins about twenty days before water is let into the river, near the end of May or in the first week of June. A well is sunk in a corner of the plot which is to serve as nursery, and water is bailed out of it, generally with the help of a lever-like mechanism called a *yettram*. The plot is ploughed over several times, and manure is introduced into the earth. Care is taken to see that the sods are well pulverised so that the surface has more or less the consistency of dust. Water is then let in, and the seeds are sown broadcast.

For the first, or *kuruvai,* crop the seedlings require about twenty-five days to be ready for transplantation. By this time water will have been let into the fields, which are ploughed several times over along with green manure as well as farmyard and chemical manures. The work of transplantation has to be quickly accomplished, and it is done mainly by women. After transplantation, a nursery is usually again ploughed over and replanted with seedlings as in the main fields. Sometimes even the well which is dug for irrigating the dry nursery is filled with earth and planted over with paddy seedlings.

Wet nurseries are prepared only after water has been let into the channels. The plot is allowed to lie for some time under water, allowing the earth to mix well with the water so that it acquires a clayey consistency. The seeds are sown broadcast after ploughing and allowed to grow till they are ready for transplantation as in the previous case. From early June till the middle of July one sees nurseries in various stages of growth. By the end of July transplantation for the first paddy crop is largely over.

The crop takes about three months to grow, and harvesting

begins around early September and continues till the end of October, depending upon when the seeds were sown and whether dry or wet nurseries were employed. In between transplantation and harvesting, weeding operations are performed. Weeding is done mainly by women and harvesting by men and women together.

There are certain stages in the agricultural cycle at which there is a heavy demand for labour. This is so during ploughing, transplanting, weeding, and harvesting. Taking the village as a whole, each of these operations extends over at least a month, with peak periods for each. Further, even when work has come to a temporary standstill in one's own village, there are always some operations being performed in neighbouring villages once the agricultural season has commenced. Thus, the demand for labour continues at a certain level practically throughout the season. It is important to bear this in mind in view of the fact that a large section of the people of Sripuram subsist primarily on casual labour of one kind or another.

Work on the second crop gets under way immediately after the first has been gathered in. Generally nurseries are prepared on unutilised plots while the *kuruvai* crop is still standing on the field. After this has been cut, the fields are ploughed over along with the stubbles, manured, and kept ready for transplantation. In the case of the second, or *samba,* crop also, sowing and the preparation of nurseries are spread over a certain interval of time. Some have their nurseries almost ready by the time the *kuruvai* is harvested, while a few begin work on them only after the first harvest has been gathered.

The *samba* season begins around early September and continues till the end of February, and thus is of longer duration than that of the *kuruvai,* taking about five months from the preparation of nurseries to the gathering of harvest. The seedlings take from five to six weeks to be ready for transplantation from the nursery to the main field. Transplantation is followed after some time by weeding, and harvests commence after the middle of January.

In some cases the *samba* may not be raised as the second crop, but as the first and only paddy crop. This, however, is done very rarely in Sripuram, where the land is fertile enough to make the raising of two crops sufficiently profitable. Where the *samba* is grown as the only crop, and not as the *thal adi,* or second crop, the preparation of nurseries is begun sometime in August and the harvest is gathered in by early January. In the three seasons considered in our study, the *samba* crop was raised as the only crop on an average of 58.87 acres, whereas on 607.89 acres it was raised as the *thal adi* or second crop.

It is customary to raise black gram, green gram, and a kind of green manure known locally as *kolinji* on the paddy fields after the second harvest. Most of the area used for growing paddy is sown with gram and green manure, but the exact acreage cannot be estimated, as accounts for these crops are not kept with the village accountant. Green and black gram are used as alternatives, and green manure seeds are mixed with either the one or the other. The acreage under green gram is roughly twice that under black gram.

The raising of black gram and green gram involves very little investment of either capital or labour. About a week or ten days before the second paddy harvest, the seeds are sown broadcast on the field. By the time the paddy stalks are cut down, the seedlings will have sprouted to a height of about four inches. The fields will have absorbed enough moisture for the gram and green manure to thrive even though watering is stopped a week before the paddy harvest. These crops do not require as much water as paddy.

Of the 105.32 acres of dry land, about 40 per cent is of the special class known as *paduhai.* Much of this land is used for raising bananas, which are one of the chief cash crops grown in the village. The cultivation of bananas requires greater care and attention than that of paddy, and more money has to be invested per acre on manure and on keeping up a continuous supply of water, either manually or through the installation of pump-sets. Also, a banana orchard is normally maintained for a period of at least two and a half years. These differences in mode of cultivation generally give a different character to relationships between lessor and lessee in the case of bananas as compared to paddy.

Work on banana gardens is begun usually in December-January, i.e., in the slack season just preceding the second paddy harvest. The land is first hoed, and then small pits are dug at intervals of four to five feet. The roots are planted in the pits along with a copious supply of manure. Within a week or so the whole garden is thoroughly ploughed over. The pits in which the roots are planted are dug sufficiently deep so that the roots do not get turned over during the process of ploughing. A couple of days later the shoots begin to appear.

After this, trenches are dug about nine inches deep and six inches wide in rows parallel to the shoots. These trenches serve to hold up water, which has to be regularly supplied, particularly during the early stages of growth. The pits are covered with ash and farmyard manure at intervals.

Once the shoots begin to sprout, the most important problem is that of keeping up a regular supply of water. This is done by bailing water, either out of a well, usually dug for the purpose, or from the river. During the wet season there is not much difficulty, but in summer, when the river is dry, a good deal of care and attention are necessary. The bailing of water is accomplished either by use of the *yettram,* which involves much labour and time, or by installing a pump-set with an electric motor, which requires investment of a different kind. Only one person in Sripuram now owns a pump-set, but such sets can be hired by others, either from this person or from Thiruvaiyar.

The first banana crop is ready in about ten to twelve months, depending upon the variety grown. A second crop is available six to seven months thereafter, and sometimes a third crop is also harvested. After the second crop, however, the trees are usually allowed to grow only for their leaves, and sometimes an entire garden may be cultivated wholly for this purpose; if leaves are cut early and regularly the fruits do not grow properly. The garden is usually ploughed and manured after the first crop has been gathered. After about two years the trees are cut down, the land is ploughed over, and a fresh garden is prepared.

Bananas are often grown in rotation with sugar cane or betel vines. Sometimes a plot of *paduhai* is given on short lease for six months or so during which period vegetables may be grown on it. Sugar cane has been introduced into the village only recently. It is grown on both *paduhai* and wet land. Sugar cane is generally planted around February or March and is ready for harvest around January. As with bananas, the growing of sugar cane requires copious supplies of manure and water, and in addition proper and careful drainage. Personal supervision is required to a greater extent than in the case of paddy.

Most exacting of all is the cultivation of betel vines. This requires not only great patience and application, but also certain specialised skills. For this reason the area under betel vine in Sripuram is only 15.72 acres, although its successful cultivation yields high returns.

Coconuts are often raised in the backyards of houses, but there are separate orchards in addition. Coconut palms do not require much attention once they have been planted, and they yield fruit after ten years, continuing to yield for forty years or so. Coconut orchards are often given on lease to outsiders, while palms growing in the backyards supply nuts for domestic consumption. Formerly coconut orchards were taken on lease by toddy contractors, but with the introduction of prohibition they are now grown primarily for their nuts.

Very few vegetables are grown in the village. Most of the vegetables used for domestic consumption have to be purchased from the market at Thiruvaiyar. They are brought there by villagers from the other side of the river Coleroon, where scarcity of irrigated paddy land leads to specialisation in vegetable farming. In most of the Brahmin houses, bananas and a few coconuts are grown in the backyards and furnish part of the domestic requirements.

III

The processes of production which have been briefly sketched necessitate the interaction of different categories of people. Production is socially organised to the extent that it involves relations between persons having more or less specific rights, duties, and obligations with regard to one another. The relations of production tend to create cleavages as well as bonds between classes of persons. These cleavages partly coincide with other cleavages in the social structure, such as those of caste, and partly cut across them.

The basic cleavage within the class structure is between owners and nonowners of the means of production. As far as agriculture is concerned, this reduces essentially to ownership or nonownership of land. Neither owners nor nonowners, however, constitute homogeneous categories. There is a considerable difference, for instance, between the big absentee landlord or *mirasdar* and the small owner-cultivator who tills the land with his own labour or that of his family; there is also a difference between the cultivating tenant more or less permanently associated with a sizeable amount of land and the agricultural labourer who works for daily wages in cash.

An analysis of relations between the different classes has to begin with a consideration of the basic principles of land tenure. These principles have been undergoing certain fundamental changes, especially during the last decade. Changes in land tenure have not become stabilised as yet, and there is a good deal of divergence between principle and practice in the sphere of agrarian relations. There are also variations from one landowner to another as to the obligations of tenure actually enforced in practice.

Land tenure in Tanjore District has a complex history, and it is necessary to have some awareness of this because of its influence on contemporary agrarian relations. In some respects legislative enactments have only brought about changes in form, allowing the substance to remain more or less unaltered. In others, however, formal changes are being followed by substantial changes in the content of relationships between the different agricultural classes.

The separation between ownership and cultivation of land, and the social and economic nexus arising out of this, has been a part of the organisation of Tanjore villages as far back as tradition goes. An *agraharam* such as that at Sripuram was often created by grafting a community of Brahmins from outside and giving them title either to remission of revenue or to ownership of land which, in any case, was tilled by separate classes of people. And, as we have seen, Brahmins were not the only people to be settled in this manner; in Sripuram the Maratha family provides an instance of Non-Brahmin landowners being settled in the village in a manner similar to that of the Brahmins.

Economic differentiation in the village was, in a sense, sharper fifty years ago than it is today. There was, certainly, greater concentration of land for productive purposes, and, what is perhaps more important, land did not pass as easily from one set of persons to another. Landowners as a class had in many ways a more homogeneous and sharply defined character than they have today. People having rather diverse social backgrounds are now in a position to invest in land, which is more in the market today than it was in the past. This in part is due to the extension of a cash economy and in part is a sequel to certain recent political changes (see Gough, 1955 and 1960; also Bailey, 1957).

There are no really big landowners in the village today. Although a complete list of land holdings, together with names of owners, is kept with the village accountant, it is difficult to give quantitative measures of the ownership and concentration of land. It is often a matter of policy for a *mirasdar* to have titles to land under the names of different members of his family, and sometimes also in the names of persons who may be outside his household.

Not every individual who has a title to land constitutes an effective landowning unit. Often the holdings of several individuals are concentrated in a unit which is managed and administered by a person who may not himself have any formal title to the land. The biggest *mirasdar* resident in Sripuram has very little land in his own name. Some of it is in his wife's name, some in her mother's name, and some even in the names of relatives who do not form a part of his household. All this land, nonetheless, constitutes a single unit for productive purposes, being controlled and managed by a single individual who is all but its *legal* owner.

Further, among title holders, those who live outside the village are almost equal in number to those who live within it, if the settlements at Melur are taken into account; if the latter are excluded, then nonresidents outnumber the residents (of Sripuram proper, that is) in the proportion of about three to two. In the case of nonresidents, particularly, it is not feasible to ascertain from the list of titles how the different title holders should be grouped into effective landowning units. Finally, many of the residents of Sripuram own land in other villages; some of them have more land in Peramur and Vishnupuram than in their place of residence. Since these facts do not permit a full quantitative analysis, discussion must be limited to qualitative and impressionistic terms.

The biggest *mirasdar* resident in Sripuram owns about 25 acres of land in the village and small amounts elsewhere. Even a generation ago there were people in the village owning 50 acres or more. Towards the beginning of the present century there were at least half a dozen families owning more than 50 acres, and one of them owned more than 100 acres in Sripuram and, in addition, considerable amounts in the adjacent villages of Peramur and Vishnupuram.

In spite of certain changes, most of the land in the village continues to be held by the old landowning class, i.e., the descendants and heirs of the people who were the landowners in the traditional system. In course of the last few decades, however, some land has passed out of the hands of this class, and the process seems to have acquired momentum over the last ten years. Partition within the family has contributed to the virtual disappearance of large estates, although this process by itself does not lead to the transference of land from one class to another.

Several factors seem to have played a part in the break-up of large estates. The old landowning class, divorced from the processes of cultivation, followed a pattern of life in which conspicuous consumption played an important part. Inordinate expenditure on marriage and other ceremonial occasions led in several instances to large estates' being encumbered by debts. Gambling and speculation in various forms contributed to the collapse of a number of landowning families in the village. The most striking case, though by no means the only one in Sripuram, is that of the Maratha family, which has been reduced within a generation from a position of great opulence to one of comparative poverty through speculation and conspicuous consumption.

To understand the process of disintegration it is necessary to reconstruct the life of the *mirasdar* as it was lived a generation ago. The tempo of life was slow and relaxed, and the burdens of agriculture were left mainly to be shouldered by tenants and cultivators. The *mirasdar* had generally very little to do with the actual supervision of agricultural operations. He spent the long day on the *payal,* engaged in gossip and convivial association, and often played cards into the early hours of the morning. Until a few years ago several men met regularly in the school building and played cards late into the night. In addition to gambling at cards, large sums of money were lost by betting at the race-course at Guindy.

Idle living and wasteful expenditure, however, go only some way in explaining the transfer of land. Other factors were perhaps even more important. From the beginning of this century onwards many *mirasdars* began to invest in the education of their sons. This was usually an expensive affair, since providing college education for a son meant maintaining him in a town or city for between two and six years. Often part of the ancestral land had to be sold to meet the expenses of education. This process continues today and, if anything, at an accelerated pace.

As the younger generation of *mirasdars* acquired Western education, many of them moved out of the village in search of suitable employment. Movement of landowners away from the village has been taking place over the last fifty years, and today most of the big *mirasdars* of Sripuram are absentee landowners. Attachment to land is generally weaker among sons of absentee landowners brought up in the city than among those who are engaged in the cultivation or supervision of their own estates. Generally the returns of the absentee landlord are less, since evasion is easier for the tenant when the landowner is not on the spot.

The absentee landowner tends to dispose of his land for two reasons. First, it is difficult for him to be in direct touch with the land, and this has obvious basic disadvantages. Second, life in the city involves greater expenditure and offers alternative avenues of investment. It has to be remembered that the old landowning class in Sripuram is one which had at no time any direct connection with agriculture, and, in addition, that it adapted itself with particular ease to the opportunities provided by Western education and urban employment. This is by no means true of the landowning class as a whole in Tamilnad. There are, as we shall see, significant differences between the old landowning class in Sripuram and a new one which seems to be emerging.

Land legislation since 1952 has progressively weakened the

position of the absentee landlord, the noncultivating landowner, and the big *mirasdar*. Although there are ways of getting round the law, the old landowning class in Sripuram now finds itself with its back to the wall. The same laws which threaten the interests of the old landowning class favour in some ways the growth of a new type of landowner, rooted to the village, tied closely to agriculture, and owning a measure of land which is adequate, but well below the ceiling.

In 1961 the imposition by law of a thirty-acre ceiling on wet land gave a final blow to the big *mirasdar* in Sripuram. Not many were directly affected by the law, since almost all the estates in the village had in their natural course of disintegration been reduced to sizes well below the ceiling. But the ceiling had a profound effect in altering the attitude to investment among the old *mirasdars* who were already in a state of decline. Land ceased to have the same unique value among them as it had in the past.

The impact of the ceiling law can be gauged from the fact that the sale of land shot up in the 1960/61 agricultural season when the law was passed in the Legislature. During this season about 150 acres of land changed hands. In the following season the amount transferred by sale was 50 acres.

Sale of land in the village shows certain broad patterns which will be discussed at some length later. One fact, meanwhile, may be indicated here. The sale and transfer of land is, to a large extent, dependent on forces which do not have their origin in the village, but operate over a much wider sphere. It is impossible to understand shifts in the composition of the landowning class by confining one's attention entirely to the village. One is necessarily drawn into an examination of changes in the structure of Tamil society as a whole.

There are certain features, even so, which seem to be specifically associated with Sripuram as a village. Many of the *mirasdars* who have acquired land through inheritance do not really belong to the village, but came to settle in it as sons-in-law. In fact, the *agraharam* at Sripuram is jokingly referred to as an *agraharam* of *mappillais* (sons-in-law). The biggest *mirasdar* resident in Sripuram today does not belong to the village, but has settled there to look after his wife's estate. It would be difficult to account for the peculiar constellation of demographic factors which has led to a preponderance of daughters over sons in the bigger landowning families of the village.

There has been considerable movement into the village of sons-in-law and maternal relatives, and away from it of sons and agnates into the urban areas in search of education and employment. This has had the consequence of giving the old landowning class in the village a somewhat fluid character. It has also disturbed to some extent the continuity of relations between landowners and tenants which constituted the bulwark of the traditional economic structure.

At the risk of too much simplification one can say that there have been three phases in the career of the old landowning class in Sripuram. The first phase was one in which it was tied more or less firmly to the village and relations between landlords and tenants were of a fairly close and durable character. In the second phase, which commenced towards the beginning of the present century, the old landowners began to look beyond the frontiers of rural society and many of them moved out, becoming absentee landlords. A third phase seems to have set in recently, in which the old landowning families, already much depleted, have become keenly aware of their insecure position and are gradually beginning to dispose of their land.

What is the character of the new landowning class which is emerging in the village? One can speak only with caution, because as yet this class is in a state of incipient growth and does not have a fixed or definable character. It is still very much under the shadow of the old class of noncultivating *mirasdars* and absentee landlords.

The separation between ownership and cultivation of land which was so sharp at the end of the nineteenth century is less today. The number of owner-cultivators was negligible in the past. Today their number is increasing, although even now most owners of land in Sripuram do not engage in cultivation. Whereas land has been sold mainly by the old *mirasdar* class, a part of it, at least, has been bought by the small cultivating tenants of the village. It is still true, however, that much of the land tends to be bought and sold by people who live outside the village and are not cultivators.

Thus, we find that ownership of land is vested in people with different social backgrounds and that landowners do not constitute a homogeneous class. One can distinguish at least three subdivisions, not all of which are themselves homogeneous. These are: (1) a section of absentee landowners resident mainly in towns and cities, with diverse social backgrounds; (2) a section of noncultivating *mirasdars* resident in the village, with a more or less homogeneous social background; and (3) a growing section of small holders resident in the village and directly engaged in cultivation or in close touch with it.

In a slightly different way the landowners can be grouped into two major divisions: rentiers and farmers. Rentiers are those who live on rents (i.e., returns on their land) without contributing any labour to the agricultural process. Farmers are those who contribute labour, either by directly participating in cultivation or through supervision. More than three quarters of the land in Sripuram today is under the ownership of rentiers.

There are intermediate types between the rentier and the farmer. Some persons lease certain parts of their land and have other parts cultivated under their own supervision. Nor is it true that the farmer, as defined above, is necessarily a resident of the village. A few persons owning land in Sripuram live in Thiruvaiyar and Tanjore and have their estates supervised by paid agents.

There are certain basic differences between rentier and farmer. The rentier does not invest in the productive process. Plough cattle, manure, seeds, and so on are supplied by the tenant to whom he leases his land. The only payment which the rentier makes is the annual land revenue payable to the government. The farmer, on the other hand, invests in the productive process and in such improvements as may be considered necessary. Improved methods of farming are likely to be applied more on land held by farmers than by rentiers.

The difference between rentier and farmer is socially an important one. Its legal importance has been shown in certain states, such as Maharashtra, by the dispossessing of the rentier of his land. Although this has not happened in Tamilnad, the rentiers there are becoming keenly aware of the weakness of their legal position in the face of changing conditions. The biggest *mirasdar* now resident in Sripuram left his city job in order to settle in the village and supervise his estate so as to establish beyond question his title to the land.

Whereas at one end of the scale the farmer tends to merge with the rentier, at the other he tends to merge with what we shall refer to as the cultivator. The cultivator is one who owns a small plot of land which is cultivated wholly or mainly by his own labour or that of his family. He does not normally hire labour, except on such occasions as transplantation and harvesting, when the labour of a single family may not be sufficient. The cultivator owns not only the land on which he works, but also the other means of production necessary to his purpose. The number of cultivators of this kind in Sripuram is small. The cultivator has this in common with the rentier and the farmer, that he owns some land; with the tenant and the agricultural labourer he shares the characteristic of being a manual worker.

IV

The majority of people who are engaged in agricultural work are nonowners of land. They work on land owned by others, and this constitutes the basis of economic and social ties between the different classes of people in the village. Among the nonowners of land engaged in agriculture it is necessary to distinguish between two broad classes, the tenants and the agricultural labourers.

It needs to be emphasized here that landowners and tenants constitute distinct entities only as conceptual categories, and not as concrete groups of individuals. One and the same person may be, and not infrequently is, both an owner of land and a tenant on somebody else's land. It is essential to appreciate this multiple class affiliation, since because of it one and the same person is often pulled by conflicting interests in different directions. This has the general consequence of preventing class interests from becoming sharply focussed and classes from being clearly ranged against one another.

It is also important to realise that social classes are dynamic categories. There is considerable circulation of personnel between the different classes. A man who is a tenant one year may, and sometimes does, become an owner-cultivator the next year. (This tends to happen in the village with increasing frequency as land passes more out of the hands of the old *mirasdar* class.) Similarly an agricultural labourer may be transformed into a tenant, and vice versa.

The different classes are not separated into watertight compartments. Individuals belong to one or more of them, and sometimes they pass from one class to another in the course of a short period. This tends to impede the development of a consciousness of class, although the conflict of interest between classes is often acute and does sometimes come to the surface. More frequently this conflict tends to be posed in terms other than those of class and to run along cleavages which are more sharply defined in the social structure, such as those of caste (see chap. vi).

Tenants as a class are the typical complement of rentiers. The general practice of the *mirasdar* in Sripuram is to give his land on lease to one or more tenants or lessees who pay him a stipulated quantity of grain at the end of the harvest. The lessee is required to meet the entire cost of cultivation, and only the demand of land revenue payable to the government is met by the rentier or *mirasdar*. Traditionally relations between lessor and lessee were of a more or less permanent character, although a change of tenant did take place from time to time.

The terms and conditions of lease vary with the kind of land and the crops grown. The major difference is between lease on wet land used for paddy cultivation and *paduhai* land used for the cultivation of bananas, betel vines, and other cash crops. Since paddy cultivation is by far the most important agricultural activity in the village, we shall consider first the nature of the relationship between lessor and lessee with regard to paddy land.

Traditionally there have been two systems for the lease of land, *waram* and *kuttahai*. Only the latter is prevalent in the village today, as it has been for the last few decades, although it is said that the *waram* system was not unknown thirty to forty years ago. It must be mentioned that the system of lease accepted as the mode in recent land legislation in Tamilnad approximates closely to the traditional *waram* system and differs in important ways from the one in practice, the *kuttahai* system.

In the *waram* system the landlord gives a plot of land on lease to a tenant and shares the harvest with him, taking a *proportion* of it previously agreed upon. The sharing of crops is done at the threshing floor. Since, in this system, the landlord takes a certain proportion of the produce, losses due to bad harvests and gains due to good ones are shared between lessor and lessee. Legislation since Independence fixed the lessee's share first at 40 per cent and then at 60 per cent. The legislation in this form is, however, largely inoperative as far as Sripuram is concerned.

In the *kuttahai* system, the lessee, known as the *kuttahaidar*, undertakes to pay a fixed *quantity* of grain for the land which he takes on lease. The quantity of grain measured out per acre to the *mirasdar* is, to some extent, variable. Small variations are determined by the quality of land, extra-economic relations between lessor and lessee, and the bargaining strength of the one with regard to the other. A big *mirasdar* who has a number of tenants at his disposal can generally bargain for a slightly higher amount than a small *mirasdar* who has only a single tenant. Also, the quantity depends on whether the tenant takes his lease directly from a *mirasdar* or from a person who is himself a lessee, as happens in certain cases.

The *kuttahaidar* contributes both labour and capital in the form of seeds, manure, plough cattle, and so forth. On very broad averages, he gives to the landlord a quantity of grain which varies between 65 and 70 per cent of the total produce. In recent times there has been a slight downward shift in the proportion given to the lessor, although it rarely goes below 65 per cent of what is produced on the land. Although these figures represent rather broad averages, and the shares given and retained have not yet become stable, it will be easily observed that there is a fairly big difference between what is prescribed by law and what operates in practice.

The relationship between lessor and lessee has a quasi-legal character, being subject to the jurisdiction of courts which derive their authority from the state. The two parties are, in theory, required to seal their relationship by signing a lease deed, a copy of which is required to be deposited with the registrar. In practice lease deeds are fulfilled more by traditional usage and sanction than by the strict execution of the written code; however, a departure from the letter of the law is allowed only within certain limits, and disputes over leases are known to have been taken to the courts.

Tensions between landlords and tenants centre around two important questions: (1) the share of the produce to be taken by each, and (2) the security of tenure guaranteed by the relationship. Attempts have been made to resolve both these questions through legislation. We have examined the nature of legislation pertaining to the first question, and also pointed to its limited success. With regard to the second question, legislation seems to have been rather more successful. Eviction of tenants is today more difficult than it was in the past.

Traditionally the relation between landlord and tenant tended to be of an enduring character. It not only lasted through the life span of the individual, but was usually handed down from one generation to another. Even today a large number of such relationships are of this kind, being based upon ties between two families which have more than a purely economic component. But in the past a landlord might evict a tenant, or have him replaced by another, for failure to meet his dues or for some other reason. In Sripuram one meets with many instances of landlords' having changed their tenants in recent years.

A series of legislative enactments, beginning with the Tanjore Tenants and Pannaiyal Protection Act of 1952, have progressively established security of tenure for the lessee and taken away from the landlord the right to evict tenants arbitrarily. The position of the landlord vis-à-vis the tenant has become weaker today in comparison with the past, although a shrewd and powerful landowner is usually able to exploit loopholes in the law to his own advantage. Whether the landlord or the tenant is in a stronger bargaining position depends partly upon caste and other social factors, in addition to those which are purely economic in nature.

The aim of recent legislation has been essentially to give security to the small cultivating tenant and to reduce the privileges of the big *mirasdar*. It does not fully protect the big tenant from eviction. A lessee is given security of tenure over wet land only to the extent of 6⅔ acres (1 *veli*). A landlord may recover from his tenant either for personal cultivation, or for lease to some other individual, any amount of wet land in excess of 6⅔ acres. Further, a *mirasdar* is himself allowed to bring under personal cultivation wet land up to a maximum of 6⅔ acres, even though this may lead to displacement.

Tenants themselves do not constitute a single homogeneous class. On the one hand are the persons who secure leases on a more or less permanent basis on several acres of land, some of which they sublet while having the rest cultivated by hired labourers. On the other are the small tenants without means or power to vindicate their rights of security, having to seek from year to year an acre or two of land from some benevolent *mirasdar*. A person may have to do many favours to a *mirasdar* in order to secure from him a few acres of land on lease. Once having secured the lease, such a person is not always in a position to make use of the legal provisions to hold fast to it for good.

An important difference exists between tenants who take their lease directly from the landlord and those who are lessees of people who are tenants themselves. The latter are, naturally, able to bargain for a higher share from those to whom they lease the land than the tenant normally gives to a landowner. The difference is retained by the tenant at first hand whose role is, thus, that of an intermediary. Subletting, however, is not a very common phenomenon in the case of paddy cultivation. What is more common is for the tenant to have his land cultivated by hired labourers whose work he supervises.

Subletting is fairly common in the cultivation of bananas and betel vines. This is, to some extent, related to the difference in techniques of production between the cultivation of paddy and the cultivation of bananas and betel vines. In the case of bananas, a plot of *paduhai* belonging to *A* is often taken on lease by *B*, payment being normally made in cash; *B* cultivates the garden, and when the first crop is ready he may lease it for one year or so to *C*, also for cash, the rate being normally Rs. 50P per plant.

It is quite common for banana orchards (as opposed to the *paduhai* on which they are prepared) to be taken on lease by wholesale merchants from outside the village. Many of the orchards in Sripuram are taken on lease by a dealer from Ariyalur, a marketing centre in Trichy district. There are others from Thiruvaiyar who also take leases on gardens located in

Sripuram. Intermediaries generally play an important part in both the production and the marketing of cash crops such as bananas.

The cultivation of betel vines also requires coöperation between a number of individuals. Since this process involves a good deal of care and attention, the person who prepares a garden is not able to maintain the whole of it with his own labour or that of his family. It is quite common for even a small betel-vine garden to be subdivided into eight or ten plots, and for some of these to be leased to others while only a few are maintained by the person who prepared them.

Coconut orchards also are often leased to outsiders. Although the lease on a coconut orchard is usually for a longer period, here also the nexus between lessor and lessee is one of cash. In fact, the leases on cash crops introduce intermediaries whose role is often more important in marketing the crops than in their cultivation. Such intermediaries generally belong outside the village and are comparable more with merchants and wholesale dealers than with tenant cultivators in the narrow sense of the term. They provide links with the urban market and bring the rural economy into close relation with the economy of the region.

V

Finally, we come to the class of agricultural labourers. These differ in several ways from lessees or tenants. The most important difference between the agricultural labourer and the tenant is the labourer's lack of security of employment. The tenant, once he acquires a lease, is assured of some work for at least one entire season; in most cases, either by traditional usage or through the sanction of law, he is able to retain his lease indefinitely.

In contrast, the agricultural labourer is often in a position of having to seek employment from day to day. Just before the commencement of the agricultural season one can see landless people waiting on the *mirasdar* and approaching him for the lease of a small plot of land. Failing in this, they may request that the *mirasdar* provide some work on his own farm, if he has any. Payments to agricultural labourers are, with certain exceptions, made in cash. The rates vary from Rs. 1.00P to Rs. 2.50P per day, depending upon the nature of work, and have shown a good deal of fluctuation in recent years.

The Tanjore Tenants and Panniyal Protection Act of 1952 sought to remedy the lack of security in the position of the *pannaiyal,* or agricultural labourer. Its success has been limited. The law lays down that a *pannaiyal,* once engaged as a farm labourer, must be provided with employment by the farmer at a certain minimum rate throughout the season. The relationship between landowner and *pannaiyal* is required to be formalised by a legal contract. Most farmers, however, evade the law by simply not entering into any formal contract whatever and by employing casual labourers for daily wages in cash.

Another important characteristic of the agricultural labourer is that he does not provide any of the capital necessary for the agricultural process. Seeds, manure, and plough cattle are supplied by the farmer. The agricultural labourer contributes only his labour. There are, however, certain marginal cases, as of the labourer who hires himself along with a plough and plough cattle; his wage rate is naturally higher than that of the one who hires only himself. Several *mirasdars* who have their land cultivated directly do not, in fact, own the instruments of tillage. They have to engage people who possess such instruments and who naturally charge a higher rate for their use. These people are sometimes cultivators or tenants in addition to being agricultural labourers.

The agricultural labourer is generally paid in cash, although for certain operations he may also be paid in kind; grain payments are quite common, almost the general rule, during harvest. Wages for agricultural labourers are rising. The amount paid, however, varies according to the nature of work and between one labourer and another. A well-to-do landowner who is in a position to provide employment for a number of people usually pays less. He may pay as little as Rs. 1.25P per day per man, while some other person may have to pay anything between Rs. 1.50P and Rs. 1.75P, depending upon the time of the year and the nature of work. If a man brings his own plough and plough cattle, he demands between Rs. 2.00P and Rs. 2.50P. A woman gets between Rs. 1.00P and Rs. 1.25P for a day's work.

In addition to cash earnings, a family of agricultural labourers earns paddy at the time of harvest. During the *samba* harvest a man and his wife earn generally about five bags of paddy, worth approximately Rs. 100.00P. During the *kuruvai* harvest the earning is rather less. Women earn most at the time of transplantation and during weeding.

The class of agricultural labourers in the village is not inconsiderable in size. It is difficult to form an estimate of how many households are engaged in this occupation, because the number changes from one season to another and because agricultural labour is often combined with other occupations. Roughly speaking, it can be said that between 20 and 25 per cent of the households in the village depend upon casual labour as a principal source of livelihood. The total number of those who are tillers without possessing any land of their own is, of course, much larger.

VI

Having given an account of the different classes engaged in agricultural production, we shall review briefly three problems already touched upon: (1) the ownership of land, its concentration, and the extent to which it is held by people outside the village; (2) the relationship between the different classes as it works itself out in the actual process of agriculture; and (3) changes in social and economic relationships as these are being brought about by legislation and other external factors.

More than half the land in the village is owned by people who live outside it. Of the five big *mirasdars* who own more than twenty acres each, four live outside the village and only one lives in it. He too does not belong to the village, but came to settle there primarily because of the insecurity of absentee landownership. He now has his land cultivated partly under personal supervision and partly through lessees.

Of the four other big *mirasdars,* three live in Tanjore and one in Srirangam. The latter owns the largest amount of land in the village and, in addition, owns some in the adjacent villages of Peramur and Vishnupuram. His estates are managed by a cultivator resident in Sripuram who gives leases to various persons and collects the rents for the owner in return for a certain commission. The owner visits the village once or twice every year.

The three landowners who live in Tanjore all have close connections with Sripuram. Two of them have domestic establishments there. One, whose widowed mother lives in the village, makes frequent visits to her both in order to collect rents and for other purposes. The second used to live in Sripuram until recently, but has now moved to Tanjore, where he has business interests. He comes almost daily to the village, where his daughter and son-in-law reside in the ancestral house and look after the estate. The third and last person never belonged to Sripuram, but has business connections at Tanjore with the second. His interests in Sripuram are looked after by an agent, as well as by several friends in the village.

It should be noted that in the case of the two persons mentioned last, income from land constitutes only one among several sources of earnings. Both are engaged in commerce and have fairly high earnings, some of which they have been investing in land. They have also purchased land in other villages recently. The ceiling law is evaded by having titles under the names of different members of the family. It follows that legislation on land is not *always* a deterrent to continued investment in it, even by people who may be regarded as absentee landowners in the broad sense of the term.

Separation between ownership of land and residence in the village usually comes about in one of two different ways. First, those who own land in the village may move out of it in search of education or employment, or for some other reason. We have seen how this has been a continuous process with the old landowning class. The consequence of this movement is that persons born and brought up in different places become by inheritance owners of land in Sripuram, which is their ancestral village. There are many who have hardly ever lived in the village and are, nevertheless, owners of land there. In a few instances land has been inherited by women who have moved out of the village after marriage.

Second, many among those who move out of the village and get tied to places far away from it tend ultimately to sell their ancestral land. Such land is often bought by persons who live outside the village, but in sufficient proximity to be able to maintain a close connection with it. These include people whose primary economic interests are other than agricultural. One finds instances of lawyers or businessmen from Tanjore investing in land in Sripuram. Sripuram attracts buyers from outside partly because of the very high quality of its agricultural land.

Since the majority of landowners do not themselves engage in cultivation, they have to enter into relations with other agricultural classes for this purpose. Two systems are prevalent in Sripuram today, the first being the *kuttahai* system, and the second the *pannaiyal* system. The former system is adopted by the majority of *mirasdars,* although some find it convenient to combine the two.

The *kuttahai* system, as has been mentioned, is one in which a lease is given on land in return for annual rents paid in kind at the end of each harvest. There seem to be two principal reasons for the predominance of this mode of relationship. In the first place, as we have seen, many of the landowners live outside the village, and personal supervision in such cases is always difficult and often impossible; absentee landlordism goes hand in hand with the *kuttahai* system. Second, the majority of *mirasdars* in Sripuram belong to a class which has been traditionally associated with pursuits very different from agriculture. Even when he is resident in the village, a *mirasdar* usually finds it more congenial to lease his land to some tenant and to have as little connection as possible with the business of cultivation, which fits ill with his style of life.

A third factor seems to play a contributory role in maintaining the separation between the ownership of land and its actual use. In recent years particularly, relations between the landowning and cultivating classes in the village have become strained, partly due to political factors which will be discussed later. Landowners are often hesitant to enter into close relations with agricultural labourers over whom their control has become uncertain. They often complain about the exacting and insolent attitudes of their labourers. To have the land cultivated directly would require a *mirasdar* to engage labourers who cannot any more be kept in check by the old sanctions operative in the past. The best escape from such a situation lies in leasing out land to a tenant with whom one's contacts are of a limited and formal nature.

A tenant or lessee, having secured a piece of land, does not necessarily cultivate it himself. Sometimes he gives it on lease to some other person for a rent higher than what he turns over to the *mirasdar*. Such a practice, apart from being gainful economically, also has political advantages. Land being very much in demand, a man is generally able to consolidate his social and political influence if he can give leases to landless persons. Such intermediaries are generally powerful people; being socially closer to the landless classes, they are able to use means to control them which are not available to the generality of *mirasdars*.

More commonly the tenant engages agricultural labourers for the purpose of raising crops on the land he has leased. His own contribution of manual labour is variable in extent. If he is a small tenant, he puts in most of the work himself, engaging a few extra hands during transplantation or harvest and in his turn doing the same kind of work for other people. If he is prosperous and has leases on many plots of land, he has the bulk of the manual work done by engaging agricultural labourers.

Sometimes a rentier may, as a special favour or in return for benefits of some other kind, give some land on lease to an indigent relative. The biggest *mirasdar* resident in Sripuram, a Shri Vaishnava Brahmin by caste, regularly gives some land on lease to his mother-in-law's sister's husband, who looks after his affairs in general. The latter, being a Brahmin by caste, does not himself till the land, but has it cultivated by casual labourers who are paid daily wages, usually in cash.

Not all landowners, of course, lease their land to tenants. Some have it cultivated directly, either with their own personal labour or by engaging servants and casual labourers. The latter procedure is what has been referred to as the *pannaiyal* system. The number of people who follow the *pannaiyal* system is limited among the old *mirasdar* class for reasons which have been mentioned earlier.

Within the village there are a few landowners who have emerged from a peasant, rather than a rentier, background. It is these people, mainly, who either adopt the *pannaiyal* system or themselves engage in cultivation. Although the number of such people is increasing, few of them even now have enough land to be able to do without being tenants in addition to landowners.

The productive process, by bringing into existence social

relations between different classes of people, gives a kind of vertical unity to the village, making landowners, tenants, and agricultural labourers dependent upon one another. People having a diversity of backgrounds and interests are brought into relationship with each other by virtue of their complementary roles in the system of production.

But these relations of production, as is evident from what has been said earlier, easily overflow the boundaries of the village. About half of the landowners live outside the village. For some of them Sripuram is merely the ancestral village whence their father or grandfather came. Some have neither lived in Sripuram nor had any connection with it through their ancestors. Although a large number of such absentee landlords reside either in Thiruvaiyar or Tanjore, there are many who live in other districts of Tamilnad and some who live in other states. Through the land which they own, and through their tenants, they constitute an essential part of the economic structure of the village.

While landowners from outside have tenants in Sripuram, some of the *mirasdars* of the village, in their turn, have tenants from neighbouring villages. In a few cases both the *mirasdar* and the tenant reside outside the village; only the land which binds them together is located within the physical boundaries of Sripuram. In such cases the *karnam*, or village accountant, provides a nexus between the landowner and the tenant.

The geographical spread of tenants as a class is much more limited than that of landowners, for the simple reason that tenants have to be in fairly close proximity to the land, whether they cultivate it themselves or have it cultivated by agricultural labourers. Most of the nonresident tenants are from Peramur, Thiruvaiyar, or some other adjacent village. Agricultural holdings being continuous in their distribution, it often happens that a plot of land which is within the revenue jurisdiction of Melur is in closer proximity to the residential area of some other village than to that of Sripuram. In such cases it is easy to see how tenants may cultivate land in Melur-Sripuram although they reside in some other village.

Similarly, residents of Sripuram sometimes take leases on land situated in Thiruvaiyar. It has already been pointed out that several *mirasdars* of Sripuram own land in the adjacent villages.

This creates further economic bonds which cut across village boundaries. The two villages of Peramur and Vishnupuram, particularly, have a considerable amount of land owned by the *mirasdars* of Sripuram for reasons which have been explained earlier. In addition, either by purchase or by inheritance, such persons have also acquired land in other neighbouring and distant villages. There are families in Sripuram having ancestral land in a village in Mysore State.

Agricultural labourers, and the land on which they work, likewise cut across village boundaries. During the slack season it is quite common to find whole batches of labourers from Sripuram working on a strip of *paduhai* located within the boundary of Thiruvaiyar, owned by a person from an adjacent village, and leased to someone else from yet another village.

Sripuram, in turn, receives casual labourers from other villages. This happens especially during the time of harvests, when people come in search of work even from fairly distant places. Nowhere are village boundaries so sharp as to exclude casual labourers from adjoining villages. It is doubtful that this phenomenon is entirely of recent origin, or that the single village was ever an economically self-sufficient unit, except in a relative sense.

It is evident that relations between the different classes have not remained static, but have undergone certain important changes. These changes, which seem to have begun towards the end of the nineteenth century, continue to work themselves out. They have assumed an increased importance since Independence.

Some of the major changes in economic structure have been associated with legislative enactments. A series of laws, beginning with the Tanjore Tenants and Pannaiyal Protection Act of 1952, have been passed in the state legislature with the objective of giving a more equitable character to agrarian relations. It is unnecessary to examine here all the social factors which have been behind the enactment of these laws, or their full social consequences, but there are two features to be borne in mind. First, these laws are in some ways the end points of certain broad economic and political changes which had been set in motion long before their enactment, and, second, the extent to which the laws are operative depends upon economic and political factors which are variable and unstable. Although some of the laws exist largely on paper, their enactment does tend to give a new direction to the attitudes of people, even when they are not fully operative in practice.

The seeds of change in the agrarian structure of the village were sown towards the end of the nineteenth century when members of the old *mirasdar* class started taking to Western education. During the early decades of the present century they were already moving out of the village in search of education and the new avenues of employment which were thrown open by it. Many of them became lawyers, teachers, and clerks and left the village to settle in some town or city. But their ties with the village were not entirely severed; they continued to own land in it, to visit it regularly, and perhaps to have a domestic establishment in the ancestral home for some time.

Till the end of the last century the economic structure of the village had a more autonomous character. The *mirasdars* mostly lived in the village and had a more direct connection with the processes of agriculture. As the younger generation of *mirasdars* moved out of the village, absentee landlordism became progressively preponderant. The character of landlord-tenant relationships underwent a gradual transformation. This phenomenon was not confined to Sripuram alone, but became a feature of Tanjore District as a whole.

When a popular government came into power after Independence, absentee landlordism was only one of the problems with which it was faced. There were other aspects of the agrarian system which drew immediate attention. Tenants, particularly in Tanjore District, were subjected to rents which seemed excessive and unjust, and they did not enjoy security of tenure. The position of *pannaiyals,* or agricultural labourers, was equally bad. It seemed appropriate that a popular government should take immediate steps to improve the position of the tillers.

A series of enactments was pushed through the Legislature with the objective of securing the rights of the tiller and curtailing the privileges of the big landowner. The most important of these were: the Tanjore Tenants and Pannaiyal Protection Act, 1952; the Madras Cultivating Tenants Protection Act, 1955; the Madras Cultivating Tenants (Payment of Fair Rent) Act,

1956; the Madras Plantation Agricultural Income-Tax (Amendment) Act, 1958; and the Madras Land Reforms (Fixation of Ceiling on Land) Act, 1961.

Some of the specific objectives which these acts sought to achieve have been indicated in earlier sections. They may be summarised here as follows: (1) there has been an attempt to bring about an equitable distribution of the produce between landowner and tenant by raising the share of the latter; (2) security of tenure has been granted by law to tenants having small leases, with the right on the landowner's part to resume holdings for personal cultivation up to a certain maximum; (3) the legal position of the *pannaiyal* has also been made more secure; (4) a ceiling has been placed on individual holdings, which cannot exceed 30 acres of wet land; (5) big *mirasdars* have been further taxed through the introduction of an agricultural income tax.

As has been earlier indicated, these laws are not all fully operative. Some of the reasons for this will be explained in a subsequent chapter. The share of the tenant continues to be well below the proportion prescribed by law, although it has risen slightly in the last five years; there has been a compromise in which, up to now, landowners have been more or less able to hold their own. As regards the security of tenure, several landowners managed to get rid of their recalcitrant tenants just before the law came into force, and sometimes even after, on some technical ground or other. There cannot, however, be any doubt that the position of tenants has been considerably strengthened in this regard. The position of agricultural labourers, on the other hand, continues to be weak and insecure in the large majority of cases.

The effect of legislation fixing a ceiling on landholdings has been of a limited nature. As has been mentioned, there were very few big *mirasdars* in Sripuram at the time when such laws were enacted. Those who had holdings exceeding the limit did not find much difficulty in dividing them between different members of the family. Nevertheless, it does seem to be true that the law has brought about some change in the attitude of people towards land. Investment in land no longer has the attraction of absolute security. One of the big *mirasdars* mentioned earlier sold part of his land the year before the law was passed, and with the proceeds purchased a house in Madras. It would be of interest to have a more detailed estimate of the change in investment pattern brought about by legislation of this kind.

The agricultural income tax has likewise affected only a small number of people. Among those resident in the village, only one of the *mirasdars* is subject to it, while three others who are nonresidents have to pay the tax. On the whole, Sripuram is a village of small landowners; however, it must not be forgotten that the wet land there is of exceptionally high quality, fetching anything between Rs. 4,000.00P to Rs. 5,500.00P per acre.

VII

It has been shown how the process of production creates relationships between different classes of people, and between the village and the outside world. Ties with the outside world are further extended through disposal of the agricultural surplus produced in the village. It may be worth while to examine briefly the marketing mechanisms through which this is brought about. Since this is a complex process, having many ramifications, only a few broad aspects will be briefly dealt with.

Much of the paddy produced in the village goes out of it for sale. The Brahmins, who constitute the bulk of resident *mirasdars,* use only *samba* paddy for domestic consumption; they eat *kuruvai* rice only in exceptional cases. The *kuruvai* is generally sold, as is also much of the *samba* produced in the fields of the big *mirasdars*. The landless people, in their turn, have often to purchase paddy from outside, since they are paid generally in cash and such grain payments as they receive do not last them through the year. They frequently buy paddy from the shops in Thiruvaiyar, and not from the village *mirasdars* who prefer to sell at wholesale rates.

It is common for big *mirasdars* to hold their stocks of grain and to release them in the market when prices rise. But in Sripuram the number of people who can make such profits is small. Most of those who are in a position to dispose of grain have limited surpluses. These are generally purchased by middlemen immediately after the harvest. There are two persons in Sripuram who actively engage in such transactions, making considerable earnings from them. One is a Non-Brahmin cultivating landowner; the other is a Brahmin who has some land of his own and also looks after the land of other people. There is a third middleman, a Non-Brahmin resident of Peramur, who has a storehouse in Sripuram where he keeps his stocks in order to release them when necessary.

Considerable profits are made by holding paddy, since price fluctuations are fairly steep. Stocks are held mainly of *samba* paddy; *kuruvai* is more difficult to preserve since it goes bad unless it is spread out in the open every ten days or so. *Samba* sells around Rs. 19.00P per bag (of 12 Madras measures) just after the harvest and may go up to Rs. 25.00P during July and August. The price of *kuruvai* fluctuates generally between Rs. 18.00P and Rs. 21.00P per bag. *Kuruvai* is eaten mainly by the poorer people.

Thiruvaiyar enjoys some importance as a centre for trade in grain. It is fairly well served by transport, and lorries connect it with every important town in the region. Some of the small producers dispose of their surplus at Thiruvaiyar, while the bigger *mirasdars* and middlemen have direct dealings with the rice mills at Tanjore.

Cash crops do not play a very important part in the economy of Sripuram. Betel vines, sugar cane, and, to some extent, bananas, however, are raised almost entirely for export outside the village. Sometimes middlemen enter into relations with producers at an early stage of production, as in the case of bananas. Most of these crops are exported via Thiruvaiyar to places outside the district. Thiruvaiyar is conveniently located to serve as a clearing-house for agricultural products raised in the village, less than a mile away.

The organisation of production and marketing is closely connected with another feature, whose nature can only be indicated here—that of credit. The cultivating tenant often finds himself in a position where he has to take loans for various purposes. He has to invest in seeds, manure, and plough cattle. His needs are particularly urgent when the agricultural season commences, because by this time his stock of grain is normally low. He may often have to borrow money to keep himself going till the harvest. Ceremonies, such as on occasions of death and marriage, are additional causes of indebtedness. Not infrequently he falls into arrears over his rent, and this, in its turn, is a threat to the security of his tenure.[1]

Various measures have been taken by the government to come to the aid of the impoverished peasant. Acts have been passed from time to time, providing temporary relief to the tenant by allowing payments of rent to be deferred, particularly during years of bad harvest. Under the old dispensation the landowner was also often the moneylender, and loans served to tie the tenant down to the soil and forced him to pay exorbitant rents. This has, to some extent, been prevented by improving the bargaining position of tenants and providing them with alternative sources of credit.

The Agricultural Department of the government and, latterly, the Package Programme have been providing credit facilities to cultivators for agricultural purposes. The loans supplied by such agencies are, however, of small amount and are subject to various terms and conditions as to their use. In addition, there is a Rural Co-operative Bank at Thiruvaiyar which has been in existence since 1955 and which caters to twenty-five villages, including Sripuram. The bank advances loans against land as well as movable property. Its facilities are utilised mainly by *mirasdars* and landowning cultivators.

The facilities offered by the Co-operative Bank are not available to the large section of tenants and agricultural labourers who have very little property to mortgage. Such people are constrained to depend upon hand loans at rates of interest far in excess of what is legally allowed. The rates of interest in such cases run between 15 and 35 per cent, depending upon various factors. A common practice is to charge interest in paddy for loans on money, the interest sometimes being as high as 3 *kalams* (worth between Rs. 30.00P and Rs. 35.00P) per Rs. 100.00P per annum.

There are some people in the village who engage in moneylending on a more or less regular basis. They do not constitute a separate class, but belong mainly to the class of landowners, i.e.,

---

[1] These matters have been discussed in much greater detail, although for a different area, by Bailey (1957).

rentiers and farmers. Not all moneylenders in the village are wealthy persons, able to squeeze high interest from their debtors. Some of them are, in fact, persons of modest means, having little wealth and less power, incapable for some reason of taking to agriculture, and eking out a bare existence on the interest on a small amount of capital, not infrequently acquired through the sale of land. Widows and old people from the *mirasdar* class often depend upon interest for their livelihood. Such people do not generally have much power or influence, and may at times have to lose both principal and interest. The rate of interest which they demand and normally receive is, nevertheless, fairly high.

In addition to these small moneylenders there are two or three men of affairs in the village who not only give loans on their own, but also negotiate loans on behalf of other lenders. They are, none of them, big *mirasdars*. Nevertheless they have considerable influence over people, both within the village and outside. They know all the ins and outs of the law courts. One of them began life as a lawyer's clerk and is now the principal moneylender in the *agraharam*. He combines moneylending with a variety of other occupations, organising cultivation on his own and others' land, supervising sales of land, and in general giving advice on matters concerning litigation.

VII

The traditional economy of land and grain was associated with the existence in the village of certain crafts and services. In fact, it is this complement of crafts and services in the agrarian economy of the village which was responsible for creating the image of the self-sufficient Indian village community. Writers as different as Metcalfe, Maine, and Marx believed that with the exception of a few commodities, such as salt and metals, the traditional Indian village produced within itself all that it consumed.

Serious doubts have been raised about the reality of this rather simplified picture of the traditional Indian village. Intensive field work by social anthropologists in recent years has tended to outmode this, among other stereotypes. As regards Sripuram, at least as far back in time as living memory goes, there is no reason to believe that the village was fully self-sufficient in the economic sphere. Even in the nineteenth century the village lacked many crafts which were necessary to its economy.

Certain crafts and services, however, continue to exist in Sripuram, and there is no doubt that these played a more important part in the village economy even a generation ago. Among artisans one finds potters, carpenters, and goldsmiths. The services are represented by barbers, washermen, pipers, and several categories of priests. Several artisan groups, such as blacksmiths, weavers, and basket-makers, are not represented in the village.

Among the artisans in Sripuram only the potters devote themselves primarily to the pursuit of their traditional craft. There are two households of potters serving the village. Among goldsmiths, only a few pursue their traditional calling, and they do this by engaging themselves in establishments at Thiruvaiyar; the others are employed in various capacities in trade and commerce. The carpenter does some work in the village, but is also engaged at Thiruvaiyar. Sometimes, the other way around, carpenters from Thiruvaiyar are engaged to work in the village.

The barbers and washermen both render services which are indispensable to the villagers. They serve a large clientele and have dealings of a more frequent and regular nature than the artisans in general. Pipers serve the temples and also perform in the houses of the more well-to-do people, particularly the Brahmin *mirasdars,* on all important ceremonial occasions. The priests, as has been indicated earlier, are of different kinds. Some serve in temples and others serve at domestic ceremonies; their clientele has a variable range.

Relations with artisan and servicing groups have lost much of their traditional character and have become more or less contractual in nature. The village artisans, in any event, do not play a very important part in the economic life of Sripuram. Most consumers' goods are bought from outside, particularly from Thiruvaiyar, and are often manufactured in industrial centres such as Trichy, Madura, and Coimbatore. Both cloth and utensils come from outside, the former mostly manufactured in the mills. Agricultural implements also are purchased from Thiruvaiyar and Tanjore. The Agricultural Department and the Package Programme have been trying to popularise the use of improved agricultural implements supplied by them.

Earthenware pots are used by many only on ceremonial occasions. Aluminium, enamel, and stainless steel utensils have largely replaced earthenware for everyday use. Only agricultural labourers and other indigent people depend primarily on clay utensils. Village handicrafts are in a state of decline, although the Khadi and Village Industries Board is making efforts to revive them. Machine-made goods imported from outside have made continuous inroads into the village economy. This may be partly due to the close proximity of Thiruvaiyar, which has a large number of shops where most of the inhabitants of Sripuram make their purchases.

Payments for individual purchases, whether inside or outside the village, are almost always made in cash. The barber and washerman are likewise paid in cash on all ordinary occasions. In fact, one of the barbers has set up a small shop on the main road which he operates more or less on the lines of hair-cutting saloons at Thiruvaiyar. Some of the younger residents go from time to time to Thiruvaiyar and have their clothes washed in one of the laundries there; this, however, is exceptional rather than general.

The barbers and washermen continue to claim, and receive, some of their traditional dues. In addition to cash payments for particular services rendered, they also get certain payments in grain during harvest. The threshing floor of every big *mirasdar* is visited by a number of persons who come to collect their traditional dues. Although there does not seem to be any obligation for every landowner to give a fixed or prescribed quantity of grain, such payments are generally not refused. Payments are made either in bundles of corn or in measures of paddy, or in both. Those who receive such payments include the barber, the washerman, and the Pandaram, as well as domestic servants, and sometimes also other dependents and clients.

The services of barber and washerman are both associated with small grants of land in the village. These grants had been made in the past by the village community, or on its behalf, for the maintenance of these essential services. No record exists of land grants in Sripuram associated with other services or crafts. The land which is associated with the barber and washerman is small in extent and has been under the supervision of one of the senior Brahmin families of Sripuram. Payments are no longer made regularly by members of this family to the servicing groups from the proceeds of the land held in trust for them.

The disintegration of village handicrafts has been accompanied by closer dependence on the outside world for consumers' goods of many varieties. There is a large Co-operative Stores at Thiruvaiyar in which shares are held by several of the residents of Sripuram. The Stores supplies articles ranging from utensils and fabrics to coffee and spices. It had a branch at Sripuram, but this was closed after some time. People from the village often show a preference for makiing purchases at Thiruvaiyar, which is within close proximity and offers a wide selection to choose from. Shopping at Thiruvaiyar has also a social and recreational aspect: for many it is a way of spending an evening.

I X

It will have been noted that economic relations even within the village have acquired a more or less contractual character. This has been made possible partly by the rapid extension of monetisation. Agricultural labourers are generally paid in cash, although rents are, as before, received in kind as far as paddy land is concerned. The artisan and servicing groups in the village are also paid in cash for specific items of work. Domestic servants used to be paid in grain; during the last decade there has been a tendency for payments to be made to them in cash.

The expansion of monetisation in the village is, no doubt, related to the growth of nontraditional occupations and the absorption of a large number of villagers in these. Proximity to Thiruvaiyar and Tanjore has, certainly, played a part in shaping this aspect of the village economy. A certain number of people, while living in Sripuram, are employed outside in clerical and other positions where payments are received in cash. There are others who live and work outside, but send regular remittances to the village. The expansion of this sector of Sripuram's economy has been due in part to the presence in its population of a large section of people who proved to be particularly receptive to Western education and the new avenues of employment to which it led.

The number of people engaged in white-collar occupations of this kind is particularly high in the *agraharam*. There are schoolteachers, accountants, and clerks employed in organisations of various kinds. Some of them work at Thiruvaiyar; others commute to Tanjore. For most families in the *agraharam* rents from land constitute only one of their sources of income.

Every month there is a regular inflow of money into the village from persons who have settled outside or are employed there. The number of remittance receivers is particularly high in the *agraharam*. The village post office receives about 120 money orders every month, amounting to a total which varies between Rs. 3000.00P and Rs. 3500.00P. In addition, people who live and work in nearby places send money to the village in other ways.

X

The discussion presented above may be summarised by drawing attention to some of the basic features of the village economy. (1) Agriculture plays a predominant part in the productive system. (2) The organisation of production is based upon relationships between different classes, characterised essentially by ownership or nonownership of the means of production, especially land. (3) The composition of the different classes, as well as their interrelations, has been undergoing fundamental changes which have been accelerated since Independence. (4) Land has come into the market; the old landowners are now scattered; new laws have been passed which seek to reorganise agrarian relations. (5) Traditional economic relationships based upon status are giving place to relationships of a more contractual nature in which the cash nexus plays an important part. (6) Village handicrafts have undergone a process of disintegration. (7) The village has become in a multitude of ways part of a much wider economic system.

Chapter V

The Distribution
of Power

Although a number of studies have been made of the economic structure of village communities (cf. Mukherjee, 1959, and Mukherjee and Gupta, 1959), very little has been achieved by way of understanding the nature of political processes as they operate at the level of the single village. This gives rise to a number of methodological problems. How does one proceed in trying to provide an intelligible account of the political structure of a village community? Which are the organs and institutions whose description should serve as a point of departure for such a study?

Political processes at the level of the village have an informal character whose analysis requires tools of a different kind from those which are conventionally in use among political scientists. In fact, it may be questioned whether the word "politics" means the same thing at the level of the village and of the state.[1] Villagers often use the English word "politics" to refer to factions and cliques among themselves; in this sense the term has a somewhat derogatory connotation.

Certain recent studies have sought to analyse political conflicts at the village level in terms of cleavages within its structure. Notable among these are studies of factions by Pocock (1957),

---

[1] There is a highly stimulating, if somewhat brief, discussion on this in Barnes (1959); see also Frankenberg (1957).

Lewis (1958), and Siegel and Beals (1960). Important though such studies are, they tend to view the village as an autonomous unit and to divert attention from broader political forces which operate from outside. Any study of political processes within the village will be incomplete unless it shows how such processes are articulated with the regional political system.

Part of our interest here concerns how broader political conflicts cast their shadow on the village community. Political alignments and cleavages in the village have to be considered not only in relation to the other features of its social structure, but also in terms of the divisions and tensions in regional society. In this sense the village may be regarded as a point at which forces operating over a much wider field converge and intersect.

There are certain manifest links between the village and the wider political system. These links assume particular importance at certain crucial periods, as during the General Elections. How does the village divide itself in the face of a political choice which is of regional and national significance? As will be seen, political choice on such occasions is generally made on the basis of a combination of factors, both local and regional in their scope.

Fortunately, some knowledge of the articulation of different political levels with each other is made possible by the existence of certain institutions and organs which operate at various levels. One of these is the political party, which links the rural electorate to the state legislature and the government. Another is the *panchayat* system, which connects the single village to the Block,[2] and the latter, in turn, to the Development District. Finally, there are political networks of various kinds which cut right across the boundary of the village.

We must, therefore, deal with organs and institutions which differ widely in their range of operation. At one extreme is the caste *panchayat* as it is still found among the Pallas of Sripuram; this is a small and more or less autonomous unit, being confined in its scope to the members of a single quarter of the village. At the other extreme is the Congress party, which is a country-

---

[2] The Block is an administrative division of the district, consisting in these areas of around fifty villages.

wide organisation and with which the village interacts only at a few points.

II

The principal objective of this chapter is to arrive at an understanding of the manner in which power is distributed in the village. We attach to the term power more or less the same meaning which has been given to it by Weber (1948, p. 180): "In general, we understand by 'power' the chance of a man or of a number of men to realize their own will in a communal action even against the resistance of others who are participating in the action." The power of the state is backed ultimately by the control and use of physical force. Power, in the wider sense which we attach to it, may be backed, in addition to physical force, by economic, ritual, and other sanctions.

It is, of course, not our intention to discuss power in all its aspects. We are not concerned, for instance, with the problem of power within the family. Rather, our concern is with power in its political aspects, and particularly in its relation to social stratification.

Political processes, in their turn, can be examined from various points of view. Here we shall examine them mainly in their relations to group structures such as *panchayats,* parties, and local elites. Organs and institutions vested with specifically political functions are coming to play an increasingly important part in rural society. This is frequently associated with changes in the distribution of power, both within the village and outside. Hence the political process is also to be seen as a mechanism through which the relations between different communities in the village are altered.

The manner in which power is distributed leads to a division of the village community into different categories: those who have power and those who do not. Within the former there are further subdivisions according to the sources from which power is derived. Thus, there are those whose power is based upon ownership and control of land as against others who derive their power from the support of numerically preponderant groups.

There is conflict between the power of the big landowner and that of the popular leader.

There is a tendency for power blocs to develop within the structure of the village. Such blocs are usually based upon a plurality of factors. Caste and class play an important part in their composition. One of the basic features of politics in the village and in the region as a whole is the increasing importance of numerical preponderance, owing largely to the introduction of the adult franchise. A popular leader can today command considerable power even though his caste and class positions may be fairly low.

Power blocs other than concrete structures such as *panchayats* and parties are rather amorphous in character. They are composed of individuals enjoying varying degrees of power and influence, though not always held together by conscious or formal bonds. In Sripuram one encounters such blocs within both the *agraharam* and the Non-Brahmin streets. In the *agraharam* there are certain individuals who take decisions in collective actions of various kinds and are consulted by others on a variety of issues. Such individuals, however, do not form a well-knit group, and their ability to exercise their will against the resistance of others is rather limited. Some of the reasons for this will be investigated later.

Power blocs in Sripuram are not only informal in nature, but their composition also tends to be fluid. There has been a good deal of change in the distribution of power, and such change is, in fact, an important feature of the system today. Changes in the distribution of power and the composition of power blocs are reflections of shifts in the bases of power. Some of the old bases of power, such as birth and ritual status, are being partly supplanted by new ones, such as numerical support, party membership, and contact with officials. Membership in political networks that cut across the village is of increasing importance to positions of power within it.

A distinction has to be made between power, which is a wide concept, and authority, which is a narrow one. Authority is power which is legitimised; it necessarily operates within an institutional framework. The president of the village *panchayat* has a certain measure of authority. He can impose his will, even against the resistance of others, in ways which are prescribed by law. Likewise members of the bureaucracy have authority. By contrast, there are leaders of factions who have power, but do not have authority. This distinction between power and authority, which derives from Weber, is particularly important in the context of the village community.

Power and authority tend to be associated with certain structures. The administrative structure reaches down into the village to the extent that both the village headman and the village accountant form part of the revenue administration. These two offices are not, however, associated with much power or authority, although the Tehsildar (a revenue official) and the Block Development officer enjoy a certain importance. Both the latter offices have their locus outside the village.

Political parties are a feature of the parliamentary system of government, which has been adopted in India. Parties tend to give structure not only to regional conflicts, but also to struggles for power which are more local in nature. It must not be assumed, however, that conflicts between parties at the regional and national levels are of the same kind as those at the local level. Parties often change the direction of their interest from one level to another, and at the local level they tend to acquire a local colour. The manner in which this comes about has been illustrated in some detail in a study of the activities of political parties in a small British town (see Birch, 1959).

There seems to be a two-way relationship between political parties and local politics. On the one hand, parties tend to operate in terms of the local idiom, choosing, for instance, candidates from the locally dominant caste. On the other hand, local conflicts tend to adjust themselves to, and fall in line with, wider conflicts between political parties. The conflict between Brahmins and Non-Brahmins at the village level acquires a new dimension when the former align themselves with the Swatantra party and the latter with the Congress or some other party.

The study of political parties is, thus, an important feature of the present work, although parties influence political life in the village mainly from outside. The analysis of the role of parties in village politics assumes particular importance in the context of Panchayati Raj. Many of those who argue for the increasing devolution of power from higher to lower levels assume at the same time that parties can be prevented from engaging in local politics. To what extent is such an assumption compatible with reality?

The study of political parties leads to the examination of ideologies. How do particular ideologies come to be identified with particular parties? What is the social base out of which parties and ideologies emerge? It is clear that parties do not always consistently adhere to their ideologies. It would be of interest to assess the extent of divergence between political ideology and political practice, and to examine the reasons behind it.

In analysing the divergence between ideology and practice, one has to take three factors into account. First, there are certain inherent contradictions between the sectional interests from which parties often draw their strength and the universalistic idiom in which they are forced to make their appeal in a secular democratic system based upon adult franchise. Second, strategic reasons demand that parties counter each others' moves, so that if one party tries to mobilise powerful sectional interests, the others have to do the same; this is why political parties try to match caste with caste as a part of their electoral strategy. Third, political ideology, which is general and abstract, is given different interpretations in the contexts of different local conditions.

Party activities at the local level are often controlled by people who do not have clear ideas about the principles for which their leaders stand at the all-India level. What, for instance, is the difference between the varieties of socialism advocated by the Congress party and by the D.M.K. (Dravida Munnetra Kazhagham)? Again, some parties, such as Congress, are associated with a much wider range of ideological principles than others— for instance, the Swatantra and the Communist parties.

The question of ideology has a wider significance in view of the recent introduction of the institutions of parliamentary democracy within the framework of a traditional society organised along hierarchical lines. It is well known that traditional Indian society was characterised by a fairly rigid hierarchical structure and that the caste system still constitutes in many ways the basic structure of Indian society. Independent India has decided to adopt political institutions which emerged under specific historical conditions and in the context of a specific ideology. To what extent is this ideology consistent with the basic structure of Indian society?

In the present study the broader problem has to be examined specifically in the context of democratic decentralisation and Panchayati Raj. Over the last five or six years there have been attempts at a progressive devolution of power from higher to lower levels. The success or failure of Panchayati Raj—the political order based on *panchayats*—depends to a large extent on the preparedness of the Indian village to utilise in democratic ways the wider powers being given to it. The most enthusiastic advocates of Panchayati Raj base their arguments on a particular image of the Indian village, namely, that it is a community in which people can meet on equal terms in order to adjust their mutual interests. To what extent is the egalitarian and consensual ideology of Panchayati Raj compatible with the segmentary and hierarchical structure of the Indian village?

III

It is convenient to begin an analysis of the power structure of the village by making a study of its *panchayat*. Although the *panchayat* as an institution is not new to the village, its character and composition have undergone considerable change in recent years. Detailed provisions were made for the constitution and working of *panchayats* first under the Madras Panchayat Act of 1950 and again under the Madras Panchayats Act of 1958.

The latter act, which has recently come into force along with the District Councils Act of 1958, provides for a three-tiered structure of Panchayati Raj. The lowest unit in this structure is the village *panchayat;* the next higher unit is the Panchayat Union Council; above that is the District Development Council. The Ministry of Community Development and Co-operation (1962, p. 7) has published official statistics which give the number of *panchayats* in Tamilnad as 12,555; of Panchayat Union Councils, 375; and of District Development Councils, 21.

The set-up of Panchayati Raj in Tamilnad as given in the same official publication (p. 6) is as follows:

> Election to the Panchayats is by secret ballot. Seats are reserved for scheduled castes and tribes having regard to their

population. One woman is coopted by the Panchayat, if no woman is elected. The Panchayats are directly elected.

The Panchayat Union Council comprises one representative from every Panchayat elected by its members, M.L.A.s in the area and three women and three Scheduled Caste members, coopted by the Panchayat Union Council, if not elected (if some are already elected, only such member will be coopted so as to make their total three each). M.L.A.s have no right to vote.

The 12 Revenue Districts have been delimited into 21 Development Districts with a Development Council in each. The Development Council consists of the District Collector (Chairman), local M.P.s and M.L.A.s, Chairmen of the Panchayat Union Councils, Presidents of Cooperative Central Banks and such officers connected with planning and development as may be nominated by Government, with no right to vote. The local M.P.s and M.L.A.s, who are members of the District Development Councils, have the right to vote.

The new *panchayat* at Melur-Sripuram started functioning in 1960, and the Thiruvaiyar Panchayat Union Council, comprising forty villages and including Melur-Sripuram, was officially launched in 1961 on October 2, the birthday of Mahatma Gandhi. When the field work was in progress, District Development Councils had not started functioning properly; consequently the present analysis will be confined to the Melur-Sripuram village *panchayat* and the Thiruvaiyar Panchayat Union Council.

A wide range of powers and functions has been conferred by the government on *panchayats* and Panchayat Union Councils:

> Panchayats have been made responsible for all development and welfare programmes at the village level. Among their functions are included construction and maintenance of all village roads, drains, improvement of sanitation, sinking and repairing of wells, repair and maintenance of ponds and tanks, protection of water for drinking purposes, construction of works for public utility. Government have transferred Porambokes, waste lands and kudimarammat to Panchayats. All unreserved forests in the village vest in the Panchayat and are administered by it.

The Panchayat Union Councils are made responsible for

construction and maintenance of roads, establishment and maintenance of dispensaries, maternity and child welfare centres, elementary schools, promotion of agriculture, cottage industries and provision of veterinary relief. Maintenance of minor irrigation works have been vested in Panchayat Union Councils. They are also entrusted with the execution of [the] C. D. [Community Development] Programme. (*Ibid.,* pp. 6–7.)

The functions and powers conferred upon *panchayats* and Panchayat Union Councils are backed by provisions for adequate resources with which to conduct their work:

> The Government have decided to pay annually to every Panchayat Union Council a land revenue assignment at the rate of Re 1 per capita out of the total land revenue (including water cess) collected in the State during the year; a local Educational Grant and a local cess matching grant. Besides, every Panchayat is paid a House Tax matching grant at the rate of Re 1 per capita of House Tax collected. Other resources of the Panchayat consist of taxes on buildings, land, professions, etc. and income from Panchayat property. (*Ibid.,* p. 7.)

It is against the background of this formal structure that we must examine the working of the *panchayat* at Melur-Sripuram and the Panchayat Union Council at Thiruvaiyar. To begin with, it has to be emphasised that *panchayats* and Panchayat Unions do not, in their present working, seem to be fully significant and effective in proportion to the powers and functions which are formally conferred upon them. There is little doubt that many of the important political decisions in Sripuram are taken outside the *panchayat*. The *panchayat* is not the only organ in the village, nor is it the most important of the ones in which power is located.

There is, as has been earlier noted, a single *panchayat* for the revenue village Melur-Spiuram. It has fourteen members, including a president and a vice-president. There is a *panchayat* room where its deliberations are held. A paid secretary looks after accounts, correspondence, and other matters.

The entire revenue village is subdivided into six wards, and elections to the *panchayat* are on a ward basis. This means that the different settlements which make up the revenue village find more or less equitable representation. Further, the three major groups of castes, Brahmins, Non-Brahmins, and Adi-Dravidas, are also more or less automatically represented, because each is dominant in one or another ward. Ward 6, for instance, is practically coterminous with the *agraharam,* and, as a consequence, one can expect the two candidates returned from it to be Brahmins.

Of the fourteen members of the present village *panchayat,* three are Brahmins, six are Non-Brahmins, and five are Adi-Dravidas. Thus, no single group commands an absolute majority. The Non-Brahmins, however, constitute the most important single group and in general they tend to dominate the affairs of the *panchayat.* Both the president and the vice-president are Non-Brahmins. The former is a Kalla from Sripuram, the latter a Vellala from Melur.

The *panchayat* president enjoys considerable power in the village, and this power is based only partly on his official position. He belongs to a family which has commanded a good deal of influence in the village, particularly among Non-Brahmins and Adi-Dravidas. Before him, his father's two younger brothers were important leaders among the Non-Brahmins. One of them was vice-president in the pre-1960 *panchayat.* The predecessor of the present *panchayat* president was a Vellala who had held office for several years. For all this, control of the *panchayat* by Non-Brahmins is of recent origin. Till the mid-forties the *panchayat* was in the control of Brahmins and the *panchayat* president was invariably a Brahmin.

The Thiruvaiyar Panchayat Union Council comprises forty village *panchayats* and one town *panchayat* (i.e., that of Thiruvaiyar). It is composed of forty-six voting members, including two Adi-Dravidas and three women who have been coöpted into it. The chairman of the Panchayat Union is an influential Maratha landowner from a village adjacent to Sripuram. The Panchayat Union is housed in a commodious building at Thiruvaiyar and has a regular administrative staff. Sripuram is represented in it by its *panchayat* president.

The Panchayat Union Council works in a more business-like manner than the village *panchayat.* This is partly because it is run in fairly close association with the bureaucracy as represented by the Block Development officer and his staff. The Block

Development office is in the Panchayat Union building, and the two organs are in many ways complementary to one another. The Panchayat Union Council generally meets once in six weeks.

The village *panchayat,* perhaps because of its somewhat greater autonomy, does not meet regularly or conduct its activities strictly in accordance with procedure. Meetings of the *panchayat* are often postponed, and sometimes meetings are held without all the members being notified in advance. Decisions tend to be taken independently by the president and to be approved subsequently by the other members. This is often just a matter of form because many of the members are afraid to incur the displeasure of the president, who is a powerful man.

The weakness of the *panchayat* as a decision-making apparatus can, in some measure, be interpreted in structural terms. The effective working of an institution such as the *panchayat* presupposes a certain measure of consensus within it. The image of the village *panchayat,* as it has been visualised by the leaders of the country, is that it works through consensus and unanimity. It is on this basis that an official handout (Ministry of Community Development and Co-operation, 1961, p. 3) states: "The institution represented not only the collective will but also the collective wisdom of the entire rural community. The principle of the panchayat was 'Panch Parameshwar,' i.e., 'God speaking through the Five.' The unanimous decision of the Panchayat was respected by the people as the verdict of God."

The question which arises here is whether the structural conditions for such consensus exist in Sripuram today. The *panchayat* is said to represent, or should represent, the collective will of the village community. But in what sense can Sripuram today be regarded as a single community?

Even a superficial examination of the village reveals the sharp cleavages which cut across its structure. These cleavages lead to opposition of interests which do not necessarily resolve themselves by harmonious adjustment. More frequently, the resolution is through the supercession of certain interests and the domination of others. The *panchayat* in Sripuram is characterised less by consensus and unanimity than by domination and unequal participation.

Although the different wards find more or less equitable

representation, they are not all of equal importance. The Non-Brahmins dominate the *panchayat* in spite of the fact that their numerical preponderance within it is not absolute. Nor do the Non-Brahmins of the village form a homogeneous unit. The dominance of Non-Brahmins in the *panchayat* is associated with the withdrawal from participation in it by Brahmins and the virtual exclusion from it of Adi-Dravidas.

Up to the 1940's the Brahmins enjoyed a great measure of power in the village. Their power was based upon ownership of land, high social and ritual status, and superior education. Numerical strength had not become a decisive factor. The *panchayat* president was a Brahmin, the *panchayat* room was in the *agraharam,* and initiative in all important matters was in the hands of Brahmins. There were, no doubt, Non-Brahmin members, but they had the position of second-class citizens.

All this began to change gradually, but with increasing momentum after the Nationalist movement in 1942. Events which followed soon after Independence made it clear that traditional social status was no longer the supreme basis of power; popular support was henceforward to be of far greater importance than it had ever been in the past. The power of the old elite was challenged by popular leaders who were newly emerging.

The challenge generally remained concealed and in the background, but sometimes it was brought into the open. On January 26, 1950, the day on which India became a republic, the present president of the *panchayat,* then an emerging popular leader, gathered together a large group of Non-Brahmins and Adi-Dravidas and marched them through the *agraharam* up to the gates of the Vishnu temple. This was something unheard of in Sripuram. For Adi-Dravidas to march through the *agraharam* was not only ritually polluting, but it also brought social humiliation on the Brahmins. A decade before the event an Adi-Dravida could be tied to a tree and beaten by any Brahmin for a smaller offence. This time, however, the Brahmins did not make any move, for they had come to realise that both the law and the balance of political power were against them.

The leaders of the *agraharam,* deprived of their position of supreme authority, were unprepared to participate in the governance of the village under the new terms and conditions. The idea of sitting in a *panchayat* where their voice might be weaker than that of the Non-Brahmins did not appeal very strongly. Hence today they try to remain aloof from the affairs of the *panchayat*.

The most influential members of the *agraharam* keep out of the *panchayat*. They are not prepared to risk an open show of strength with the other elected leaders. Of the three Brahmins represented in the *panchayat*, only one enjoys some position in the *agraharam*, and that is derived from the influence of his father-in-law. When important functions are arranged in the *panchayat*, the Brahmins generally keep away. The traditional ruling group in the village is alienated from its new structure of authority. Yet this structure is being vested with an increasing range of functions.

The Adi-Dravidas are unable to participate fully in the affairs of the *panchayat* for a different reason. While the Brahmins have largely chosen to withdraw from participation, the Adi-Dravidas by and large find themselves excluded because of their low economic, social, and ritual position. When they do attend meetings of the *panchayat*, they are required to sit separately. Often they are informed about a meeting only after it has been held, and their thumb impressions are later secured on the relevant documents.

There are several reasons why the Adi-Dravidas are not able to assert their rights and participate as full members of the *panchayat*. In the first place, their economic position is still very weak, and they are largely dependent on Brahmin landowners and Non-Brahmin tenants for their source of livelihood. They have to depend in a variety of ways on the patronage of the *panchayat* president and other important Non-Brahmins.

Some of the Non-Brahmins, and particularly the Kallas, have a tradition of violence which makes the Adi-Dravidas hesitant in challenging their authority. Clashes have taken place in neighbouring villages between Kallas and Adi-Dravidas, on one occasion culminating in the murder of a Kalla landowner by an Adi-Dravida. The Kallas took reprisal by beating up the Adi-Dravidas in the village where the murder took place. They even tried to storm the court-room at Tanjore and to take the alleged murderer out of court custody in order to deliver justice to him on their own terms. Ministers of the state government had to intervene before the matter was settled. The Kallas of this area are not only numerically very strong, but they are highly organised and feared for their violent ways. The Adi-Dravidas in Sripuram are afraid to challenge the decisions of the *panchayat* president, who is a Kalla.

In any case, the spirit of challenge takes time to develop among people such as the Adi-Dravidas, who have been accustomed for generations to take their social and political inferiority for granted. Even today the majority of Adi-Dravidas would feel embarrassed if a Brahmin *mirasdar* were to enter their *cheri*. When one of the big *mirasdars* of the village wished to purchase a tree which had been felled in the *cheri,* and suggested that he would like to see it, his Adi-Dravida tenants and servants begged him not to go there, and said that they would carry the tree to his backyard. Generally when an Adi-Dravida sees a Brahmin *mirasdar* coming along the main road, he crosses over to the other side and waits for the Brahmin to pass. A Brahmin does not normally give anything directly into the hands of an Adi-Dravida; he either tosses it to him or throws it on the ground for him to pick up. I have seen Adi-Dravidas refuse to take coins or bundles of straw directly from the hands of Brahmin *mirasdars.*

Adi-Dravidas feel embarrassed and tongue-tied in discussing social and political matters on equal terms with their *mirasdars*. This does not, however, prevent them from driving very hard bargains with them on economic matters. Another duality in the behaviour of the Adi-Dravida expresses itself in the difference between individual and collective action. An Adi-Dravida who would feel embarrassment at accepting anything from the hand of a *mirasdar* may take courage to march through the *agraharam* when he is in a group. Of course, an Adi-Dravida does not behave in the same way towards every Brahmin. Much depends on the economic status of the latter and the nature of personal relations between the two.

Political attitudes among the Adi-Dravidas are far from being unambiguous or organised. Nor are they by any means homogeneous. One of the most striking differences is that between the generations. The younger generation of Adi-Dravidas are, on the whole, more rebellious, militant, and politically conscious. They have been more exposed to radical political propaganda, particularly through the film industry. There are a few such hotheaded young Adi-Dravidas in the *cheri* attached to Melur who are referred to as "Communists" by the Brahmin *mirasdars*. The older ones, on the other hand, are politically less conscious and are less predisposed to challenge the traditional structure.

In the hierarchical traditional structure, social distances were clearly defined and were more or less rigidly maintained. There was hardly any scope in this structure for people at the two ends of the hierarchy to sit together and discuss their private quarrels on equal terms. As long as the traditional structure persists, the old habits of mind are likely to continue. These habits of mind hardly provide an adequate basis for equality and consensus.

The new popular leaders who control the *panchayat* at Sripuram differ from the traditional elite of the village not only in caste, but in other regards as well. Some of the *panchayat* leaders are unlettered; neither the president nor the vice-president knows English. This contrasts sharply with the old elite, which placed a high value on education. The members of the old elite, several of whom have been to college, tend to regard with contempt the newly emerging popular leaders.

Economically also there are wide differences among the members of the *panchayat*. At one end there is a fairly big *mirasdar*, owner of a rice mill and son-in-law of a person with important business connections at Tanjore. At the other end there are small tenants and agricultural labourers. The *panchayat* president himself owns some *paduhai* land and is able to maintain a fairly high standard of living. It is difficult for people with such wide differences in economic background to meet on equal terms.

As we have noted, the *panchayat* at Sripuram is dominated by a few Non-Brahmins, among whom the president occupies an important place. Although these persons enjoy a measure of popular support, they lack many of the qualities which are necessary for efficient administration. They have neither the education nor the experience to master technical details. Often they are at a loss to account for funds. The *panchayat* at Sripuram has, in fact, been going through a crisis because of irregular accounting. This is alleged by some to have been caused by defalcation, but apparently it was also due to mismanagement and lack of experience.

The college-educated Brahmin *mirasdar,* particularly if he has had some experience of working in a city office, commands an advantage in this regard. He can balance accounts more easily, and he is in a better position to grasp the rules of procedure and to use them to his advantage. He can hold his own against the Block Development officer on technical matters much more effectively than a semiliterate popular leader with a peasant background.

Soon after the constitution of the new *panchayat,* it was faced with a crisis brought about partly by procedural irregularities. The influential Non-Brahmin leaders came to one of the prominent Brahmins in the *agraharam* and appealed to him to take over the affairs of the *panchayat.* They assured him unconditional support and coöperation. The person they approached is one of the big *mirasdars* of the village, college-educated and with the experience of several years' employment in a bank at Madras. His administrative competence and knowledge of affairs are beyond the reach of any of the present members of the *panchayat.* In addition, his father is an influential lawyer at Thiruvaiyar. In spite of repeated persuasion, however, he declined the offer and continued to keep himself aloof from the *panchayat.*

The *panchayat* president of Sripuram represents a kind of rural leadership which is becoming increasingly important and influential. He is not one of the elders, being in his middle thirties. He has powerful connections both within and outside the village. He belongs to the Kalla caste, which is the dominant caste in the area. He has had little formal education and cannot be considered a big *mirasdar.* He owns some *paduhai* land, part of which is rumoured to have been illegally acquired. He has the reputation of having been engaged with success in a number of brawls. He is feared considerably for his physical strength and the strength of his supporters.

The family background of the president is of some importance. His grandfather came and settled in Sripuram in the early years of the present century. His father and the father's two younger brothers built up an influential position in the village as toddy contractors in the days before prohibition. The father ran a toddy shop at Sripuram, and this not only made him prosperous, but enabled him to build up an enormous patronage, particularly among the Adi-Dravidas of the village.

To be successful in business as a toddy contractor one must have a firm control over men. One has to settle issues not only with troublesome clients, but also with the police. Bribery, threat, and physical violence are necessary in order to hold one's ground, and at the same time they enable a person to build up patronage. Adi-Dravidas often used to be chronically indebted to the toddy seller. A successful man of affairs would use these obligations as a basis for creating enduring loyalties. Fear and patronage went hand in hand in developing the influence of the president's family.

The enforcement of prohibition did not destroy the old bonds which had been earlier created. The president and, before him, his father's two younger brothers continued to have their hold over a large section of the Adi-Dravidas. The president's sister's husband also enjoys a position of importance. Together they constitute the "strong men" of the village, and even the Brahmins tend to treat them with circumspection.

Sometimes the services of the *panchayat* president are used by Brahmin *mirasdars* in ways which help to strengthen his power. A few years ago one of the big Brahmin landowners who lives at Tanjore was having trouble with a tenant at Thiruvaiyar. He wished to bring under personal cultivation a certain plot of land which the tenant was not prepared to vacate. The *mirasdar* called the *panchayat* president, as the acknowledged strong man of the village, gave him some money, and asked him to do the needful. The latter collected together a large group of people, mainly Adi-Dravidas, and squatted on the land belonging to the *miras-dar*. The tenant took fright and decided to quit. The president thereupon marched his band of followers to one of the coffee shops at Thiruvaiyar and treated them to coffee and snacks out of a part of the money paid to him by the *mirasdar*. Situations such as this enable him to make some money, and, what is more important, they make it possible for him to distribute patronage. Needless to say, in the case just cited the president was not acting in his official capacity; in fact, the incident took place outside the boundaries of Sripuram.

It is not uncommon to see the president marching at the head of a band of followers towards some coffee shop at Thiruvaiyar. His services are requisitioned by a variety of people, and they have to be paid for. Those who use his services are, some of them, powerful people on their own right, as for instance the local M.L.A. (Member of the Legislative Assembly). They can always be approached for favours in return.

When somebody gets into trouble with the police he can count on the president's help. If it is a minor case, the president is able to intervene directly, or through some influential person, and get a release. Or he may help in providing bail. Sometimes he can get witnesses from among his followers to provide false evidence. Thus, the leader has his place in an elaborate network of patronage. What he does for his followers in the village, others higher up do for him. Officials are rapidly coming to realise the importance of popular leaders of this kind, who have easy access to M.L.A.'s and party men who are themselves, to a large extent, dependent on the support of such people.

The *panchayat* president is an important agent in mobilising support during elections. He commands a fairly large block of votes, a fact which gives him a certain position in the eyes of prospective M.L.A.'s and local party bosses. Candidates who have to fight elections prefer to collar the support of "vote banks" such as the *panchayat* president instead of canvassing support directly from each individual voter. The president of the Sripuram *panchayat* campaigned for the successful candidate in the last General Elections. The candidate, after his electoral success, came to the village and rode triumphantly through it in an open jeep with the president at his side. He later addressed a meeting in the *panchayat* room in the course of which he referred to the president as his "elder brother." Occasions such as this have a profound effect in boosting the position of the local leader. Power is, in more ways than one, contagious. Those who move with the powerful are regarded by others as being themselves powerful.

Within the village the president keeps up his position as a strong man. He lives fairly well in a two-storeyed brick and mortar house, having a radio and fluorescent lights. He entertains visitors well, particularly if they come from the town. He is of robust build and carries himself with an air of importance.

Generally he prefers to move along with a small band of followers. He dresses much more carefully than the average Non-Brahmin peasant.

The president has a reputation for violence. People are afraid to cross his path. During the last General Elections there was some altercation between him and a Non-Brahmin youth from the village who was canvassing for a rival candidate. The president took off a slipper and beat the boy with it in public, in the presence of the polling officer. Many persons spoke strongly against this, but nobody took any action.

Political power is usually viewed as being based on economic dominance, social status, numerical support, or "personal" qualities of leadership. The role of organised violence in maintaining power, particularly at the village level, tends to be overlooked. Studies made in the United States show how systematic use is made of physical violence by "bosses" in running their political machines (see, for instance, Whyte, 1943). Although it is doubtful whether one can speak of the existence of political machines in the American sense of the term in this country, "bossism" nonetheless seems to play an important part.

It is difficult to furnish data on the role of the *panchayat* president of Sripuram as a political "boss." There is a strong belief among many villagers that he is in a position to intimidate the *panchayat* secretary into distorting records and falsifying accounts, although it is virtually impossible to verify such beliefs. His personal influence over officials seems to be limited, but he has contacts with other persons whose influence at that level is considerable. The area of direct influence of the *panchayat* president is, after all, confined mainly to a single village and its environs.

Along with many other leaders of the area, the *panchayat* president began his political career during the Nationalist movement which swept through the country in August, 1942. As a young man he took part in anti-British demonstrations, cutting down telegraph wires, stoning police vans, and so on. As a consequence he spent a short term in prison.

After Independence the prestige of those who had participated in the "August movement" ran high. Those who made sacrifices for the country came to be invested with a halo. Some of them were granted small plots of land by the government. They came to be known as "August *tyagis*," the term *tyagi* signifying a person who has renounced something, or made a sacrifice. The *panchayat* President's role in the August movement gives him a position among local leaders of the Congress party. It would, of course, be wrong to assume that all those who took part in the movement did so exclusively for ideological reasons, or that the *panchayat* president is deeply committed to the policies of the Congress party.

In order to appreciate fully the political influence of the *panchayat* president, one has to move outside the sphere of the village and examine wider structures and networks of power. The *panchayat* president, by virtue of his office in the village, is a member of the Panchayat Union Council. This is a body of wider scope, having considerably greater powers than the village *panchayat*. To take one example, members of the Panchayat Union Council have a say in the appointment and transfer of primary-school teachers. They have at their disposal large sums of money which can be used for giving contracts to the right kind of people, from whom favours can be asked in return.

The chairman of the Thiruvaiyar Panchayat Union Council is an influential *mirasdar* and a scion of the princely Maratha family. Although not well educated according to the standards of Brahmins, he enjoys a fairly high social status by virtue of his family background. He is a member of various boards and committees, and also of the Rotary Club at Tanjore, where all the notabilities of the district come together. He stood for election to the state Legislature in 1957 as an Independent candidate, but was unsuccessful.

The chairman of the Panchayat Union Council moves frequently between Thiruvaiyar and Tanjore. He has a jeep, which is an important status symbol and which enables him to give rides to his followers and henchmen. For the ordinary villager it is always flattering to be given a ride in a jeep by an influential man with important political connections. Those who have the use, even occasionally, of the chairman's jeep are likely to vote for him, or for the candidate backed by him. A jeep is also a powerful instrument in an election campaign.

In the 1962 General Elections the chairman backed the Congress candidate and worked along with the president of the

Sripuram *panchayat* for the campaign. The two were thus brought into closer contact with each other and with influential party members. After the election was won, it was in the chairman's jeep that the newly returned M.L.A. went in a triumphal procession through Sripuram and neighboring places.

It thus seems fairly evident that the power of village leaders such as the *panchayat* president derives only partly from support within the village. To a considerable extent it is based on the strength of ties with influential people outside the village. The two sets of factors tend to reinforce one another. Party leaders from outside acknowledge the *panchayat* president because he is a leader of the village, and because he controls a sizeable block of votes there. His stock in the village goes up when he is seen moving with party bosses and the chairman of the Panchayat Union, and when the M.L.A. refers to him in a speech in the village as his "elder brother."

It is also clear that the *panchayat* president does not derive all his power from his official position. In fact, power and authority overlap only to a limited extent. It would be interesting to find out to what extent the demand for this person by political "bosses" from outside would fall if he were to step out of office. Judging by the fact that many of the members of the village *panchayat* have practically no power, one would be inclined to argue that the office of president is only one factor in the political influence of its present incumbent.

The village *panchayat* is, thus, dominated by its president and a few other persons, not all of whom are its official members. The official members of the *panchayat* do not, in fact, constitute either a solidary or a powerful body. Many important decisions are taken outside the *panchayat,* which is in some ways used as an instrument to give a seal of authority to such decisions. Meetings of the *panchayat* tend to be irregular and brief. The village *panchayat* does not provide a forum for free discussion and debate. Its social composition is too heterogeneous for this to be possible.

IV

In addition to the statutory village *panchayat* there is in the village another *panchayat,* of a more limited scope. The Pallacheri at Sripuram has its own *panchayat,* which works independently of the official *panchayat* of the village. The *cheri panchayat,* as it operates today, is a somewhat modified version of the traditional body known as the *kuttam,* which functioned as a powerful instrument of social control in the *cheri* until a decade ago. A comparison between the *cheri panchayat* and the official village *panchayat* provides some insight into the relationship between social structure and the distribution of power.

The *kuttam* was a very old institution among the Pallas. It consisted of a group of elders, known as *nattanmaikkarans,* who were responsible for organising collective action, settling disputes, and maintaining social order in the community. The *kuttam,* with its *nattanmaikkarans,* was exclusively a caste affair and its jurisdiction did not generally extend beyond the boundaries of caste. Non-Brahmin castes such as the Kallas also had *nattanmaikkarans* among them, but in Sripuram it was only among the Pallas that they had any functions until recently.

The *kuttam* in the Pallacheri was reorganised in 1951 on the initiative of a Non-Brahmin Congress leader from Thiruvaiyar. It is of some significance that the first General Elections in independent India were held in 1951/52. The old *kuttam* was directed by four *nattanmaikkarans* whose offices were hereditary. It was decided in 1951 that the new *panchayat* should be constituted on democratic and elective principles.

In 1951 the traditional body comprising the four hereditary *nattanmaikkarans* was dissolved and in its place a new association called the *sevai sangam* was established. It acquired 100 *kuzhis* (⅓ acre) of land, and an assembly hall was built, the expenses being met partly by subscriptions raised from among members of the *cheri* and partly from funds provided by the Thiruvaiyar Congress Committee. The *sevai sangam* constitutes the *de facto panchayat* of the Pallacheri.

The new *cheri panchayat* consists of eleven persons elected from among the residents of the Pallacheri by all adult male members of it. Incidentally, it does not include any of the four traditional *nattanmaikkarans.* The *panchayat* conducts most of its business in the presence of a general assembly of the members of the *cheri.* Any member of the new *panchayat* found guilty of misconduct is deposed and is replaced by some other person by a show of hands in the general assembly. The assembly, thus, plays an important part in the day-to-day working of the *panchayat*.

The *panchayat* or *sevai sangam* meets once a month on the night of the new moon. The meetings are attended not only by the eleven elected members, but also by most of the adult male residents of the *cheri*. This is in contrast with meetings of the village *panchayat,* from which nonmembers are generally excluded. A meeting of the *sevai sangam* is more of a social occasion where discussions tend to take on a rambling character. Nonmembers give more or less free expression to their views on a variety of subjects. Such meetings do not have the purposive or deliberate character associated with formal official bodies. Those who participate, having a similarity of social background, are in a position to talk to each other on more or less equal terms and in the same idiom.

The authority of the *cheri panchayat* is considerable, although the resources at its disposal are limited. Since it has no official recognition, it does not receive any share of the official revenue allotted to the statutory *panchayats*. Funds are raised by subscription and also through the fines which are imposed from time to time for various kinds of breaches of custom.

The *cheri panchayat* adjudicates disputes of various kinds, following procedures which are more or less traditional in character. Both parties are allowed to present their arguments, and in controversial cases witnesses are called. After hearing both sides of the case, the *panchayat* gives its verdict through its leader. Every attempt is made to arrive at a unanimous decision, and avoidance of divisions or voting is sought. If a unanimous decision cannot be reached, the matter is sometimes placed before the *panchayat* of an adjacent Pallacheri, and the decision of the latter is usually accepted as final. The emphasis on unanimity is significant; it can be achieved effectively only when the adjudicators have a commonness of social background.

Fines are levied for a wide variety of offences. For petty thefts, cash fines of small amounts are imposed. Higher fines are levied for adultery and other sexual offences. Rape is regarded as a very serious crime, and a special punishment is imposed in addition to fines. The culprit has his face smeared with soot, a bucket containing mud is placed on his head, and he is made to go around the *cheri* in this guise, while a drum is beaten along the route. This is considered the most degrading form of punishment.

The *cheri panchayat* does not have any legal authority. It is, nevertheless, able to functon, because moral sanctions have a certain force in a homogeneous community such as the Pallas are. This does not mean that disputes are invariably settled within the *cheri*. Sometimes they are taken to the courts outside, or they may even be taken to some influential *mirasdar* for settlement. The fact that disputes are, nonetheless, brought before the *cheri panchayat,* and usually are settled there in spite of the absence of formal legal sanctions, testifies to the strength of collective sentiments among the Pallas.

The two *panchayats,* the one confined to the *cheri* and the other embracing the entire village, are in striking contrast. The village *panchayat* has formal authority and large resources at its disposal. Even so, it works in a very half-hearted manner. Meetings are irregular and are not widely attended. Decisions are often taken outside the *panchayat* and later imposed upon it. There is a strong emphasis in it on carrying out developmental activities such as maintenance of roads, improvement of sanitation, and protection of water for drinking purposes.

The weakness of the village *panchayat* seems to arise from the imposition of a democratic formal structure on a social substratum which is segmental and hierarchical in nature. Although the formal structure of power is democratic, the value system within which it operates is inegalitarian. Formally, members of the *panchayat* have equal authority, but in its exercise the extent of this authority varies sharply with caste, class, and other factors. We have noted that in practice the Adi-Dravida members of the *panchayat* are made to sit separately if, indeed, they are invited to attend its meetings.

The effectiveness of the *cheri panchayat* follows from its social homogeneity and the pervasive nature of the moral bonds which unite its members. There is a correspondence here between the structure of the *panchayat* and the community which it represents. It is owing to this that the institution has a vitality even though it is devoid of a legal basis.

These comparisons lead to a further and more general question. To what extent is it possible to build up democratic structures based upon consensus in the absence of an egalitarian system of values? It is often pointed out that village *panchayats* in ancient India were based upon consensus. There is no doubt that a far greater measure of consensus prevailed in Sripuram even a generation or two ago than is found there today. But this consensus was based upon a tacit recognition of the superiority of some groups and the inferiority of others. It was a consensus imposed, in a sense, by the former on the latter. Today, when the basic hierarchical values of caste society are intended to be thrown overboard by the introduction of Panchayati Raj, the consensus which existed in former times tends to evaporate.

V

A closer study of the village shows that there are within it at least three spheres of power. These spheres broadly correspond to the three main subdivisions of the village, namely, the *agraharam,* the Non-Brahmin streets, and the *cheri*. Each subdivision has, to a certain extent, its own community life, with its own leaders and men of influence. Needless to say, these spheres tend to overlap in many areas and the leaders of one community may have influence over others. But by and large the three spheres tend to maintain a measure of autonomy.

The *panchayat* president, who has some formal authority as far as the whole village is concerned, and considerable power in the Non-Brahmin streets as well as the *cheri,* has practically no voice in the internal affairs of the *agraharam*. He is never consulted over any collective undertaking confined wholly to the *agraharam*. If there are disputes in the *agraharam,* they are never taken to him for advice or adjudication. His advice, rarely sought, has very little value as far as social life in the *agraharam* is concerned. Most people in the *agraharam* would be surprised if it were suggested to them that they should take their problems to the president and solicit his help or assistance. Sometimes, of course, he may be used by a Brahmin for settling an issue with a Non-Brahmin or an Adi-Dravida. An instance of this has been cited earlier, but such issues do not, strictly speaking, relate to the internal affairs of the *agraharam*.

There are several influential people among the Brahmins, but their influence is confined largely to the *agraharam*. As we have seen, the more influential people in the *agraharam* generally keep out of the village *panchayat*. This does not mean that they have no interest in wider political processes. One of them is, in fact, an active member of a national party, but his political connections outside the *agraharam* are with people at Thiruvaiyar and Tanjore.

The members of the *cheri* likewise have their own internal organisation which is, to some extent, autonomous. They tend to settle their internal affairs among themselves. Membership in the village *panchayat* does not mean very much to them as yet. Sometimes, as we have seen, disputes are settled in a larger gathering of Pallas. It thus appears that the political system of the village lacks a unified character and is heterocephalous in nature.

It has to be indicated once again that the different structures of power within the village are not fully autonomous, but exert some influence on one another. Thus, Adi-Dravidas occasionally bring their disputes to some influential Brahmin *mirasdar*, or solicit his intervention on some internal affair of the *cheri*. But the process works only in one direction. No Brahmin would go to an Adi-Dravida leader and seek his advice or help on matters which pertain exclusively to the *agraharam*. Further, such interventions by Brahmins in the internal affairs of the *cheri* are too few and occasional to be aptly described within the framework of patron-client relationships.

One of the influential Brahmin *mirasdars* is from time to time approached by some of the Pallas for intervention in their disputes. His advice is generally sought when the matter involved has some technical legal aspect on which nobody in the *cheri* is competent to speak with authority. The persons who approach the *mirasdar* are not always his lessees, or his clients in the narrow sense of the term. The *mirasdar* tries to adopt as far as possible a noncommittal attitude. It is, to some extent, an accident of character that the biggest *mirasdar* in the village, who is also a Western-educated man, seeks to avoid involvement in village politics. But his influence is, in any case, so weak and tenuous that were he to assert himself, he might lose even the limited moral authority which he now commands.

Although the *mirasdar* has no real authority among the Pallas, it would be of some advantage to one of the parties if it could claim his support. This might, in effect, act as a deterrent to the opposite party and bring about a compromise. But if the opposite party were to take its own course of action in spite of the *mirasdar,* he would have no sanctions to apply. Having no sanctions to apply, he prefers as far as possible to remain uncommitted.

Sometimes Non-Brahmins also come to the same *mirasdar* for his help. Recently a Kalla woman, who was having some trouble with the *panchayat* president and his relatives, approached him. In such cases the *mirasdar* tries to be even more noncommittal. The most he can do, in his own estimation, is to give expert or technical advice on matters about which the average villager is ignorant. To go beyond this might jeopardise his own position and influence.

Some of the Non-Brahmin leaders likewise have a certain measure of influence in the internal affairs of the *cheri.* In this regard the Non-Brahmin leaders seem to have greater influence and to use their influence with more confidence than the Brahmins. It has been already indicated how the *panchayat* president owes part of his influence to the support of a large section of Adi-Dravidas. This support is maintained by the distribution of patronage in various ways.

In a way it is easier for a Non-Brahmin leader to build up and maintain support among the Adi-Dravidas than for a Brahmin. The structural distance between Brahmins and Adi-Dravidas is much greater than that between Non-Brahmins and Adi-Dravidas. Ritual and other social considerations prevent Brahmins from having too close connections with Adi-Dravidas. The latter cannot enter the *agraharam,* but have to approach a Brahmin through his backyard. The Brahmin, in his turn, is prevented from visiting the *cheri* by ritual considerations. Non-Brahmins, on the other hand, have more direct connections with Adi-Dravidas.

In fact, traditionally Brahmins did not have much direct connection with Adi-Dravidas. They gave their land to Non-Brahmin tenants who, in their turn, engaged Adi-Dravida labourers. In other ways also Brahmins were often dependent on Non-

Brahmins for dealing with Adi-Dravidas. When an Adi-Dravida misbehaved, a Brahmin *mirasdar* might ask his Non-Brahmin tenant to fetch the miscreant from the *cheri,* tie him to a tree, and give him a beating. Physical force, which was one of the most effective sanctions against the Adi-Dravidas, was not often used directly by Brahmins, being brought to bear through their Non-Brahmin tenants and servants. This enabled the latter to build up considerable influence over the Adi-Dravidas. Brahmins are generally not suited by their style of life to use physical force as effectively as the Non-Brahmins. To a large section of Brahmins, particularly to those who have been to school or college and have worked in an office, nothing is more repugnant than being involved in a brawl. Such inhibitions do not normally circumscribe the power of the Non-Brahmin peasant.

VI

The *agraharam* itself does not have a strong or unified leadership. There are cleavages between the old and the young, the orthodox and the progressive, the Shri Vaishnavas and the Smarthas. These cleavages rarely lead to open or violent conflicts. Brahmins, on the whole, tend to feel increasingly the need to be united in the face of the non-Brahmin challenge to their power and authority. What is lacking, however, is an effective leadership which can command respect from the different sections of Brahmins and take the initiative in organising collective action.

The reason for the absence of such a leadership lies perhaps in the amorphous character of the *agraharam*. The social composition of the *agraharam* evinces two important features which have already been referred to. First, it is extremely heterogeneous in caste composition; this is in contrast with the dominance in many *agraharams* of a single lineage, making relatively easy the existence of a unified leadership. Second, the population of the *agraharam* has a rather shifting character; many of the old notabilities have gone out, and they have been replaced by new persons who do not have proper roots in the village.

Even fifteen years ago the *agraharam* had an influential leader whose voice was universally respected. His influence was not confined to the *agraharam,* but extended to the Non-Brahmin streets. Within the *agraharam* he was universally known as the *mutta,* which is a term of respect, meaning an elder. The *mutta* was in the direct line of descent of one of the ancient families of the village, the Periam family. He and his ancestors had contributed both money and land to the Vishnu temple at Melur, and had taken active part in many collective undertakings in the village. The land which was associated with the services of the village barber and the village washerman stood in the *mutta's* name.

The *mutta* himself was a moderately big landowner, although there were others who owned more land than he. He was also a man of moderate education, knew some English, and was a member of the managing committee of the well-known high school at Thiruvaiyar. The *mutta* took keen interest not only in the activities of the *agraharam,* but also in agriculture, and visited his fields regularly, a thing which is not done by many influential Brahmins today. This enabled him to maintain close touch with the Non-Brahmins, who till the end treated him with the respect and deference due by tradition to an elderly Brahmin *mirasdar*.

There is nobody in the *agraharam* today who commands the same respect from every quarter as the *mutta* did. In an agrarian economy landownership is an important source of influence and authority. But in order to be fully accepted as a leader in an *agraharam* one has to combine landownership with other qualities such as, for instance, learning and scholarship—both traditional and modern—and membership in an ancient and well-established family or kin group.

Most of the big landowners of Sripuram, as we have seen, live outside the village. Their interests are too widespread to allow any deep involvement in the politics of the village, or of the *agraharam*. Only one of the big *mirasdars* resides in the *agraharam,* and he is a relative newcomer. Because he is a *mappillai,* or son-in-law, of the village, his position both within the *agraharam* and in relation to the tenantry is weaker than that of a person who has been born and bred in the village and has his ancestral home there. Particularly when he first came to settle in the village, around 1948, it required much tact and accommodation on his part for him to gain full acceptance in the *agraharam*. The position of a son-in-law is always a delicate one.

The person referred to has, in spite of his position as a relative outsider, been able to establish some influence in the *agraharam* and in the village as a whole. He is often referred to simply as the *mappillai*, not only in the *agraharam*, but also among Non-Brahmins and Adi-Dravidas. He is one of the more influential persons in the *agraharam*, but he does not enjoy the same unequivocal support that the leaders of a generation ago did. As we shall see, there are other reasons for this in addition to his being an outsider.

What applies to the *mappillai* is also true to a large extent of a number of other people in the *agraharam*. It has earlier been mentioned that the *agraharam* at Sripuram is characterised by the presence of a fairly large proportion of sons-in-law. In one way or another they all share the uncertain status of the *mappillai*. They do not provide the best material for the recruitment of village leaders.

In addition to the sons-in-law, there are others who have recently settled in the *agraharam* for a variety of reasons. They include clerks and schoolteachers who are employed at Thiruvaiyar and other places. Such people settle in Sripuram mainly because of its proximity to Thiruvaiyar and the presence in it of a large *agraharam*. They do not fully constitute a part of the village, and sometimes they live in it only for a short while before moving to some other and more convenient place. The presence in the *agraharam* of people of this kind gives to it a somewhat amorphous character.

Thus, in order to understand why the *agraharam* lacks a unified, cohesive, and well-organised character, the two points mentioned above have to be borne in mind. First, the old families have disintegrated and emigration has largely deprived the village of those who might have been its natural leaders. This is true of a large number of Brahmin villages in the district, in which many *agraharam*s have become virtually empty. Sripuram, it is true, still has a fairly large and populous *agraharam*. But—and this is the second point—those who have replaced the older families have neither the position nor the interest to supply the village with the kind of leadership which formerly existed.

There is another factor which is important with regard to the character of leadership in the *agraharam*. This is the balance between traditional and modern attitudes and habits of mind. A Western education and some knowledge and experience of life in the cities, and of the ways in which the bureaucratic machinery is run, are important qualifications for leadership. Thus, when the *mappillai* first came to settle in the village, leaving his job at Madras, he was able to organise many things which would have been difficult for the traditional leaders of the *agraharam* to achieve. He was one of the persons responsible for bringing electricity to the village. He took the initiative in having a metalled road constructed between Sripuram and Peramur, and inviting M. Bhaktavatsalam, who was then Home Minister to open the road. The traditional leaders of the *agraharam* have very little aptitude for organising activities of this kind.

The *mappillai* is generally consulted on all important matters concerning the *agraharam*. He is often approached for advice, or for intervention with officials. He presides over prize-distribution ceremonies and other social gatherings in the *agraharam*. On all matters regarding choice of courses for higher education his advice and opinion are sought. But generally he tries to act with caution and to avoid taking decisions for other people. He was persuaded to be chairman of the managing committee of the Vishnu temple at Melur, but resigned after some time.

In spite of his many advantages, however, the Western-educated man suffers from a number of limitations. Especially if he happens to be a newcomer, his actions are noted, discussed, and criticised by the elderly and more orthodox people in the *agraharam*. The Brahmins have a certain tradition of living which is dominated by a fairly vast body of ritual and social etiquette, and although very few individuals carry out the traditional code of conduct in all of its detail, deference has to be paid to it in principle. Anyone whose actions might be construed as a challenge to the traditional values has to pay the price of social criticism and censure.

When the *mappillai* first came to settle in Sripuram, his actions were delicately measured against the yardstick of tradition by the orthodox elders of the village. He dressed and carried himself in the manner of the city-bred man rather than the villager. People tried to draw him out in various ways and to make him declare his position in regard to rituals, tradition, and Hinduism. Being an intelligent and tactful person, he provided answers which enabled him, at least to some extent, to make himself acceptable.

In ritual and ceremonial matters, however, and in matters pertaining to the organisation of the temple, there are other persons in the village whose voice carries greater weight. These are the elders who are *vaidic* in their style of living and have been settled in Sripuram for several generations. Although they are mostly small landowners, they have the advantage of being able to claim Sripuram as their ancestral village. On all ceremonial occasions they are given precedence. Temple offerings are first given to them and then distributed to the others. Their advice and opinion are sought on social and ritual matters, and they take the initiative in organising religious functions.

Thus, the *agraharam* does not possess a very strong or unified leadership. This is in keeping with the amorphous nature of its social composition. It is also a consequence of the exodus from the village of some of the most influential elements of its population. Finally, conflicts in values between the generations, and in particular the rapid pace of change, lead to a separation between leaders with a traditional and a modern outlook. Although the absence of a strong leadership within the *agraharam* does not lead to open or violent conflict, still there is a lack of strong and effective social control and organised collective action.

The Non-Brahmins have gradually emancipated themselves from the domination of the Brahmins over the last two decades. Among the Non-Brahmins caste plays an important part in determining leadership, and the two most prominent castes are the Kallas and the Vellalas, the latter constituting the largest single Non-Brahmin caste in the village. Landownership is important, although it is possible for an influential Non-Brahmin tenant to distribute patronage without himself owning any land. (It has to be remembered that there is no big Non-Brahmin landowner in the village.) Western education has not spread sufficiently among the Non-Brahmins of Sripuram for it to play a decisive part in the determination of power.

The Kallas are a fairly closely knit group. They are dominated by a small kin group centering around the *panchayat* president. The Vellalas are also an influential caste, having deep roots in the village. One of them had been *panchayat* president for more than a decade before being replaced by the present incumbent. Some of the prominent Vellalas are medium-size landowners. They also take a good deal of land on lease from Brahmin *mirasdars*.

The political strength of the Non-Brahmin leaders depends, in addition to caste, on economic factors. All the important Non-Brahmins, whether Vellalas or Kallas, are fairly well-to-do by Non-Brahmin standards. Ownership of land, however, is by itself neither a sufficient nor a necessary condition for the acquisition of power. What seems to be more important is the ability to dispense patronage, and ownership of land is one of the means for achieving this end. Each of the Non-Brahmin leaders has a certain following, whether from his own caste or from among the Adi-Dravidas. His power depends to a great extent on the ability to keep up this following.

Numerical support is an important basis of power among Non-Brahmins. Such support is derived in the first place from membership in a numerically preponderant caste, and in the second from control of extensive patronage. Organised violence is of some importance in the maintenance of power among Non-Brahmins. The reputation of Kallas in this regard, both in the village and in the region, has already been indicated. The Brahmins of Sripuram, in contrast, depend very little on organised violence as a basis of power within the *agraharam*.

Finally, connection with influential people outside the village ensures an important position within it. The chain of patronage cuts across the boundaries of the village. The *panchayat* president, as we have seen, has important connections outside Sripuram. A few of the other Non-Brahmins, particularly among the Vellalas, have similar connections. Such connections depend upon caste, class, party membership, the holding of an office such as that of the *panchayat* president, and the personal relations associated with patronage.

Among the Adi-Dravidas, who are a more homogeneous group, leadership depends more on kinship ties and personal factors than on social stratification. The Pallas are the dominant community, and the Paraiyas, Chakkiliyas, and Thottis have very little political influence, being insignificant in number. The Adi-Dravidas are rapidly becoming aware of their political importance. This importance comes visibly to the forefront at the time of elections, when party leaders and prospective M.L.A.'s come to them for votes. As yet the Pallas of Sripuram are not sufficiently well organised to be able to exploit on a permanent basis the strength which they owe to their numbers.

It is, however, becoming increasingly clear to them that M.L.A.'s and even state Ministers are accessible to them. The Congress party treats them with special consideration, and the government gives them preferential treatment. Some of the younger people in the *cheri* are pushing themselves into the fore-front so as to procure for themselves and their community the full benefits which the government and the ruling party seem to be prepared to give. Meanwhile these persons are still dependent on the patronage of the *panchayat* president, through whom such approaches generally have to be made. In some of the neighbour-ing *cheris* a few of the younger Adi-Dravidas have distinguished themselves for their militant attitude towards Brahmin *miras-dars*.

VII

Some idea has been given of the distribution and centres of power in the village. It has been seen that an analysis of the power structure of Sripuram takes us outside the village. Not only do political relations extend far beyond the village, but what happens within it is understood very inadequately if one ignores the broad political forces which operate in the region as a whole.

Political parties require study, since they provide links between the regional distribution of power and alignments within the village. Parties as organised groups do not have a central position in the village, or even a sustained or continued existence there. They act upon it mainly from outside. Most persons living within the village do not belong to any particular party. Party member-ship and support, nevertheless, throw an important light on cleavages in the structure of the village, although the exact nature of political alignments may be difficult to predict. Political parties assume special importance on certain occasions, as during elec-tions.

There are three political parties which have some kind of existence in Sripuram. These are the Congress, the D.M.K., and the Swatantra party. Other parties, such as the D.K. (Dravida Kazhagham), exercise some influence from outside. The Communist party was at one time an important force in the area, but it is now virtually inoperative. The Congress party was the first to take root in the village. The other parties have sprung up only in course of the last four or five years.

The roots of the Congress party go back to the days before Independence when the Nationalist movement first began to spread to the villages. As early as the 1920's there were members of the Congress party in the village, and a few of them attended annual sessions of the National Congress. One of the members of the village, in fact, became a prominent Congressman of the state and served as a Minister in the state government between 1937 and 1939. Thus, traditions of association with the Congress party go back to at least two or three generations in the case of some of the families of Sripuram.

For some years before 1957 there was a village committee of the Congress party, which had then some forty to fifty members in Sripuram, each paying a subscription of Rs. 25P. The president and the treasurer of the local committee were both from the *agraharam;* the secretary was a Non-Brahmin. The village committee is now practically defunct. The president is no longer in the village, and the treasurer has shifted his allegiance to another party. The secretary continues to be associated with the Congress.

Even before 1957 the Congress party in Sripuram did not lead a very active existence. The treasurer collected subscriptions periodically, and the secretary arranged meetings when some notability could be persuaded to visit the village. The members continued paying their subscriptions because of their past association with the party, which was at that time the only one in the village, and because of its identification with the Nationalist movement.

Until 1957 the Congress party in Sripuram had its membership both among Brahmins and Non-Brahmins. The Brahmins had taken the initiative in establishing the party, and the Non-Brahmins had joined it in increasing numbers since 1942. After 1957, and particularly after 1959 when the Swatantra party held its first convention, Brahmin support of the Congress party in the village underwent a rapid decline. Today there are only a few Brahmins in Sripuram who retain their connections with the Congress. There are several Non-Brahmins who continue to be members of the party, but it does not have a permanent organisation in the village.

Today the Congress party office at Thiruvaiyar directs affairs within the village mainly through a few influential Non-Brahmins. The party also has a base in the *cheri,* where the *sevai sangam* flies a Congress flag. Party activities assume special importance during elections, when meetings are arranged in the Non-Brahmin streets by the *panchayat* president and a few others. There is only one Brahmin who takes some part in these meetings. He has been associated with the Congress party for more than thirty years.

The first convention of the Swatantra party was held in 1959 and one of the Brahmin residents of the village went to Bombay to attend it. This person is the same college-educated and influential *mirasdar* referred to above as the *mappillai.* After his return from Bombay he set about organising the party in the district, and he is at present the treasurer of the Swatantra party for Tanjore south. The Swatantra party has made considerable impact on the village during its brief career.

There are in the village about sixty registered members of the party. Almost all of them are from the *agraharam.* There are some four or five members from the Non-Brahmin streets; most of them have some personal attachment to the treasurer who shifted to this party. After the formation of the Swatantra party most of the Brahmins transferred their allegiance from the Congress party to the new one. This happened not only in Sripuram, but throughout Tanjore District and Tamilnad as a whole.

It cannot be said that all the sixty registered members of the Swatantra party have definite or clearly formulated political views. Some have joined it because of personal attachment to the local treasurer, and more particularly to the founder of the party, C. Rajagopalachari, the veteran Brahmin leader of the Nationalist movement. A number of women have enrolled themselves because their husbands are members of the party. There are in all about a dozen people in the village who identify themselves closely with the Swatantra party. All of them are from the *agraharam.*

The Swatantra party, in spite of its relative newness—or perhaps because of it—seems to have a sharper focus than the Congress. The Congress has such a vast tradition and organisation, and has been associated with so many shades of ideology, that very few people find any difficulty in identifying themselves with it, aside from those in certain small sections of society. The Swatantra party has a more limited appeal. Ideologically it is identified with a competitive social and economic order having a minimum of state regulation, and socially with the better-educated and economically more advanced groups.

In Sripuram the Swatantra party has its centre in the *agraharam,* among the more educated persons. The Congress was dominated by the same category of people a generation ago, but today its leadership has passed to the relatively uneducated Non-Brahmins. There has not been very much effort on the part of the local organisation of the Swatantra party to convert it into a mass party. It is doubtful to what extent such efforts would meet with success.

In the *agraharam* there are several subscribers to *Swarajya,* the English-language weekly of the Swatantra party. Articles in the *Swarajya* are carefully read and widely discussed in the *agraharam.* For the majority of people who are not sufficiently familiar with English, the Tamil monthly *Kalki* plays a somewhat similar role. It publishes regularly political articles by C. Rajagopalachari, the founder of the Swatantra party and its principal theoretician.

The D.M.K. (Dravida Munnetra Kazhagham) also is of recent origin, having started a separate career in 1949. Its roots in the village go back only four or five years. It shot into prominence during the 1962 elections, in which it emerged as one of the strongest opposition parties in any state.

In Sripuram the activities of the D.M.K. centre around its reading room, situated in one of the Non-Brahmin streets. The association of the D.M.K. with a reading room, which one finds in Sripuram, is characteristic. A large number of reading rooms in the neighbouring towns and villages are associated with the D.M.K. They are often named after the leaders of the party, some of whom are popular film stars or are otherwise associated with the film industry.

The D.M.K. in Sripuram does not seem to have any formal

organisation. This is in keeping with its generally decentralised and flexible character. The affairs of the party in the village are conducted by two young men who run the reading room, organise meetings which leaders of the party are invited to attend, and conduct election campaigns. The Tamil film industry, which is closely associated with the D.M.K., and the well-known oratorical powers of the party leaders have created a certain following for the D.M.K., particularly among young persons.

It is characteristic that the affairs of the D.M.K. in Sripuram are managed by two young Non-Brahmins, for the party has its strongest support among the young and until recently was almost wholly associated with the Non-Brahmins. This is in contrast with the Swatantra party, whose social locus, as we have seen, is rather different, while the Congress party has a wider appeal than either.

Although the D.M.K. places much emphasis on the establishment and maintenance of reading rooms, it is not associated, at least in the rural areas, with the intelligentsia as the Swatantra party, to some extent, is. It has, certainly, a wider popular appeal. The D.M.K. has also been in the past associated with violence, and in this regard also its political style is rather different from that of the Swatantra party. Finally, the D.M.K. combines separatism with some form of socialism in its political ideology.

The differences in social composition and political ideology between the D.M.K. and the Swatantra party have been fairly sharp until recently. In Sripuram there was hardly any contact between the two parties before the 1962 elections, which brought about an informal alliance between them. The comparatively sophisticated and well-to-do Brahmins who dominate the Swatantra party at Sripuram had until then regarded the local D.M.K. leaders as being socially beyond the pale and politically misguided.

VIII

Within the village, political parties lead a more or less inactive existence under ordinary conditions. Occasions such as the General Elections bring them periodically to the centre of social life. The 1962 elections provided considerable excitement in the village. Several of the residents took part in the campaign, and many of them followed the developments with keen interest. Throughout the month of February, 1962, the General Elections provided one of the major topics of conversation, particularly in the *agraharam* and the Non-Brahmin streets.

During elections political parties find themselves in active competition with one another. The competing parties set themselves more and more actively to the task of mobilising support. As the election campaign mounts, people tend to identify themselves progressively with one party or another. The cleavages within the village community are more sharply focussed, and the links between political interest and social structure are brought to the surface.

Elections to the Parliament did not draw as much interest as those to the state Assembly. The pace of electioneering seems to have been set by candidates for the state Assembly, with the parties placing less emphasis on the campaigns of their candidates for Parliament. Voting for Parliament followed by and large the pattern set in the voting for the Assembly, although, as will be seen later, there were certain significant differences.

Three parties set up candidates for the Thiruvaiyar Assembly constituency of which Sripuram forms a part. These were, the Congress, the D.M.K., and the P.S.P. (Praja Socialist Party). The P.S.P. did not in this area organise its campaign in a big way, and it was clear from the beginning that the fight was to be between the Congress and the D.M.K. The P.S.P. had never had any organisation in Sripuram, and its candidates did not attract much attention there.

All the three candidates for the Assembly constitutency were of the Kalla caste. The sitting member was also a Kalla returned on a Congress ticket; he was, however, not seeking reëlection. His predecessor, also a Kalla, had been returned as an Independent candidate in 1952, but lost his seat in 1957 to the Kalla Congressman.

As the election fever mounted, it became clear that in Sripuram the campaign for the Congress party was to be led by the *panchayat* president and a few other influential Non-Brahmins. Rallies were organised in the village, speakers were invited from outside, and the *panchayat* president was frequently seen moving about in one of the Congress party jeeps. Processions and rallies within the village were generally led by the president, and included a fairly large proportion of Adi-Dravidas.

The D.M.K. election machinery at Sripuram had its centre in the party reading room. The campaign was led by the two young men who were in charge of the affairs of the party in the village. Several meetings were held in the reading room, and the D.M.K. candidate for the Assembly addressed a meeting there a few days before the election.

The Brahmins in Sripuram, since they identify themselves mainly with the Swatantra party, did not initially take an open stand vis-à-vis the campaign. They discussed in general terms the prospects of the Swatantra party in the state as a whole and its chances of leading an effective opposition in the Assembly. Since in this area the party had not set up a candidate either for the Assembly or for Parliament, the Brahmins took time to decide on the position they should adopt.

Support for the Congress party was ruled out as far as the majority of them were concerned. The Congress had alienated itself from the Brahmins by its restrictive legislation, its replacement of the older Brahmin leadership by a Non-Brahmin one, and, in the Tanjore area, by its open alliance with the anti-Brahmin D.K. Finally, Rajagopalachari, the one leader in Tamilnad who drew the unquestioned loyalty of the majority of Brahmins, had launched a crusade against the Congress. Thus, with a few exceptions, most of the residents of the *agraharam* took a stand against the Congress.

But the only effective alternative to the Congress, the D.M.K., was one which did not appeal immediately to the Brahmins. The differences in social composition, ideology, and political style between the Brahmins of Sripuram and the hard core of the D.M.K. there have already been referred to. Till the end of 1961 the Brahmins as a group had scarcely considered it conceivable that they should identify themselves with the D.M.K.

Towards the end of 1961, however, the Brahmin leaders of the Swatantra party of Sripuram and Thiruvaiyar began seriously to consider organising support for the D.M.K. The word had been given by Rajgopalachari to all his followers that they should vote for D.M.K. candidates in the absence of Swatantra ones. The leader of the Swatantra party in the village took his stand in support of the local D.M.K. candidate. A proposal to vote for the P.S.P. was briefly considered and rejected, as it would merely split votes and strengthen the chances of the Congress candidate.

About a fortnight before the election a meeting was arranged in the D.M.K. reading room at Sripuram as part of the campaign. The D.M.K. candidate was to address the meeting, and the Swatantra party leader from the *agraharam* was requested to take the chair. The meeting was attended by a fairly large number of Non-Brahmins. A few Brahmins also came, but the attempt at establishing good will was not successful. The social distance between the two groups stood out conspicuously, and this was perhaps the first occasion on which they had tried to come together on such terms. The Brahmins formed a separate cluster and stood apart, leaving soon after their leader had finished his speech.

Gradually a few Brahmins began to canvass votes for the D.M.K. in the *agraharam*. The older and more orthodox Brahmins were at first a little reluctant to lend their support to this party which had not in the past adopted a very friendly attitude towards them. The rival Congress candidate, however, was freely using the services of D.K. leaders, who made open attacks against the Brahmins in their speeches. This seems to have tipped the scales and led many of the Brahmins to vote for the D.M.K.

In the end it seems that most Brahmins in the village did vote D.M.K. for the Assembly seat. The Non-Brahmin votes were split, the majority perhaps going in favour of the Congress. The Adi-Dravidas also seem to have voted largely for the ruling party. The Congress retained the seat by a fairly clear majority.

Our analysis of the General Elections, thus, throws additional light on the relations between politics and social structure in the village. (1) It shows that political parties play an important role in maintaining, or in altering, a given distribution of power within the village, although they may operate mainly from outside. (2) It shows the relevance of existing cleavages within the structure of the village to the nature of political alignments. (3) It shows, finally, that although political alignments follow preëxistent cleavages, the relationship between political party and social segment is a dynamic one, i.e., subject to change over short periods of time. Thus, the Brahmins, who had initially been associated with the Congress party, shifted their support to the D.M.K., although such a contingency could hardly have been foreseen a year before the elections.

IX

In the foregoing pages we have given an account of the distribution of power in Sripuram and the operation within it of political systems which articulate the village with the outside world. If the account may seem at times to lack a certain formal order, it must be pointed out that the problem of power is far more difficult to treat in structural terms than, for instance, the problem of caste. It must also be added that many of the political forms which are emerging in Sripuram today are new and in a state of flux, and have not yet acquired a crystallised character. Thus, the ambiguities of the account reflect to some extent the ambiguities inherent in the political process.

We have considered in turn, *panchayats,* community power structures, and political parties. Each of these was treated in brief and somewhat sketchy terms. It might have been possible to give more detailed accounts of the *panchayat* or the community structures by confining ourselves wholly to the village. This, however, would have done violence to the nature of the political process, which is dependent to such a large extent on external forces and networks which ramify in every direction.

Although it had at first seemed desirable to discuss *panchayats,* community structures, and parties separately and in turn, it has not been possible fully to achieve this ideal. The discussions on these different units and systems have often run into one another. This is largely because the systems themselves interpenetrate to a very great extent, and it is my hope that the account given will provide some idea of the nature and extent of this interpenetration.

Social networks play an important part in the interlinkage of different structures of power. We have seen, for instance, how the *panchayat* president is linked to clients in the village and patrons outside. Some of these ties cut across the boundaries of caste as well as party or the *panchayat* system. The *panchayat* president has political links not only with Adi-Dravidas inside the village, but also with Non-Brahmins outside. Further, he has ties with both Congress and D.M.K. politicians outside the village. Similarly, the Brahmin *mirasdar*, referred to as the *mappillai*, has ties outside the village with Brahmin Congressmen as well as Non-Brahmin members of the Swatantra party. The *panchayat* president has connections not only with politicians of different parties belonging to a variety of castes, but also, through them and in his own right, with officials of the government.

The politicial system in Sripuram shows a highly dynamic character. Power relations within the village have been changed or reversed, new institutions and organs have been set up, and political ties of diverse kinds have been expanding beyond the village.

In the traditional set-up, power within the village was closely linked with landownership and high ritual status. Until a generation ago the Brahmin *mirasdars* enjoyed decisive dominance. Today the Non-Brahmins play a much more important part in organising collective activities in the village. The control of the *panchayat* has been wrested by them from the Brahmins. Nor is caste the only factor today in the control of political organs. Party membership, contacts with officials, and ties of patronage are factors which play an increasingly important part.

New organs and institutions have ben created in the country, and these affect political life in the village in a fundamental manner. In these organs membership and control are based on principles which are very different from those which operated in traditional society. The control of the traditional *panchayat* was based upon landownership and ritual status. Members of the new *panchayat* are democratically elected. Ascriptive criteria were of paramount importance in the control of the traditional structures of power. The new system provides greater scope for manipulation and personal initiative.

The system of Panchayati Raj, with its three-tiered hierarchy, has become an important locus of power. It enables the *panchayat* president of Sripuram to have contacts with party bosses, the chairman of the Panchayat Union Council, and the Block officials. Ministers of the state governments have a stake in village *panchayats,* and one of them was received on his visit to the village by the *panchayat* president in the *panchayat* hall. Thus, the *panchayat* system enables the president of the village *panchayat* of Sripuram to have access to ministers of the state government. When the minister visited Sripuram, a petition for better housing facilities was presented to him by the Adi-Dravidas of the village *through* the panchayat President.

Political parties are also a part of the emerging social order. It is true that there are no well-organised units of political parties having a sustained existence in Sripuram. On the other hand, the D.M.K. has a reading room in the village and an office-bearer of the district unit of the Swatantra party is a resident of the *agraharam*. Further, party units impinge upon the village from outside, particularly during elections. Party loyalties give a new dimension to old cleavages and alignments. Party membership also enables the villagers to enter into networks of power which cut right across the boundaries of village, caste, and class.

A most important feature of the new political order is the emergence of networks of interpersonal relations which ramify in every direction. The creation of new political opportunities and new bases of power has provided congenial conditions for the development of elaborate networks of patronage. Such networks serve to link the village with territorial units of increasingly wider scope, and they also provide interlinkage between caste, class, *panchayat,* and political party.

Chapter VI

Conclusion:

Caste, Class, and Power

In the three foregoing chapters we have discussed three important aspects of the social structure of Sripuram. These are its caste structure, its class system, and the distribution of power within it. An attempt was made to treat each system separately without considering in detail its interrelations with the others. This attempt, involving as it did a process of abstraction, was only partly successful. The discussion on the distribution of power, for instance, led inevitably to a consideration of the caste and class components of leadership.

In reality, of course, caste, class, and power are closely interwoven. They can be treated separately, and particularly the last two, only by a process of abstraction. It is necessary, however, to make this abstraction in order to reduce the diversity of empirical data to a few fundamental categories. It is also necessary to consider the three systems separately in order to understand their relative importance in the process of change. As has been emphasized from the beginning, change is a fundamental feature of the social structure of Sripuram today.

Caste, class, and power refer in different ways to the phenomenon of social stratification. There are some, it is true, who have argued that class is *not* a form of social stratification, but is rather to be understood in terms of social conflict. (See Dahrendorf, 1959, pp. 63, 76.) We have seen, nonetheless, that in the context of Sripuram landlords, tenants, and agricultural labourers form a rank order which is more or less tacitly recognised by all. It is, therefore, proposed that we continue to follow the conventional usage and regard the class system as an aspect, or a dimension, of social stratification.

Marx, with whose name the study of class is particularly associated, is not himself fully consistent in the use of the concept. By and large he uses the term "class" in the wider sense to refer to owners and nonowners of the means of production. Sometimes, however, he uses it in a narrower sense to refer to structures which are characteristic of capitalist society.

Again, in writing about people whose material conditions of existence are similar, or identical, Marx adds: "In so far as there is merely a local interconnection among these small-holding peasants, and the identity of their interests begets no community, no national bond, and no political organisation among them, they do not form a class" (n.d., p. 124). These remarks have a particular bearing on agrarian societies, for there ownership or nonownership of the means of production does not necessarily constitute a basis for communal or political action.

Classes, thus, do not necessarily constitute communities, although they may, under specific social and historical conditions, be organised for communal action. Whether classes remain as mere categories or are organised into groups depends, to a large extent, on the action of political parties. The Communist party, for instance, tried in the early fifties to organise the *kisans* (i.e., tenants and agricultural labourers) in the Tanjore area for political action. This attempt died out after a brief outburst of violence, but its memory even now colours the relations between classes.

In the Marxian analysis conflict occupies a central position in the definition of class and class relations. Dahrendorf, in fact, defines class almost exclusively in terms of conflict: "Class is always a category for purposes of the analysis of social conflict and its structural roots, and as such it has to be separated strictly from *stratum* as a category for purposes of describing hierarchical systems at a given point of time" (1959, p. 76). But the definition of class used here does not imply the existence of conflict as a necessary or continuous element in the relations between classes.

In the context of the agrarian social structure of Sripuram classes are hierarchically arranged social categories, based broadly upon ownership or nonownership of the means of production. Classes are subdivided in terms of (1) the types of ownership and control and (2) the types of services contributed to the process of production. Thus, a distinction is made between sharecroppers and agricultural labourers. Further, rentiers, farmers, cultivators, sharecroppers, and agricultural labourers constitute distinct categories only at the conceptual level. They do not, in reality, comprise discrete groups, since it is frequently found that a single person is both a rentier and a farmer, a sharecropper and an agricultural labourer.

Although there are points of tension between the different agricultural classes, it would not be correct to characterise their mutual relations as essentially those of conflict. One reason for this is the high degree of overlap in reality between the different classes. The individual often has divided loyalties, being at the same time a landowner and a manual worker, a tenant and an agricultural labourer.

Another important factor is the existence of conflicts based on other alignments, some of which tend to assume greater importance than those of class. The division of the village into Brahmins, 'Non-Brahmins, and Adi-Dravidas provides, as we have seen, fundamental cleavages in its social structure. Tensions often follow these cleavages rather than those of class. As we shall see, however, there is a considerable measure of overlap between caste and class, so that a particular conflict is often as much a conflict between Brahmin and Non-Brahmin as between landlord and tenant.

The distribution of power, again, creates a hierarchy which is different from the hierarchies of caste and class. It is, moreover, far more difficult to locate. Power cannot be defined adequately in terms of formal criteria, and frequent shifts in the power structure give to it a much more fluid character than is associated with either caste or class. Further, many features of the power structure cannot be seen at all in terms of a hierarchical arrangement—as, for example, the conflicts between two rival parties.

II

Caste and class resemble each other in some respects and differ in others. Let us first note these points of similarity and difference before seeing how the two systems are interrelated in their actual working. The relations between class and power will be examined subsequently, and, finally, the role of caste in party politics.

Castes have been defined earlier in terms of distinctive styles of life. In the terminology of Weber (1948, pp. 186–191; 1958, pp. 39–40), they constitute status groups. "In contrast to classes," Weber writes, *status groups are normally communities. They are, however, often of an amorphous kind.*" (1948, p. 186.) It should be pointed out that castes constitute communities only at the local or narrow regional level. Thus, the Shri Vaishnavas of Sripuram, or even all the Brahmins of that village, can be spoken of as a community. It would be inexact, however, to speak of all Brahmins, or even all Shri Vaishnavas, as constituting a community.

Castes, as status groups, are defined essentially in terms of styles of life. Property and occupation enter as important elements in the style of life of a status group, but they need not be decisive. Thus, the Shri Vaishnava Brahmins of Sripuram, who constitute a status group or community, include people with different occupations and economic positions. There are rentiers among them, as well as clerks and schoolteachers. Such occupational differences do not significantly disturb the unity which characterises the style of life of the Shri Vaishnavas of Sripuram as a community.

Too much diversity of occupation or economic position may, however, disrupt the unity of a status group. Although a given style of life may be compatible with more than one occupation, the number and range of such occupations are not unlimited. It is doubtful whether the Shri Vaishnava Brahmins would continue to be a single status group if a large section of them took to menial occupations. As we have seen, the cleavage between Smarthas and Kurukkals is, to a considerable extent, related to their different economic positions.

Social honour in the caste system is very closely tied to ritual values. Styles of life which are highly esteemed are generally associated with a large number of ritual restrictions. Thus, there are restrictions among Brahmins on the eating of various kinds of food. Together with this there are ritual prescriptions with regard to the manner of dress, the caste mark, and so on. These restrictions and prescriptions symbolise different styles of life and serve to mark out the different status groups which are their bearers. Although status groups are a feature of societies of different kinds, nowhere are they so sharply defined as in the caste system. This is in large measure owing to the attachment of elaborate ritual values to the pursuit by different castes of different styles of life.

Another distinctive feature of the caste system as a system of status groups is its extreme proliferation, or the multiplicity of castes. Social classes, defined in terms of ownership or nonownership of the means of production, tend to be reduced to a few broad divisions—ultimately, according to Marx, to two. Status groups, on the other hand, show a tendency to multiply. Nowhere has this tendency manifested itself in a more extreme form than in the caste system. Various estimates place the number of castes in India as between two and three thousand. We have seen how in Sripuram within a single street, the *agraharam*, there are twelve named endogamous divisions.

Classes and status groups have been contrasted by Bottomore (1955, pp. 58–59) in the following terms: "The difference, broadly, is between a hierarchy of a *small number* of organised or partly organised economic groups whose relations to each other are antagonistic, and a hierarchy of *numerous* groups, more correctly described as aggregates of individuals of equal social prestige based on similarities which are not exclusively economic, and whose relations to each other are not primarily antagonistic but are partly competitive and partly emulative." (Italics added.)

Each subcaste or *jati*, however, should not be considered as a discrete entity in any absolute sense of the term. It has been shown how a subcaste has a distinct entity only in relation to another subcaste of the same order of segmentation, and merges itself within a wider group in relation to one of a higher order of segmentation. Besides, the general tendency among castes today is one of fusion, rather than of fission.

Classes, as such, are not defined essentially in terms of social honour, although class positions do tend to be associated with differential honour. Classes, as we have seen, are defined in terms of property, of ownership or nonownership of the means of production. Property by itself does not create social honor, although it is generally a precondition to it. Thus, when a Vellala acquires land, he does not automatically move up in the scale of social honour; for this he is required, in addition, to Sanskritise his style of life.

Classes are—in principle and, to some extent, in practice—open; castes are not. One may change one's position from tenant to landowner, or from agricultural labourer to owner-cultivator. One cannot, however, change from a Vellala into a Brahmin or from a Palla into a Vellala. The free mobility which is, in principle, permitted within the class system, is, in reality, limited by various factors. Thus, the son of a rentier has much greater chances of himself becoming a rentier than the son of an.agricultural labourer. It is, however, not impossible for the latter to become a landowner, and cases of this have been instanced in an earlier chapter.

Movement upwards or downwards within the caste system is, in theory, inadmissible, although there is some movement in practice. We have seen how Kallas transform themselves into Maravas, and Ahamudiyas into Vellalas. Yet there are significant differences between social mobility in the caste system and social mobility in the class system. In the latter it is the individual who moves up or down, whereas in the former entire communities change their position (see Srinivas, 1962).

Mobility in the caste system is a much slower and more gradual process than in the class system. The style of life of a community has a complex and pervasive character, and it takes a long time to bring about a change in it. Property, in contrast, can be acquired and lost more easily and over shorter periods of time. This applies particularly to the contemporary economy of Sripuram, where the cash nexus is of considerable importance and where land has come into the market.

Movement between the different agricultural classes in Sripuram has been taking place at an accelerated pace. Towards the end of the nineteenth century landowners formed a more or less closed category, as did agricultural labourers. Practically the only way of acquiring land was by inheritance. Today there is considerable buying and selling of land. One of the consequences of this is that a growing section of people tend to become completely detached from the agrarian class structure of the village. These are the ex-rentiers who, having sold their land, have taken to typical "middle class" occupations such as those of teacher and clerk.

The caste system enjoyed both legal and religious sanctions in traditional Indian society. Different castes were assigned different rights, not only in economic matters, but over a wide range of social phenomena. In traditional society punishment differed not only according to the nature of the offence committed, but also according to the caste of the offender.

Classes, in contrast, are *de facto* categories. They do not enjoy the kind of legal and religious sanctions which were associated with castes (or, for that matter, with estates in feudal society). It is true that inequalities before law, which were associated with the different castes, have been completely removed, or almost so, in course of the last hundred years. Nonetheless, old habits of mind, conditioned by a legal and religious structure which for centuries upheld these inequalities, continue to play a part in the relations between castes in contemporary society.

III

Today, as we have seen, there is a certain amount of divergence between the hierarchy of caste and that of class. Both the systems have been undergoing some modification, the caste system because of the general trend towards westernisation and secularisation, and the class system because of the extension of a cash economy and because of land having come into the market.

In traditional society, and even fifty years ago, there was much greater consistency between the class system and the caste structure. One can even say, with some risk of oversimplification, that the class system was largely subsumed under the caste structure. This means, in effect, that ownership and nonownership of land, and relations within the system of production, were to a much greater extent associated with caste than is the case today. The disintegration of village handicrafts and the emergence of new "caste-free" occupations have also contributed towards dissociating class relations from the caste structure.

Sripuram, as has been mentioned earlier, constituted an *agra-*

haram village. Much of the land in it was owned by a community of Brahmins who, in addition, owned land in other villages. The Non-Brahmins, in general, owned very little land. Yet there was, even in the nineteenth century, one notable exception. This was the Maratha family which at one time owned a little less than half the land in the three villages of Sripuram-Melur, Peramur, and Vishnupuram taken together.

The Maratha family, however, stood in some ways outside the framework of the local social structure. It was grafted onto the village from outside, and it differed in many ways from both the Brahmins and the Non-Brahmins. It may even be said to have differed more from the Non-Brahmin peasantry in its style of life than from the *mirasdar* Brahmins. By kinship and culture it was related to the princely family of Tanjore, and it always maintained a certain distance from both Brahmins and Non-Brahmins in the village. In fact, it is difficult to place the Maratha family within the local caste structure of Sripuram.

Ignoring, then, the Maratha family, it is certainly true to say that in the nineteenth century more land was held by Brahmins and more Brahmins were landowners than is the case today. It is generally believed that the entire land in the three villages was divided into twenty shares. Of these, nine and a half shares were held by the Maratha family, and the rest, in different proportions, by the six major Brahmin families or lineages. Even to this day one of these Brahmin families bears the title of Kakkarai ("one-fourth share") Shastri.

Most of the residents of the *agraharam* till the end of the nineteenth century belonged to one or another of these six families and were coparcenaries in the village land. The connection between the Brahmins and their ancestral land has been indicated earlier. Learned Brahmins were often settled in the village by the ruling prince, and were endowed with land for their sustenance. Such land almost invariably became ancestral property and passed by inheritance from one generation to another.

It follows that, since service either as domestic or temple priest was adopted by only a few families in the *agraharam*, land must have been the main support of the others. The alternative avenues of employment such as teaching and clerical work which are open to Brahmins today provided very limited opportunities at the turn of the last century. Further, many Brahmins living in the village today are supported by cash remittances sent by relatives employed in the city. Such ties between city and village were also of a rather more limited nature five or six decades ago.

Thus, in the second half of the nineteenth century the *agraharam* was dominated by the six Brahmin lineages which, along with the Maratha family, owned most of the land between them. Some of the older families have left the village altogether, but whatever genealogical material is available shows that land was more widely held in the *agraharam* than at present. Towards the beginning of the present century the terms *"mirasdar"* and "Brahmin" were almost synonymous in Sripuram. This is no longer the case today.

Although most of the Brahmins owned much of the land in the village, they did not themselves cultivate it. The land was leased to tenants who were mainly Non-Brahmins. It is probable that more land was cultivated under the direct supervision of Brahmin *mirasdars* some fifty or sixty years ago than is today. There is, however, little doubt that tenancy played a major part in agrarian relations in the past, as it does at the present.

The Non-Brahmins, with the exception of the Maratha family, owned very little land in the village at the turn of the century. Much of the land which they now own has been acquired over the last fifty years, and particularly since Independence. As a group, they were tenants rather than noncultivating owners or owner-cultivators. They tilled land taken on lease from the Brahmin *mirasdars* either on the *waram* basis or, more commonly, according to the *kuttahai* system.

Even so, as far back as the nineteenth century some of the Non-Brahmin peasants of Sripuram owned land in the village. Their names figure in the settlement register dated 1897. It is not easy to go back much further than this with any measure of certainty as far as the Non-Brahmins are concerned. Family records are not maintained among them (with, of course, the notable exception of the Maratha family) as is done among some of the Brahmins.

Such land as was owned by Non-Brahmin peasants in the village in the nineteenth century was very small in amount, and landownership was confined to a small number of Vellalas and perhaps one Padayachi family. Gradually, however, Non-Brahmins began acquiring land as Brahmins began to dispose of it. The simple picture which we have of the nineteenth century, when Brahmins owned land and Non-Brahmins did not, began to acquire a more complex character. More Vellalas and Padayachis became landowners, and the Kallas also began to acquire land from the beginning of the present century onward.

Nonetheless, the land which was sold by the older Brahmin *mirasdars* was not all bought by the Non-Brahmin peasantry of the village. There is today no single Non-Brahmin in the village who can be compared with the big Brahmin *mirasdars,* whether of the past or of the present. The only big Non-Brahmin landowner is an outsider who never had any direct connection with the village.

Thus, although the number of *mirasdars* among Brahmins and the size of their estates came to be reduced, there did not emerge a corresponding class of *mirasdars* among the Non-Brahmins of the village. Most of the Non-Brahmins of the village who now own land there are small holders. They are not rentiers, but farmers and peasant cultivators. A Vellala in Sripuram, even if he owns twice as much land as a Brahmin, has, in general, a much closer connection with the cultivation of it than the latter. Thus, ownership of land has not effectively brought the upward-moving Non-Brahmin peasant very close to the Brahmin *mirasdar.*

For the rest, most of the Non-Brahmins engaged in agriculture continued to be tenants, as in the past. Even when a Non-Brahmin peasant acquires land, he does not immediately cease to be a tenant. On the contrary, he will try to acquire more land, if not as private property in the capacity of an owner, then on lease in the capacity of a tenant. We have seen earlier, however, that Non-Brahmins do not have the monopoly of being tenants. There are tenants, technically speaking, even among the Brahmins, but their position is exceptional. The case of tenants among Adi-Dravidas will be considered later.

Thus, the Non-Brahmin peasant castes, such as the Vellalas, the Kallas, and the Padayachis, occupy a position in the agrarian class system which is, on the whole, different from that of the Brahmin *mirasdar.* By and large, they constitute the tenantry, or an important section of it, even though some Non-Brahmins are themselves owners of land. A growing number of them have been acquiring land in small parcels, but ownership of land does not automatically transform a Vellala or a Padayachi into the proto-type of the Brahmin *mirasdar*.

The Non-Brahmin peasants, who may be broadly characterised as tenants, include at one end the small landowner; at the other end of the class structure they shade off into the category of agricultural labourers. Many Non-Brahmin tenants, in fact, work as farm servants or day labourers in addition to cultivating the land which they have secured on lease. This is in sharp contrast to the Brahmins, who do not provide even a single recruit to the class of agriculturral labourers.

As a class, agricultural labourers overlap to the largest extent with the Adi-Dravidas. Over a large area of the agrarian econ-omy, the traditional arrangement seems to have been thus: the Brahmin *mirasdars* owned land which they leased to Non-Brahmin tenants who had it cultivated by engaging Adi-Dravida labourers. This, of course, is a highly simplified picture, and even in the traditional economy there were exceptions to the simple correspondence between Brahmin and landowner, Non-Brahmin and tenant, and Adi-Dravida and agricultural labourer. These exceptions have increased considerably over the last fifty years. The class system can no longer be seen simply as an aspect of the caste structure.

Of the eighty-two Palla households in the *cheri* at Sripuram, only about half a dozen are those of tenant cultivators with some security and permanence of tenure. The rest depend mainly upon agricultural and other forms of casual labour for their livelihood. Even the few tenants hold small leases and have to supplement their earnings by working as labourers. In one or two cases the lease is a reward from a Brahmin *mirasdar* for long years of dutiful service as labourer or servant.

The number and proportion of Adi-Dravida tenants in the neighbouring *cheris* seem to be greater. Several Brahmin *miras-dars* have tenants among Adi-Dravidas from one of the five other *cheris* which are within the physical boundaries of Sripuram-Melur or from some other adjacent *cheri*. In some cases the relation between Brahmin *mirasdar* and Adi-Dravida tenant goes back several generations.

Over the last fifteen years there has been an increase in the number of Adi-Dravida tenants. As Non-Brahmin tenants become more demanding and aggressive, with the shift of political power in their favor, Brahmin *mirasdars* tend to show a greater preference for Adi-Dravida tenants, who are, on the whole, less militant and more respectful of traditional authority. A Brahmin *mirasdar* is generally in a stronger bargaining position with an Adi-Dravida lessee than with a Non-Brahmin. His bargaining position, in relation to the latter is, in fact, often very weak.

A Non-Brahmin tenant is much more likely to take disputes with his landlord to the courts. Adi-Dravidas can be more easily intimidated, and they are, in any case, distrustful of the courts for a variety of reasons. They do not have the influence which they feel to be necessary to push matters through the courts, and they are hard put to raise the money necessary for initiating court proceedings. Non-Brahmins, of the whole, are more familiar with court procedures and are less easily controlled by the traditional authority of the Brahmin *mirasdar*.

The threat of court proceedings is an important consideration in contemporary landlord-tenant relations in Sripuram. It has been shown earlier (chap. iv) that the proportions in which the produce should be shared between landlord and tenant have been stipulated by law, and that the law in this regard is not observed in practice. The landlord takes a much larger share than he is allowed by law, and he is always uneasy when threatened with court proceedings. Court proceedings, however, would affect not only the Brahmin *mirasdars,* but also the more influential Non-Brahmins who often sublet their land and therefore extract even higher rents than do Brahmins. Thus, although the threat of court proceedings on account of fair rents always hangs in the air, it has so far not been carried into effect in any significant way. The reasons for this will become clearer when the relationship between ownership of land and political power has been analysed.

Even without going to court, or threatening to go to court, Non-Brahmin tenants give considerable trouble to their Brahmin *mirasdars*. They may refuse to give the stipulated quantity of grain, or not give it on time. They have the strength of organised numbers behind them, and also of political power. A recalcitrant Adi-Dravida tenant may be beaten with impunity on the instruction of his *mirasdar,* but not so an influential Vellala or Kalla tenant.

Many Brahmin *mirasdars* now feel that they will be better served by Adi-Dravida tenants than by Non-Brahmins, but they are not fully free to make substitutions. In the traditional system, when Brahmins were in full control of affairs, their tenants were mainly Non-Brahmins. Legislation against the eviction of tenants, passed since 1952, now makes it difficult for Brahmins to get rid of their troublesome Non-Brahmin tenants. Thus, even when a Brahmin *mirasdar* wishes to bring about change in the old relations, he is often prevented by law from doing this.

There are, nonetheless, ways and means by which the law may be evaded. In the early fifties, when it became clear that some legislation against eviction was in the offing, the shrewder among the Brahmin *mirasdars* got rid of their troublesome Non-Brahmin lessees and had them replaced by Adi-Dravidas. Even after the laws were enacted, tenants could be evicted for arrears of payment or on other technical grounds, provided the *mirasdar* happened to be a sufficiently shrewd and powerful person. Today, a sizeable proportion of Brahmin *mirasdars* in Sripuram have one or more Adi-Dravida tenants, whether from the *cheri* attached to the village or from an adjoining one.

There are a number of reasons why Adi-Dravidas were not preferred as tenants in the traditional system. The landless Palla is notorious for being unthrifty and improvident. In the past, whatever surplus income he made often went to the liquor seller. He rarely saved, and he had very little movable property to speak of. From people of this kind it is usually difficult to extract rent when it falls due. Arrears tend to mount, and the only sanction which the *mirasdar* has at his disposal is to have his Palla beaten or put in jail, neither of which is of profit to him in the long run. A Non-Brahmin tenant, owning some movable property, would rather sell his utensils, or mortgage his wife's ornaments, than court imprisonment for nonpayment of arrears.

Concepts of purity and pollution also acted against the development of direct relations between Brahmins and Adi-Dravidas in earlier times. The relationship between landlord and tenant, particularly in the traditional system, was often a close and personal one. Exchange of goods and services extended beyond what is strictly involved in the relation between owner and tiller of land. The tenant was often called to do odd jobs in the *mirasdar*'s house, where he had relatively easy access.

The Adi-Dravida, by reason of the pollution attached to his person, was debarred from many of the activities which a Non-Brahmin tenant by convention performed for his *mirasdar*. He had access only to the outer backyard of the Brahmin's house. If the Brahmin needed him urgently, he could not himself go to the *cheri* to fetch him. Even today an Adi-Dravida tenant cannot, after harvest, deliver the grain directly to the house of his Brahmin *mirasdar*. He has to stand at the head of the *agraharam* and call out for his landlord, who then sends somebody to carry the grain in.

It is thus that Adi-Dravidas are associated more closely with Non-Brahmins than with Brahmins. Non-Brahmins engage Adi-Dravidas as labourers and servants, and in some cases sublet to them land which they have themselves acquired on lease from Brahmins. In such cases there is a threefold hierarchy of Brahmin landowner, Non-Brahmin tenant, and Adi-Dravida subtenant. Although the Non-Brahmin makes some profit out of such a relationship without contributing either land or labour, his position, being that of an intermediary, is a very weak one in the eyes of the law.

Thus, though the majority of Adi-Dravidas are agricultural labourers, there are some who are tenants at second hand. There are also some among them who are tenants at first hand, holding their lease directly from Brahmin *mirasdars*. A few have even become owners of land. As far as the *cheri* attached to Sripuram is concerned, this is an entirely new phenomenon. Some Adi-Dravidas belonging to the adjoining *cheris* have owned small parcels of land for the last few decades.

With the purchase of land by Adi-Dravidas, the class system has further dissociated itself from the rigidity of the caste structure. The term "Adi-Dravida" is no longer synonymous with "nonowner of land," as it was a few decades ago. But the acquisition of land by Adi-Dravidas is a recent phenomenon. In the Sripuram *cheri* only three Adi-Dravidas have purchased land, and that only in course of the last three years. In the revenue village as a whole not more than a dozen Adi-Dravidas own land.

On an average each of them owns about one acre, so that even the owners of land among the Adi-Dravidas have to supplement their income by engaging themselves as tenants or else as agricultural labourers.

The relationship between the caste structure and the class system has, evidently, been a dynamic one. In the traditional system caste and class overlapped to a very large extent. There is even today a considerable measure of overlap between the two systems. But the class system has gradually been dissociating itself from the caste structure. One can achieve a variety of class positions with different degrees of probability, whatever one's position in the caste structure may be.

IV

Although relations between classes have been undergoing change, this change has not kept pace with changes in the distribution of power. Ownership of land has shifted only in a small way from the old rentier class to the emerging class of farmers and owner-cultivators. Power, on the other hand, has shifted much more decisively from the traditional elite of the village into the hands of the new popular leaders.

Not only was there greater congruence between caste and class in the traditional system, but both were more congruent with the power structure than today. The powerful families in the past were the big landowning families. These included the principal Brahmin families and, among Non-Brahmins, the Maratha family. Today political power, whether in the village or outside it, is not as closely tied to ownership of land as it was in the past. New bases of power have emerged which are, to some extent, independent of both caste and class. Perhaps most important among these is the strength of numerical support.

One can, of course, view either caste or class as an independent locus of power. In fact, the concept of dominant caste has been widely used to show how power in the village or the district has been controlled by one or more castes. There can be little doubt that in traditional society power was largely subsumed by the structure of caste, and this was certainly true of Sripuram also at the turn of the century. Today, however, power is no longer a monopoly of any single caste in the village. It has, to some extent, detached itself from caste, and one has now to consider the balance of power between different castes (or groups of castes). This balance is unstable in nature, and factors other than caste play an important part in maintaining it and changing it from day to day.

Class also may be viewed as an independent locus of power, but only in a limited way. In Sripuram classes have never been communities; they have not been organised for political action; and they have never had the necessary coherence for acting as political units.

In addition to caste and class there are important loci of power which belong specifically to the domain of politics. The emergence of such loci—the *panchayat* system, parties, and political networks—has largely been a feature of the political modernisation of India. We have tried to achieve some understanding of the nature of the new loci of power, their sources of strength, and the processes by which they become differentiated from the traditional structure.

The popular leaders of the village today are not necessarily big landowners. The *panchayat* president who is a key figure in village politics owns some land, but this is not his principal source of power. We have seen how his power depends upon a plurality of factors, among which his contacts with politicians and party bosses outside the village and his position in an elaborate system of patronage are important ones.

Two factors have contributed in a big way to changes in the distribution of power in the village. The first of these is the decline in the influence of the old *mirasdar* class for a variety of reasons. The second is the growth of an elaborate political machinery, linking M.L.A.'s, party bosses, and village leaders and making it possible for people to acquire power in ways which were not open before the introduction of adult franchise and Panchayati Raj.

The power of the big landowners in Sripuram (and, to some extent, in Tanjore District as a whole) has been progressively curbed over the last several decades. It is not unlikely that this weakening of power has been confined to the old *mirasdar* or rentier class of landowners, and that the farmer and owner-cultivator classes have held their own or even strengthened their political position. Since Sripuram has been dominated in the past by rentiers and absentee landowners, it is to this class that we now turn our attention.

The power of the *mirasdars* in Sripuram was considerable at the beginning of the present century. There were several among them who each owned more than thirty acres of land. Most of them lived in the *agraharam,* and they were united by bonds of kinship and caste and by a common style of life. The rest of the village looked up to them for their livelihood and for help and guidance on a variety of matters. In addition to agriculturists, the artisan and servicing castes also depended to a large extent on the patronage of the *mirasdars.*

Several factors were responsible for the power and influence of the old landowning class in Sripuram. There was, to begin with, a greater measure of unity among them as a class than there is today. Landowners were united, not only in terms of economic interest, but by a common style of life. In a majority of cases they were born in the village, had grown up there, and had known each other from childhood. Their relationships with each other, as well as with their tenants, were of a close, intimate, personal character.

Today not only has the proportion of landowners resident in the village gone down, but fragmentation has greatly reduced the size of individual or family holdings. Together with this, the cost of living has gone up, since landowners have very often to support one or more children studying outside. This makes it very difficult for the *mirasdar* to meet his traditional obligations to tenants and to artisans and servicing groups. Formerly at festivals such as Deepavali and Pongal, as well as on other occasions, landowners were expected to give liberally to a host of dependents. Today most of them cannot easily afford to do this. As their ability to distribute patronage becomes weakened, their power and influence over tenants and dependents also tend to wane.

Along with this, one has to consider the fact that a large section of landowners have left the village and settled elsewhere. Absentee landowners do not generally have either the opportunity or the interest to maintain control over affairs in the village. They do not have any close or enduring ties with their tenants. They do not distribute patronage or in any appreciable way influence political life in the village. Many of them know the village, and are known by its inhabitants, only superficially.

Thus, the landowners as a class have become fragmented and scattered. Some of them cling to the traditional ways of life and continue to reside in the village. Others have acquired Western education, secured urban employment, and developed interests outside the village. The former unity of the landowners—and, along with it, a part of their strength—has been destroyed.

Political and legal factors have further undermined the position of the old class of rentier *mirasdars*. Earlier, the landowner had a fairly free hand in fixing rents, as well as in evicting tenants. Land legislation in recent years has considerably strengthened the position of tenants at the same time as it has curbed the powers of landowners. A tenant can no longer be evicted at the pleasure of the *mirasdar*. The latter is, thus, deprived of one of the most powerful weapons in his armoury. The political climate in the state as a whole is changing, and the class of rentier *mirasdars* in Sripuram has begun to feel that the tide is against them.

The emerging leaders of the village are, thus, not members of the old landowning class. They generally belong to the class of small owner-cultivators. Their power is, to a large extent, based upon numerical support within the village and political contacts outside it. These two factors, as we have seen, tend to reinforce each other.

Members of the old *mirasdar* class feel ill at ease in the face of changes in the ideological climate. The introduction of democratic forms of government, and more particularly of adult franchise, has created in the minds of people a new consciousness of their own political importance, irrespective of caste, class, and other social factors. Villagers, however low their social or economic position, have by now had the experience of being courted during elections by important political personalities from towns and cities. The support of the masses can no longer be taken for granted. And in this matter the new political leaders, the contact men, have an edge over *mirasdars* of the older type.

There is always a certain barrier which deters the old *mirasdar* from approaching his tenants and servants for votes in an attitude of supplication. There is a sense of pride which keeps him from competing for popular support with people who had till recently taken his superiority for granted. The campaign for popular support demands many compromises which do not come easily to the rentier *mirasdar,* who still preserves a very keen sense of personal prestige.

There is a feeling of estrangement between the old elite of the village and the masses. The *mirasdar,* who is often a Brahmin, cannot go to the *cheri* to canvass votes from the Pallas. The new Non-Brahmin leaders have an advantage over him in this regard. Non-Brahmins in general have long had much closer contacts with the Adi-Dravidas in the village. It is easier for them to assume an air of equality when approaching the latter for votes or political support in general. The very structure which in the past ensured the superiority of the *mirasdar* by keeping others at a distance from him now acts as an obstacle when he is faced with the demands of an egalitarian ideology.

Popular leaders of the kind who now dominate the village *panchayat* began to come to the forefront after 1942. As the Congress developed more and more into a mass movement, young people with initiative and drive, and with the ability to organise support, moved into the limelight. Gradually the skill to organise people became an important factor. The self-esteem of members of the old *mirasdar* class often stood in the way of their developing such a skill. Particularly today there is a distinct tendency on the part of the college-educated *mirasdar* to regard local politics as something dirty, requiring the prospective leader to rub shoulders with people of all descriptions.

The new popular leader in his turn began to expand his contacts both within and outside the village. Lack of funds was not always a very serious handicap, since the party as well as various agencies of the government could be tapped for money. The development of democracy, with its elaborate paraphernalia of parties and local self-government, has made politics a paying business for those who have initiative, drive, and popular support. Being a part of this elaborate political machinery gives to the individual a certain standing, irrespective of his caste or class position.

As more and more specialised political agencies develop, the political system itself tends to acquire a weight of its own. In the traditional system there were no parties, legislatures, or Panchayat Union Councils in and through which the individual could acquire power independently of his position in the class or caste structure. No doubt, membership in the party, the Legislature, or the Panchayat Union Council is even today largely dependent upon caste and class. But the relations between caste, class, and power have become more complex and more dynamic in contemporary society, and the introduction of adult franchise in particular has opened up new avenues for the acquisition of power.

Thus, there is a certain divergence between economic and political power in the village today. The big *mirasdars* are no longer the ones who are politically the most powerful. Those in whom political power is vested in the village today cannot accurately be described as big landowners. To what extent are the ones who have acquired political power also on the way to acquiring control over land? This is a question to which no satisfactory answer can be provided under the terms of the present analysis. Although it would be useful to view the relationship between political and economic power in terms of dynamic criteria, there is no doubt that there may be considerable lags between the two over a particular period of time.

One should not, however, emphasize too much the divergence between political and economic power. In order to acquire and retain political power it is necessaary for a person to have some economic standing. Although political power has shifted from the class of rentier *mirasdars,* it has not gone into the hands of landless labourers.The latter are still largely in a state of subordination. In the *panchayat* and outside they have very little say in matters which affect the village as a whole.

Although not big *mirasdars,* most of those who enjoy political power in the village have some land or other source of income. A person who is politically influential has to distribute patronage to his followers. He has to entertain guests from outside and keep up a certain standard of living. It is not possible for a landless labourer, or for one whose income is very small and uncertain, to meet the demands which are made by followers on a leader and a man of influence.

While a moderately secure economic position is an important condition for the acquisition of power, political power, in its turn, brings certain economic advantages. The *panchayat* president receives funds from the party, or from leaders higher up, and part of this he can divert to his personal use. He also has certain discretionary powers in the use of *panchayat* funds, and it is widely believed in the village that he is able to use these powers to his own personal advantage. Members of the *panchayat* and, particularly, of the Panchayat Union Council have authority to give contracts for jobs of various kinds, and the giving of contracts usually brings in its wake reciprocal benefits.

Contacts with officials in government departments is an important source of economic advantage for the villagers today. One can obtain credit facilities for various purposes and an increasing range of benefits through government departments. Political connections often help to break through the rigid demands of a bureaucratic structure. The *panchayat* president of Sripuram, who has contacts with important political leaders, is in a position to use these contacts to gain many administrative advantages.

Although numerical strength has become an increasingly important basis of power, by itself it does not count for very much. What is required, in addition, is organisation, and in this regard people with some social and economic standing play an important part. Small tenants and landless labourers, and those who are on the border line between them, have as yet very little power. Far from being able to manœuvre for benefits and privileges, they are generally not even able to get for themselves what they are entitled to by law.

Sometime after the Payment of Fair Rent Act was passed in 1956, some of the small tenants in Sripuram made an attempt to have it enforced. The Brahmin *mirasdars* found themselves in a difficult situation, as they had by then lost the power to enforce their decision against strong opposition from the other villagers. But on this issue they were joined by the farmers and owner-cultivators, the new men of power in the village, because the latter, largely as intermediaries, had as much to lose as the rentiers, or perhaps more, by the enforcement of the act.

Although legally the position of small tenants has been strengthened considerably, there are still many loopholes in the law which can be used to advantage by an enterprising *mirasdar*. The law allows the latter to resume for personal cultivation land up to a maximum of 6⅔ acres. Even the big *mirasdar* often has his land under the names of several members of his family, any one of whom rarely has more than the stipulated maximum. It is always possible to take advantage of this provision in the law to evict tenants if their demands are pitched too high.

In actual practice some compromise is generally reached. The *mirasdars* by and large have allowed their tenants to keep a slightly higher share of the produce than they did before 1956. But their success in getting round the law was due in no small measure to the support which they received from the politically powerful owner-cultivators and big tenants.

In Sripuram tensions between people occupying different positions in the agrarian system tend to be seen as issues between individuals. There is a good measure of discontent all around. The agricultural labourer feels that he has no security; the small tenant feels that he is being cheated; the landowner feels that his rights are being increasingly curtailed and that peasants are being taught by politicians to make unreasonable demands. But, by and large, conflict, bargaining, and adjustment are not organised, and are matters between one individual and another.

Agricultural labourers do not have much experience of organised political action. In the main, their efforts to improve their position in any big way have been thwarted. In a neighbouring *cheri* a number of agricultural labourers got together and made a threat to their landowner of stopping work unless their wages were increased. The landowner, a Non-Brahmin with high political connections at Tanjore, secured a lorry to transport labourers from outside to work in his fields. The local agricultural labourers were starved into capitulation.

Generally in Sripuram the individual agricultural labourer tries to bargain for a slightly higher wage for himself. Wages are sufficiently variable and dynamic to allow each person the hope that he may be able to make a certain gain for himself. And, most important, the agricultural labourer wishes to keep himself in the good books of the *mirasdar* in the constant hope of being able to gain from the latter a piece of land to cultivate on his own as a tenant.

The agricultural labourer has been tied for generations to a particular way of life, and he does not normally fix his aspirations beyond a certain level. A secure and stable source of livelihood for himself and his family is his immediate objective. As he generally sees it, the best and the most obvious way of achieving this is by acquiring a lease through the favour of some *mirasdar*. The idea of patronage, as an exchange of favour for service, is an important legacy of the traditional system. The thought of organising political action does not come easily to the landless labourer, particularly if he happens to be of the older generation.

Lessees or tenants are of various kinds, and their attitudes depend upon their legal position, the amount of land which they hold on lease, and whether they own any land themselves. An individual often has a plurality of roles; he may be a lessee vis-à-vis somebody and have, in addition, lessees of his own. In such cases his attitudes will be shaped by a delicate balance of specific personal interests. Tenants with big leases may identify themselves more closely with landowners than with small tenants.

Not all lessees have a very secure legal position. The more powerful ones among them are often intermediaries; as such, their position is ambiguous. Intermediaries do not have the same economic interests as tenants who are tillers of the soil. In fact, the intermediaries would generally stand to lose by a lowering of rents. As a result, there is limited scope for the two to come together for common political action.

Thus, classes—as categories of persons having similar positions in the system of production—are not politically organised for a variety of reasons. The separation of the different classes is, in reality, not sharp enough for each to have a feeling of identity in opposition to the others. Individuals have multiple positions, and their loyalties are divided. There are risks involved in challenging established economic interests. The agricultural labourer may find it difficult to secure employment, and the tenant may find himself evicted through manipulation by the landlord of some loophole in the law.

V

Political conflicts seem to have followed more closely the cleavages of caste than those of class. The division of society into

Brahmins, Non-Brahmins, and Adi-Dravidas has been of more immediate relevance in mobilising political support than its division into landowners, tenants, and agricultural labourers. To a large extent, of course, conflicts between castes subsume within them conflicts between classes, since there is a considerable measure of overlap between the two systems.

One important difference between caste and class is that castes, at least at the level of the village, constitute communities, whereas classes do not. In Sripuram all Brahmins, for instance, live in one place; all landowners do not. As a community of persons living together, constantly interacting with each other, and being shaped by the same general values, Brahmins are more likely to develop common political attitudes than are landowners or members of any agrarian class.

In the traditional set-up political power in Sripuram was in the hands of the Brahmins. The Non-Brahmins, with the exception of the Maratha family, did not enjoy much political power. Major decisions affecting the village as a whole were in general taken and implemented by the Brahmins. This, as we have seen, has changed considerably. Power has now gone into the hands of Non-Brahmins, and Brahmins tend to play a smaller part in deciding the fate of the village.

One of the most important political phenomena of the past three decades, in Sripuram as well as in Tamilnad as a whole, has been the shift of power from Brahmins to Non-Brahmins. This has not necessarily or always meant a shift from landowners to tenants or cultivators. The new men of power in Sripuram cannot adequately be characterised as tillers of the soil. More important, they owe much of their power to connections with influential Non-Brahmins outside the village who in many cases happen to be big landowners.

In Sripuram the transfer of power from Brahmins to Non-Brahmins was symbolised by the shift of the *panchayat* office from the *agraharam* to the Non-Brahmin quarters. This was associated with the replacement by a Non-Brahmin of the Brahmin *panchayat* president in the mid-forties. Today guests of the *panchayat*, including state ministers, are received in the new *panchayat* office and do not have any occasion to visit the *agraharam*.

The relationship between caste and political power has to be examined in the context of change, because change has been an important feature of this relationship over the last few decades. Further, such changes as have been taking place within the village are, in many cases, reflections of shifts in power in regional society. It is necessary, therefore, to undertake a broad survey of the changing role of caste in the politics of Tamilnad over the last forty years in order to place in their proper perspective the events which are taking place in Sripuram today.

The Brahmins have occupied a rather ambivalent position in the politics of Tamilnad since the end of nineteenth century. Their changing fortunes in Sripuram reflect their general decline in the state as a whole. Yet the superior position which Brahmins enjoyed in traditional society had been further strengthened during the earlier years of British rule, when they added Western education to the high economic position and ritual status which was already theirs.

Till the outbreak of World War I, Western education in Tamilnad was almost a monopoly of the Brahmins. This was particularly true of the Tanjore Brahmins. It had the consequence, at least initially, of further widening the gap between Brahmins on the one hand and Non-Brahmins and Adi-Dravidas on the other. We have seen how this happened in Sripuram. The Brahmins turned themselves towards urban life, and there was a corresponding loss of interest in agriculture. The Non-Brahmins, on the other hand, remained firmly rooted to the village and its agrarian economy.

Western education not only brought social prestige on its own right, but also opened the way to new economic opportunities. The new urban jobs—clerical, executive, and professional—became a virtual monopoly of the Brahmins. Brahmins in important executive and managerial positions used the ties of caste and kinship to recruit more Brahmins. The Non-Brahmins found themselves virtually excluded because of their belated start.

Western education, and employment in important managerial and administrative positions, brought the Brahmins close to the new rulers of India, the British. Brahmins entered the highly prestigious and powerful Indian Civil Service, and government bureaucracies of all kinds became their strongholds. They also dominated the professions of law, medicine, and education. Since nationalist awakenings first found expression among members of the professions and the urban middle classes in general, the leadership of the Congress party came to be dominated by the Brahmins.

The Non-Brahmins, however, did not for long remain reconciled to their inferior position. Those among them who were able to acquire Western education soon set about organising themselves politically and appealing to the British for a more equitable distribution of opportunities. The Justice newspaper, a vehicle of Non-Brahmin demands, was launched in 1917, and at about the same time the Justice party. The stage was set for the struggle for power between Brahmins and Non-Brahmins.

In the early decades of the present century in Tamilnad the Brahmins dominated the Congress party, by far the most influential national political organisation. The Non-Brahmins, including Muslims and Christians, rallied round the Justice party. The latter gained important advantages by coöperating with the British over the Government of India Act of 1919, which the Congress decided to boycott. The struggles between Brahmins and Non-Brahmins were initially confined largely to the urban middle classes, but they soon pervaded wider areas of society.

The leaders of the Non-Brahmin movement expressed the fear that the transfer of power for which the Congress was agitating might lead to the domination of the people by a small elite composed of Brahmins. They argued, therefore, for preferential treatment of Non-Brahmins to make up for the advantages which the Brahmins had secured over them in the fields of education and employment.

After the Congress boycotted the Government of India Act of 1919, the leaders of the Justice party managed to have discriminatory measures favouring the Non-Brahmins built into the administration. Posts in the government as well as seats in the institutions of higher learning came to be reserved for Non-Brahmins. For those aspiring to pass into the new middle classes it became important at every stage whether they were Brahmins or Non-Brahmins. Discrimination continues against Brahmins to this day and is a major factor in their feeling and consciousness of unity.

In the twenties the Brahmins began to lose ground in education and administration. In the thirties the Self-Respect movement started carrying anti-Brahmin feelings to the masses. Newspapers were started in English (*The Liberator*) and in Tamil (*Swaya-mariyadai*) in which Brahmins were denounced for their arrogance and the pursuit of their narrow group interests. Brahminism as a way of life came in for attack for its bigotry and duplicity, and for the exploitation which it practised and encouraged.

Attempts were made to do away with the service of Brahmin priests. The Purohit Maruppu Sangam ("Association for the Elimination of Priests") was formed, and Self-Respect marriages (without the service of Brahmin priests) began to be performed. A general attitude of hostility towards Brahmins came to be built up on the social plane, and feelings ran high against them.

The leading figure in the attack against Brahmins over the last thirty-five years has been the one-time Congress leader, E. V. Ramaswami Naicker. In the thirties and early forties he spearheaded the Self-Respect movement and trained a band of educated young men with idealistic fervour as his disciples. In the forties he formed the Dravida Kazhagham (D.K.), a militant organisation devoted to anti-Brahmin and anti-North Indian activities. In 1949 some of the ablest young men split from the D.K. and formed a separate party, the Dravida Munnetra Kazhagham (D.M.K.), which has now emerged as the leading opposition party in the state. Though also rooted in anti-Brahminism, the D.M.K. is more moderate in its programmes, even admitting Brahmins within its folds. It claims to be hostile not to Brahmins as such, but to the elements of obscurantism and exploitation in the Brahminical way of life.

The wave of anti-Brahmin feeling which swept through the state found its echo in Sripuram. At Thiruvaiyar leaders of the D.K. burnt copies of the Ramayana and threatened violence to the Brahmins in political speeches. Films preaching the D.M.K. ideology and heaping scorn on Brahmins drew large audiences from the village at cinema halls in Thiruvaiyar and nearby places. The Brahmins found themselves politically isolated and the target of attack from forces of various kinds, some of them politically organised.

The Congress itself, which in the early decades of the present century was largely dominated by Brahmins, gradually passed under the control of Non-Brahmins. In 1942 the "August movement" provided a major breakthrough for the Non-Brahmins, whose support became increasingly important, if for no other reason than the strength of their numbers. After Independence the political influence of the Brahmins dwindled rapidly. Today in Tamilnad the ministry and the Legislature as well as the Congress party are dominated by Non-Brahmins. The Congress has, to some extent, been forced to transform the character of its leadership in order to hold its own against parties with a Non-Brahmin background such as the D.K. and the D.M.K. With the replacement of C. Rajagopalachari by K. Kamraj in the fifties, the political influence of the Brahmins has been more or less effectively neutralised.

Political events of the last forty years have given the Tamil Brahmins a strong feeling of identity as a minority. The traditional quarrels between Smartha and Shri Vaishnava, let alone Thengalai and Vadagalai, have been largely forgotten. In general the feeling is strong among the Brahmins of Sripuram that they should be united if they are to survive. This feeling of unity among the Brahmins, their consciousness of a common destiny, is in considerable measure a response to the political challenge of the last forty years.

In the village the Brahmins have gradually come to accept their social and political isolation. They have been singled out for attack by leaders of the D.K. and the D.M.K., through the press and the films. Their social exclusiveness, once jealously guarded in the interest of "culture," refinement, and ritual purity, has now been turned against them. Although there has been bitterness against landowners and moneylenders, it has never been organised in the way in which hostility towards Brahmins has been. The anti-Brahmin movement is not in its practice an attack against a particular economic class, but against Brahmins in general, whether they are landowners, schoolteachers, clerks, or temple priests.

It is the anti-Brahmin movement rather than class conflict between the landowners and the landless that has dominated political life in this area over the last forty years. No doubt, the anti-Brahmin movement has been viewed by many in the idiom of a class struggle. And, in fact, the Communists in the early fifties drew the support of the D.K. to launch their attack against the landowners, who in the Thiruvaiyar area often happened to be Brahmins.

The Brahmins have not fared very well in the hands of the Congress party, or the government either. We have seen that discriminatory measures against the Brahmins have been built into the administration since the twenties. The Congress party, when it came into power after Independence, continued with the policy of preferential treatment of the backward communities. A Brahmin today, as before, finds the odds against him when applying for a job in the state government or a seat in some technical institution.

As victims of discrimination in various forms, the Brahmins tend to develop a high degree of political consciousness. When the results of the degree examinations were published in 1961, two Brahmin boys from Sripuram sought admission in various engineering colleges in the state, but were unsuccessful. Their parents and the community as a whole held this against the discriminatory policy of the government. In various ways the Brahmin from Sripuram is thwarted in the pursuit of his career. Rightly or wrongly, he attributes his misfortune to the government and the ruling party, from which he becomes progressively alienated.

The Brahmins, thus, are in a political situation which is, in many ways, unique. From being a political elite in the first part of the present century, they now find themselves in the position of a political minority. The forces of democracy have turned the tables upon them. What has happened in Sripuram is only one instance, and to some extent it follows from what has been happening in the state as a whole. But although the Brahmins have lost much political ground, they have not entirely withdrawn from political activities within the state. We shall examine presently the changing relationships between the Brahmins and a variety of political parties.

The political fortunes of the Non-Brahmins have also been rather varied, and perhaps even more complex that those of the Brahmins. We have noted that the Non-Brahmins first organised their political interests around the Justice party. The Justice party, however, was a platform for only a small section of the Non-Brahmins—the urban, educated middle classes among them. Its impact on the rural masses was negligible, and it became virtually extinct after its rout in the 1937 elections.

The Justice party served one important purpose. It served to bring into focus the conflict of interests between Brahmins and Non-Brahmins, and to organise this conflict politically on a state-wide basis.

The Non-Brahmins had, in the meantime, found a new sense of identity and a new ideology in the Self-Respect movement. This movement called upon Non-Brahmins to rid themselves of their ritual dependence on Brahmins and to stand on their own feet. It tried to create for the first time a feeling among Non-Brahmins that they were equal to the Brahmins, if not superior. And the Self-Respect movement was not confined to the cities; it spread to the rural masses. Even as late as 1961, Self-Respect marriages were being conducted in Sripuram, among both Non-Brahmins and Adi-Dravidas, without the service of Brahmin priests.

The political fate of the Non-Brahmins was not decided by the defeat of the Justice party in the elections of 1937. The Congress, which was sucessful in the election, began to draw increasingly upon the Non-Brahmins for its leadership. We have seen how in Sripuram the 1942 movement paved the way for the emergence of Non-Brahmins to positions of influence in the Congress. What happened in Sripuram was taking place in the state as a whole. Independence in 1947, and the first General Elections in independent India in 1951/52 saw the Non-Brahmins forge further ahead in their control of the Congress and of politics in Tamilnad as a whole. By the mid-fifties the Non-Brahmins were in a commanding position in the Congress party, the state Legislature, and the cabinet. They have more or less effectively maintained their control till now.

Non-Brahmin control is not confined among political parties to the Congress alone. New parties which arose as successors to the Justice party made their appeal to Non-Brahmins in particular. The Congress, at least, has expressed itself in a universalistic idiom, and has not come out explicitly for any particular community, however much it may have been favoured or controlled by that community in practice, and neither has it come out openly against any.

In the mid-forties the D.K. emerged as a champion of Non-

Brahmins and Adi-Dravidas. It has been militant in its approach, openly preaching violence and directing its attack and virulence against Brahmins in particular. By the mid-fifties, however, with the Non-Brahmins gaining effective control over the Congress, the D.K. had become a spent force as a separate political entity. In 1951/52, when the veteran Brahmin leader C. Rajagopalachari was still at the helm of Congress affairs, the D.K. supported the Communists. In 1957 and 1962 the D.K. joined hands with the Congress, taking active part in its campaigns, particularly in the districts of Tanjore and Trichy.

Although the D.K. has become politically a spent force, this is by no means true of its offshoot, the D.M.K. The D.M.K. separated from the D.K. in 1949. It has been, on the whole, less militant than the parent body and less aggressive in its attitude towards Brahmins. In theory, at least, membership is open to Brahmins, although they have not shown much keenness to join the party.

In spite of the relatively moderate policies of the D.M.K., its anti-Brahmin background must not be lost sight of. Many of the present leaders of the party had their apprenticeship under Ramaswami Naicker and have a number of anti-Brahmin activities to their credit. Through the medium of films the party leaders have made attacks on religious orthodoxy and on the Brahminical social order with which orthodoxy has been associated. Sporadically the party members are known to have participated in outrages against the Brahmins. In practice the leadership of the D.M.K. has been almost entirely Non-Brahmin.

There is one other party whose position in relation to the caste structure must be examined. This is the Swatantra party, which has entered the field recently. In Tamilnad the Swatantra party is known fairly widely as the "Brahmin party." This is due, in part, to the fact that its founder and most influential spokesman is C. Rajagopalachari. There is also considerable correspondence between the aims and policies of the party and the social situation of the Brahmins in contemporary Tamilnad. This is not to deny that even in Tamilnad the Swatantra party has many Non-Brahmin members and leaders.

Having examined the correspondence at the state level between caste groups on the one hand and political forces and parties on the other, we turn briefly to a consideration of the situation at Sripuram. Party loyalties there show in many cases a close correspondence with membership in one or another caste group. In many ways such loyalties follow the lines of caste much more closely than those of class.

The most striking case of correspondence is the one between Brahmins and the Swatantra party. Many of the Brahmins of Sripuram are members of this party, and most of them express support for it. In the village the party has made practically no headway among the Non-Brahmins, not to speak of the Adi-Dravidas. Not only do others see the Swatantra party as a Brahmin party, but the Brahmins themselves tend to feel that it answers specifically to their needs.

One day, while on my way to Thiruvaiyar, I observed the Brahmin Swatantra party leader of the village engaged in what appeared to be a very confidential conversation with an important Non-Brahmin businessman from Tanjore. I casually asked my companion, a Brahmin from Sripuram, whether the Non-Brahmin businessman was a member of the Swatantra party. His answer, a mixture of surprise and bitterness, was characteristic. "Don't be absurd," he said. "He hates Brahmins like anything. Do you think he will join the Swatantra party?"

The identification of the Brahmins with the Swatantra party is a conscious one. It cuts across the boundaries of class, occupation, income, education, and generation. Whether he is a *mirasdar* or a server in a coffee shop, college-educated or relatively unlettered, an orthodox elder or a "progressive" young man, the Brahmin in Sripuram feels it his duty to be loyal to the Swatantra party. Exceptions are very few and are based mainly on personal association with the Congress.

Although the Swatantra party in Tamilnad has been largely identified with the Brahmins, this does not mean that it has no relationship with class factors. Its appeal in Tamilnad has so far been largely confined to landowners, business people, and professional men; it seems to have made little headway among industrial workers or landless labourers. In Sripuram, however, what strikes one particularly is its much closer identification with the Brahmins than with any specific economic class.

The Brahmins' uniformity of political opinion and their

massive support of the Swatantra party are a consequence of their political experience in the state as a whole over the last forty years. Singled out for social criticism, political attack, and administrative discrimination, they feel a strong sense of urgency to be united politically and to support the party of their leader, Rajagopalachari, irrespective of differences which may exist within their ranks. Brahmins in Sripuram, when questioned about their support of the Swatantra party, emphasize the need for unity at all cost.

In Sripuram the relationship of the Brahmins to the Congress party is now a purely negative one. It is, nevertheless, important, because their attitude towards the Congress has led them to support parties to which they would be otherwise hostile. We have noted that in the 1962 elections the Brahmins of Sripuram voted for the D.M.K. candidate for the Assembly seat. This support was based explicitly on hostility towards the Congress and not on any appreciation of either the policy or the leadership of the D.M.K.

The importance of caste loyalties among Brahmins manifested itself in an interesting manner in the 1962 elections. The Brahmins of Sripuram, for the reasons just mentioned, had taken a more or less collective decision to vote against the Congress. For the Assembly seat they voted almost *en masse* for the D.M.K. candidate, who, like all the other candidates for the seat, was a Kalla by caste. For the Parliamentary constituency, however, the Congress had put up a Brahmin candidate, C. R. Pattabhiraman, the son of a very distinguished Tamil Brahmin, Sir C. P. Ramaswami Iyer. In spite of their firm resolve to vote against the ruling party, a large section of the Sripuram Brahmins changed their mind at the last moment and voted for the Brahmin Congress candidate.

Non-Brahmins have a choice of associating themselves with a number of political parties. In Sripuram and the surrounding area, the most important of these are the Congress and the D.M.K. The Swatantra party has made practically no headway among them, although it has done so in other areas. The D.K. has a number of sympathisers, but since it does not contest elections on its own, it is not always possible to separate its supporters from those of the Congress.

In Sripuram during the 1962 elections Non-Brahmin support was divided between the Congress and the D.M.K. But it is very difficult to infer any pattern on the basis of this. Those who voted for the Congress, or even took part in its election campaign, might in many cases switch over their support to the D.M.K., depending upon a variety of personal and local factors. Political opinion among the Non-Brahmins of the village is not as sharply defined as it is among the Brahmins. This is, no doubt, due largely to the much lower proportion of literacy and education among them, and to their greater diversity.

Class differentials among the Non-Brahmins of Sripuram do not today play a very important role in determining party support, although they may do so elsewhere. There seems to be a generational difference, but this, too, is not very sharp. On the whole, the older, better-established Non-Brahmins in the village tend to support the Congress. The D.M.K. is run by younger people, some of whom are sons of fairly well-to-do farmers and owner-cultivators.

The Adi-Dravidas are, on the whole, supporters of the Congress. Thus, Congress support cuts across both caste as well as class. Support of the Congress by the Adi-Dravidas is closely related to the policies which the ruling party has been following. Indeed, there is some criticism by both Brahmins and Non-Brahmins that the Congress has been nursing the Adi-Dravidas at their expense and with the political objective of keeping itself in power by ensuring massive support from the Adi-Dravidas.

By virtue of their position as Scheduled Castes, the Adi-Dravidas enjoy a number of privileges which are embodied in the Constitution of India. In addition, they are believed to enjoy certain political advantages in Tamilnad in particular. Both Brahmins and a section of Non-Brahmins think that Congress ministers and M.L.A.s are generally more easily accessible to the leaders of the Adi-Dravida community and that they tend to take a more sympathetic view of its grievances. This attitude is often interpreted in terms of political motivation. To what extent the sympathetic attitude of the Congress leaders at the top actually benefits the rank and file among the Adi-Dravidas is, however, open to question.

Although it is quite likely that the government would continue to provide benefits to the Scheduled Castes irrespective of the party in power, these benefits tend, in practice, to be attributed to the Congress party. Leaders of the Congress, in their turn, do not hesitate to claim for themselves the credit for improving the position of Adi-Dravidas. The latter, being largely illiterate, are not always able to see the finer distinction between the government and the ruling party, and tend to support the Congress. In the 1962 elections most of the Adi-Dravidas in Sripuram voted for the Congress.

It should be reiterated that the Adi-Dravidas enjoy their special position by virtue of their caste, and not their class position, although it is true that the two overlap to a considerable extent. Adi-Dravidas who own land, although they are few in number, enjoy special benefits in spite of their economic position; a landless Non-Brahmin is not entitled to these benefits. It is thus caste, and not class, which is decisive in shaping the political attitudes of the Adi-Dravidas.

It will have been noted that political attitudes and party support are least clearly defined among Non-Brahmins. This is, to some extent, explained by the fact that they constitute the largest and the most heterogeneous of the three principal divisions. Whereas Brahmins as well as Adi-Dravidas evince a degree of political unity and cohesiveness, internal conflicts are common among the Non-Brahmins. Power tends to be divided between several dominant castes which operate at the district level, or at the level of the Assembly constituency. These dominant castes today all belong to the Non-Brahmin division.

The last three elections have made it clear that local politics is controlled fairly effectively by one or more dominant castes which have to be taken into account even when the state cabinet is being constituted. District dominance of castes is a well-known phenomenon and can easily be demonstrated by making a study of the caste composition of candidates who have sought election from different constituencies. Padayachis in North and South Arcot, Mudaliyars in Chinglepet, Kallas in certain areas of Tanjore, Gaundas in Coimbatore and Salem, and Vellalas in Tinnevelly dominate local politics and also find representation in the leadership of the state.

The tie-up between dominant caste and political representation can be illustrated with reference to the Thiruvaiyar Assembly constituency. In the three General Elections held after Independence only Kalla candidates have been returned. The Kallas constitute about thirty per cent of the electorate in this constituency.

Not only has the sitting member always been a Kalla, but the overwhelming majority of candidates who have contested the Thiruvaiyar seat have been of this particular caste. In the 1951–52 elections the Congress party set up a distinguished Muslim candidate who was defeated by an Independent Kalla. In 1957 the Congress won the seat by putting up a Kalla candidate. In 1962 there was a triangular contest between Congress, D.M.K., and P.S.P., and all three parties put up Kalla candidates. It is now more or less generally acknowledged that any candidate to be successful from this constituency has to be a Kalla. Party affiliation, though important, does not constitute a guarantee for success. The Thiruvaiyar constituency demonstrates a pattern which is fairly general in Tamilnad.

V I

We have in the foregoing examined the three principal dimensions of social stratification—caste, class, and power—and have sought to bring out their interrelations. An attempt was made to view these interrelations in dynamic terms. Granting that change has been pervasive in nature, it seems to have affected the different subsystems in different degree. Changes in the distribution of power seem to have been of a more radical nature than those in the caste structure.

Within the caste system there has been a general trend towards the contraction of structural distance between proximate segments. Thus, marriages take place today between the two subdivisions of the Brihacharanam segment, commensal relations are common between Smarthas and Shri Vaishnavas, and the Brahmins in general show a greater measure of unity in their style of life in comparison with the past. This contraction of structural distance is largely a consequence of the two closely related processes of secularisation and westernisation.

Contraction of structural distance has not, however, taken place in a uniform manner at every level. Thus, the cleavage between Brahmins and Non-Brahmins may, in some ways, be regarded as having deepened. This holds true particularly of political relations.

Whereas in the caste system the tendency has been towards a certain convergence of adjacent segments, the class system has shown increasing mobility. Ownership of land passes more easily from one set of people to another, and new classes tend to develop. Further, the class system has progressively detached itself from the caste structure, although there is still a high degree of correspondence between the hierarchies of caste and class.

The distribution of power has acquired a very dynamic character over the last two decades. In some ways the traditional relationship between caste and power has been reversed. Whereas in the past power was concentrated in the hands of Brahmins, today the village *panchayat* is controlled by Non-Brahmins and the traditional elite is being pushed into the background.

Power has also become independent of class to a greater extent than in the past. Ownership of land is no longer the decisive factor in acquiring power. Numerical support and a strategic position in the party machinery play an important part. Adult franchise and Panchayati Raj have introduced new processes into village society. The struggle for power has become a pervasive phenomenon. This may partly be due to the fact that today much more power is accessible to the common man than was ever the case in the past. Mobility in the caste system has always been an extremely slow and gradual process. To acquire land and move up in the hierarchy of class also takes a generation or two. Shifts in the distribution of power under the new set-up are, by comparison, quick and radical in nature.

VII

Viewed over a period of time, the social world of Sripuram is seen to have expanded considerably and still seems to be in a process of expansion. Enough evidence exists to show that Sripuram has never been a wholly self-sufficient unit in the thousand years or so of its history. But the degree of its articulation with the outside world has increased at a rapid pace over the last six to eight decades.

There has been much movement of population to and from the village. Subcastes, lineages, and kin groups have become widely dispersed. Territorial dispersal is particularly marked among the Brahmins. Among them networks of kinship and affinity not only cut across the boundary of the village, but also of the district and the state. Western education and the availability of professional and white-collar jobs in towns and cities throughout the country have been the principal factors behind the territorial mobility of the Brahmins.

The village has become articulated with the outside world not only through the dispersal of its population, but in other ways also. The economic system of the village has become more closely integrated with the wider economy. Economic relations today transcend more easily and more extensively the boundary of the village. Land has come into the market. Every year some amount of land is bought and sold in the village. Many of the buyers live in other villages or in adjacent towns. The cash nexus plays an increasingly important part in the village economy. Money comes into the village every year, every month, through the sale of land, through the sale of agricultural produce, and by way of cash incomes from white-collar jobs and remittances from relatives outside. Much of this money is spent in the purchase of mass-produced consumers' goods.

The village is also becoming progressively politicised. It is being drawn more tightly into the web of district and state politics. The new *panchayat* system links the village to a hierarchy of territorial units. Political parties relate local tensions and conflicts to wider ones. Political networks of various kinds link individual villagers to party bosses, M.L.A.'s, and government officials.

Social mobility, economic change, and political modernisation lead to the creation not only of new relations, but also of new values, new attitudes, and new aspirations. Some of the contours of the traditional structure tend to be blurred, and new ones tend to emerge. It has been shown how, for instance, the process of political modernisation provides scope to the individual to enter into networks of interpersonal relations in which village, caste, and other traditional bonds are not wholly decisive.

In a sense the traditional structure had a simpler character. It was made up largely of systems of groups and categories whose boundaries were relatively clear and well defined. The caste structure provided the fundamental cleavages in the village. The entire population was divided first into Brahmins, Non-Brahmins, and Adi-Dravidas, and these divisions were further subdivided. Membership in one or another of these subdivisions was the basis of the individual's identity, not only in ritual contexts, but also in the economic and political spheres.

The caste structure subsumed within itself, to a much greater extent than it does today, both the organisation of production and the distribution of power. The division of the village into landowners, tenants, and agricultural labourers corresponded to a much greater extent with its division into Brahmins, Non-Brahmins, and Adi-Dravidas. Class positions had only a limited autonomy. Being a landowner was, to a large extent, only one aspect of being a Brahmin. Similarly, being an Adi-Dravida fixed, by and large, one's position as an agricultural labourer.

Today class positions have acquired a certain measure of autonomy. The class system has in part detached itself from the caste structure, although, as we have seen, class positions in the village are by no means entirely, or even largely, "caste-free." Numerous factors have contributed to the dissociation of class from caste. Land has come into the market and is in process of changing hands; not all Brahmins are now landowners, nor are all landowners Brahmins. New occupations have emerged which take the villager right out of the productive organisation of the village. The penetration of a cash economy and the increased geographical mobility have also loosened the economic system. Finally, political and legislative changes have altered the bargaining positions of the old economic classes.

Just as there was greater overlap in the past between the broad hierarchies of caste and class, there was also greater correspondence between the caste structure and the distribution of power. In the village, caste was traditionally the only important locus of power: this was, no doubt, because class itself was largely subsumed under caste. In Sripuram important decisions concerning the village as a whole were taken largely by Brahmins; Non-Brahmins played some part in implementing these decisions; and Adi-Dravidas had very little say in matters not specifically concerned with their internal system.

Although in the past power in Sripuram was largely controlled by the Brahmins, the Non-Brahmins also enjoyed some power; however, as far as village affairs were concerned, Non-Brahmins enjoyed power largely by delegation. In a general way they were engaged by Brahmins for keeping the Adi-Dravidas in order. Brahmin *mirasdars* had in the past very little direct dealings with the Adi-Dravidas. The *cheris* were inaccessible because of ritual considerations. When an Adi-Dravida was to be punished, this was done either directly by the Non-Brahmins, or by Non-Brahmins acting under instructions from Brahmin *mirasdars*.

The materials presented in this chapter and the preceding one make it clear that power has, to a considerable extent, detached itself from the matrix of caste and has, in a manner of speaking, become more "free-floating" than it was formerly. Two things have happened which are of considerable importance. First, the older balance of power between caste groups has been altered; Non-Brahmins have wrested a good deal of power from the Brahmins. Second, new loci of power, based on factors other than caste, have been built up over the last few decades.

It must not be inferred from what has been said above that there is little relationship today between caste and power. The point is that because power has been partly disengaged from the matrix of caste and has acquired independent loci, the relationship between the two is now much more complex than before. One's caste continues to be an important basis of power, and an important factor in taking political decisions, although other factors are also acquiring importance.

The growth of new political organs and institutions and the entire process of political modernisation are likely to render still more complex the relations between caste and power. In this context the question as to whether a caste continues to be a caste when it acts in a political context seems a little naïve. Clearly, castes as status groups do continue to have a virile existence. The question is not whether, as status groups, they provide a basis for political mobilisation—for this they evidently do—but what other factors in addition to caste are of importance to the distribution of power, and how such factors interact with one another and with caste.

In the sum, the processes of economic change and political modernisation have led the productive system and the organisation of power to acquire an increasing degree of autonomy. In the concrete, the overlap between the hierarchies of caste, class, and power has been progressively reduced. A new economic order is emerging in the towns and cities which is not based upon caste in the same way in which the traditional order was. The economy of the village is drawn increasingly into the orbit of this new economic order. Similarly, the new political order is at least formally independent of caste, and it too has an important effect on the social life of the village.

It would seem that a certain measure of "discreteness" is enjoyed by each of the three orders considered: caste, class, and power. One can vary independently of the other—up to a point. But the limits within which variation is possible in one of the orders, the two others remaining the same, cannot obviously be determined here. This can be done only on the basis of comparable studies carried out in different parts of the country.

Caste has been the fundamental institution of traditional India, and its importance has been particularly great in the area considered. Traditionally, most important cleavages and alignments have been embedded in the matrix of caste. With the change from a static, traditional social order to a more dynamic one, the economic and political systems gradually detach themselves from caste and acquire a relatively autonomous character. To what extent they have done so in the different parts of the country would be an interesting question to answer by empirical research. An attempt has been made here to provide an analytical scheme for the study of social change in India.

REFERENCES

Bailey, F. G.
   1957   *Caste and the Economic Frontier.* Manchester.
Baliga, B. S.
   1957   *Tanjore District Handbook.* Madras.
Barnes, J. A.
   1959   "Politics Without Parties," *Man,* LIX, 13–15.
Béteille, André
   1964   "A Note on the Referents of Caste," *European Journal of Sociology,* V, 130–134.
   1965   "The Future of the Backward Classes: The Competing Demands of Status and Power," *Perspectives, Supplement to the Indian Journal of Public Administration,* XI, No. 1, 1–39.
Birch, A. H.
   1959   *Small-Town Politics.* London.
Bottomore, T. B.
   1955   *Classes in Modern Society.* London.
Census of India.
   1962   *Census of India, Paper No. 1, 1961.* New Delhi.
Dahl, Robert A.
   1961   *Who Governs?* New Haven, Conn.
Dahrendorf, Ralf.
   1959   *Class and Class Conflict in an Industrial Society.* London.
Dumont, L.
   1957a   *Une Sous-Caste de l'Inde du Sud: Organisation Sociale et Religion des Pramalai Kallar.* Paris.
   1957b   "Hierarchy and Marriage Alliance in South Indian Kinship," *Occasional Papers of the Royal Anthropological Institute,* No. 12.

Evans-Pritchard, E. E.
  1940   *The Nuer.* Oxford.
Frankenberg, Ronald.
  1957   *Village on the Border.* London.
Gough, E. Kathleen.
  1955   "The Social Structure of a Tanjore Village," in
          M. MARRIOTT (ed.), *Village India.* Chicago.
  1960   "Caste in a Tanjore Village," in E. R. LEACH (ed.),
          *Aspects of Caste in South India, Ceylon and North-West
          Pakistan.* Cambridge.
Hemingway, F. R.
  1906   *Madras District Gazetteers: Tanjore.* Madras.
Hutton, J. H.
  1961   *Caste in India.* Bombay.
Iyengar, S. Sundararaja.
  1933   *Land Tenures in the Madras Presidency.* Madras.
Kumar, D.
  1962   "Caste and Landlessness in South India," *Comparative
          Studies in Society and History,* IV, No. 3, 337–63.
Lewis, Oscar.
  1958   *Village Life in North India.* Urbana, Ill.
Mannheim, Karl.
  1936   *Ideology and Utopia.* London.
Marx, K.
  n.d.   *The Eighteenth Brumaire of Louis Bonaparte.* Moscow.
Ministry of Community Development and Co-operation.
  1961   *Panchayati Raj.* Delhi.
  1962   *A Digest on Panchayati Raj.* Delhi.
Mukherjee, P. K.
  1959   *Economic Surveys in Under-developed Countries.* Bom-
          bay.
Mukherjee, P. K., and Gupta, S. C.
  1959   *A Pilot Survey of Fourteen Villages in U. P. and Punjab.*
          Bombay.
Pocock, David.
  1957   "The Bases of Factions in Gujarat," *British Journal of
          Sociology,* VIII, 291–342.
Popper, Karl R.
  1957   *The Poverty of Historicism.* London.
Sastri, K. A. Nilakanta
  1955   *The Colas.* Madras.

Siegel, Bernard J., and Beals, Alan R.

1960   "Pervasive Factionalism," *American Anthropologist,* LXII, No. 3, 394–417.

Sivertsen, Dagfinn.

1963   *When Caste Barriers Fall.* New York.

Srinivas, M. N.

1952   *Religion and Society among the Coorgs of South India.* Oxford.

1962   *Caste in Modern India and Other Essays.* Bombay.

Thurston, Edgar.

1909   *Castes and Tribes of Southern India.* 7 vols. Madras.

Weber, Max.

1948   *From Max Weber: Essays in Sociology,* ed. by H. H. GERTH and C. W. MILLS. London.

1958   *The Religion of India.* Glencoe, Ill.

Whyte, William Foote.

1943   *Street Corner Society.* Chicago.

LOCATIONS OF SRIPURAM AND (*inset*) TANJORE DISTRICT.
SETTLEMENT PLAN OF SRIPURAM.

INDEX